from Otto and G
July 20

CW00971459

berlin before the wall

A Foreign Student's Diary With Sketches

Hsi-Huey Liang

Routledge

New York   **London**

Published in 1990 by

Routledge, an imprint of
Routledge, Chapman and Hall, Inc.
29 West 35th Street
New York, NY 10001

Published in Great Britain by

Routledge
11 New Fetter Lane
London EC4P 4EE

Copyright © 1990 by Routledge, Chapman and Hall, Inc.

Printed in the United States of America

All rights reserved. No part of this book may be reprinted or
reproduced or utilized in any form or by any electronic,
mechanical or other means, now known or hereafter invented,
including photocopying and recording , or in any information
storage or retrieval system, without permission in writting form
the publishers.

Interior designed by Andrea H. Meyer

Library of Congress Catalog in Publication Data

Liang, Hsi-huey
        Berlin before the wall: a foreign students' diary with sketches/
by Hsi-huey Liang
        p. cm.
    ISBN 0-415-90168-5
    1. Berlin (Germany)— Description. 2. Liang, Hsi-huey,
-—Journeys— Berlin (Germany) 3. Chinese students
— Berlin (Germany)— Diaries. 4. Germany
— Politics and government— 1945- I. Titile.
DD860.L52 1990
943.1'550875— dc20   89-70036
                                                  CIP

British Library Cataloguing in Publication data also available.

To the Memory of
JAY H. CERF
(1923–74)

CONTENTS

Introduction

Arrival (Fall 1953)

November

Arrival in Berlin, pp.16-17
A visit to RIAS (Radio in the American Sector), pp. 18-20
Political cabaret, pp. 21-22
Berliners remembering the coming of the Red Army, p. 23

December

A German veterans' journal, p. 28
Conversation with the Schmidt family about the Nazi years, pp. 28-29
The Free University, p. 30
First visit to East Berlin, pp. 31-32
Professors Otto Suhr, Hans Herzfeld, Walther Hofer and others, pp. 32-34
At the movies: a Burt Lancaster film, p. 34
The Friedrich Meinecke Institut, p. 35
A session of the Berlin city parliament. Meetings with veteran socialists, pp. 37-38
Auto license plates in Berlin, p. 39

Winter 1953-1954

A conversation with my landlady: an unrepentant Nazi?, p. 43
A political conversation in a pub, pp. 43-44
East European refugees, pp. 44-45
Walks in the working-class district of Wedding, pp. 45-47

January

Sightseeing in East Berlin, pp. 49-50
New York Times correspondent Walter Sullivan, pp. 50-51
Supper with kindly neighbors who are very poor, pp. 51-52
Visit to Berlin-Spandau: a vocational school, the Siemens factory, pp. 52-54
The Heinrich Zille Klause, pp. 55-56
Tea with the Indian military mission, pp. 56-57
The Central Refugee Camp, Berlin-Marienfelde, pp. 57-59
Arthur Fleischer, home-town historian, p. 59
Lunch with a Siemens director, pp. 60-61
Ernst Gries, anti communist resistance fighter? pp. 62-65
Dr. Lachmann, an old fellow-student of Hajo Holborn, p. 65
Another visit to the Zilleklause, p. 66
At HICOG: preparation for the Four-Power Conference, p. 67
Lost-and-found office at police headquarters, p. 68
Movies: "Pünktchen und Anton," "Ein Leben für Do," pp. 68-69
Anti communist propaganda leaflets, p. 70
Film about Hitler, "Bis 5 Minuten nach 12," pp. 70-71
Tea with the Schmidt family: memories of the good old prewar days, pp. 72-73

Epilogue

INTRODUCTION

This book has no plot and no dénouement. It was not written with the intention that it be published, and if today it has some historical interest, this is entirely due to the passing of time and the importance that Berlin held in world affairs some thirty-five years ago.

The year 1953-54 was when I became a historian, thanks to travel grants and fellowships from Yale University and my good fortune in having professors in New Haven who taught and inspired me: Professors Holborn, Krieger, R. Turner, Vernadsky, Rudin, and a visiting Swede by the name of Höjer. In deference to our craft, this record of what I saw and thought in Berlin at the height of the Cold War has not been changed beyond the elimination of some stylistic and grammatical slips. I have no wish to improve the image of the narrator in this diary because it was so long ago anyway, and because I trust that anyone who sees his or her name mentioned here will forgive me my mistakes of judgment when I was young. Only one name has been changed. This plea for forbearance also applies to the pictures I drew of them, some from memory at the end of the day, others stealthily under the table when I sat demurely pretending to take notes.

To help younger readers find their bearings quickly, I should explain that Berlin eight years after the end of the Second World War was just beginning to recover from the worst havoc of destruction. The city stood under four-power occupation (as it still does today) but, though the Berlin Wall was not built until 1961, there was already much contrast between the Western sectors (American, British, French) and the Eastern sector (Russian). Political tensions were high because of the recent Soviet blockade of West Berlin (1948-49), which the Allies defeated with the famous airlift, and because of the workers' uprising in East Berlin a few months earlier (17 June 1953).

To help older readers who may be puzzled by the things I did in Berlin, I should explain that I am the son of a Chinese diplomat, born in Berlin when Hindenburg was German president. I subsequently lived in a number of different countries in Europe and in China until in 1951 I arrived in the United States to do graduate work in history. It was not very wise for someone whose best chance for a stable future lay in America to leave that country for a research trip to Europe a mere two years later, for there was no assurance I would be allowed to return to the U.S. But the topic of my thesis project was too important to me: I wanted to explore the living conditions—and through them, the mentality—of the lower classes in one of the grandest capitals of Europe that I had known as a child. As I look back today, this curiosity was probably stirred by the appalling discovery of abject poverty in wartime China. Young people often are drawn to the study of the wretched of this earth in their search for a universal humanity. The thesis that I finally wrote for Yale (1959) was not terribly original, but I treasure to this day what I learned as I trudged the streets of Berlin in search of workers or people who knew about workers' problems, and still others who could teach me about this fascinating city.

As readers will see in the following pages, two of my teachers in Berlin were not Germans but Americans: Jay and Carol Cerf. I owe them both a lifelong debt for their friendship during that year. A doctoral student and teaching assistant in political science at Yale, Jay was a few years older than me. More important, he also had served in the Navy Air Force and was a hundred times more savvy than I about life and politics. In Berlin, where we really got to know each other, Jay was always much more popular with the Germans we met than I was because he was so much the American that postwar German youth admired and longed to be like: cheerful, open-minded, and self-confident, a mid-westerner from Chicago, as willing to learn from others as he was ready to tell people where he stood, unashamedly American in his way of speaking German and never ambiguous in his opinions. Carol was his perfect complement: delicate in appearance where Jay exuded robust good health, she was quiet and observant, utterly devoted to her husband and at the same time indispensable as the soother of ruffled feathers when Jay's forthrightness occasionally went too far. Jay was in Berlin on a Fulbright fellowship to prepare his doctoral thesis on the East German youth organization, the Free German Youth (Freie Deutsche Jugend, or FDJ). While Carol took care of their infant son Randolph and dug into West Berlin archives for him, Jay went out to interview refugees from East Germany just as I went out to interview old socialist workers, and often we went together.

I hope the entries in this diary express my gratitude to all those who helped me grow during my year as a student in Berlin. My brother Dehwei is thanked for sending me seventy-five dollars to pay for the jeep I bought in Berlin. I also thank my student assistant Claire Venghiattis (Vassar '89), who helped with the editing of this diary and Jad Davenport (Vassar '90), who photographed the illustrations, and at Routledge my two obliging editors, Jay Wilson and Michael Esposito.

H.H.L.
Vassar College
Poughkeepsie, N.Y.
October 1988

ARRIVAL
Fall 1953

Inside a cafe in Steglitz

Reisetagebuch!
Finder erhält Belohnung!
Travel Diary. Hsi-Huey Liang,
c/o The Graduate School, Yale University
New Haven, Conn., U.S.A.

6 November 1953

This trip to Germany began on 16 November (a Monday) when I embarked on the M.S. "Italia" of the Home Lines bound from New York to Hamburg on a ten-day voyage. It was right here on boarding ship at eight in the morning that I entered Germany, for the entire deck crew including Captain Tormoehlen was German. (Only the machine crew was Italian.) Announcements were made in German and in bad English. "Luncheon is served for passengers of the tourist class. Thank you.— Die Passagiere werden gebeten zum Mittagessen Platz zu nehmen. Danke schön." This announcement startled me and sent me scurrying off to the dining hall as we steamed towards open sea, thus missing my chance to see the Statue of Liberty.

The passengers were almost all Germans or German-Americans. My roommate (who spent most of his time in another cabin since ours was too hot), was a 28-year old sailor named Walter Hahn, who had jumped ship in New York two years before and worked illegally as a carpenter before turning himself in to the authorities. There was old Mr. Kofoe, a ship boiler mechanic of Danish descent now living in California, going to Denmark for a last visit. He was very popular. He used to get into arguments with our steward, Herr Carl Roeder, who liked to tease him by telling him that everything German was better. There was an American oil company employee who was (as were most people on this ship) rather rough on the edges but in his own way interesting (mustache, loud sports clothes, a drinker, huge gold cufflinks). There was Mr. Kamm, an old man who went around trying to teach people the most elementary things in a didactic way. I got annoyed with him because of his interminable chatter and his pro-Nazi leanings. He pointed out one passenger to me as a pure Aryan girl— she was blonde and blue-eyed— and he wanted me to believe that only old Jews were put in concentration camps where they unfortunately "died of hunger due to the Allied blockade." This cantankerous German nationalism annoyed me no end. I overheard the conversation between two German women, about 28 or 30 years old, with a sea officer, in which they talked of their longing for Germany all the time they had been in the States. They deplored the destruction of the "Kraft-durch-Freude" ships and took much pride in Germany's material recovery. Mr. Wlasek (a cattle dealer from Wisconsin) tried to tell me that all the wars in Europe had been England's fault (did he mean the economic rivalry theory for the 1914 war?), and another man, a guest-farm keeper in New Jersey, told me he just hated all Jews. Poor Mr. Kofoed went around deck in his old sweater and *Bommelmütze*, muttering curses about the master race.

There was entertainment almost every night, but it never had much life since the average age on board must have been over 60. Still, I was interested in a "Gesang für Jedermann" program, in which a trio of accordion, bass and mandolin made political jokes. One was a song, "Wir waren alle in der Partei" (All of us were party members), followed by a stanza, "Wir sind alle denazifiziert" (We've all been de-Nazified),"and again "Wir sind alle in der Partei," namely, the CDU, SPD and whatnot. Another joke: Germany has a new army. The Salvation Army! Only this time the barracks are a little farther away. Its flagbearer has done his duty and is tired. As he lets the flag slump, the man behind him cries: "Raise the flag! Die Fahne hoch!" OK says the flagbearer, "Im gleichen Takt: eins, zwo, drei– Die Fahne...!" The tittering which ends the story is an impudent wink at the Allies.[1]

Otherwise the ship was very boring. A slight rough sea on Sunday. I met a young official of the Hapag Lloyd Reisebüro in Essen who told me that in his opinion democracy had taken good root in Germany and that the Germans may have learnt their lesson at long last. But he thought them politically naive.

The trip only became interesting when we got into Hamburg. The sky was overcast and it was foggy and bitterly cold. Our ship slowly slid up the river Elbe, the water brown and muddy. The pilot came aboard at 4 a.m., customs officials in Cuxhaven at 6 a.m. The customs officials were very courteous and lenient. No thorough checking. Off the ship and on a bus by 12 o'clock. Hamburg is a busy city, to judge by what we saw on the way to the Hauptbahnhof. No British troops in evidence and lots of new German cars. Volkswagen cars and small, very light trucks, also made by VW, and many small Italian cars. British and American cars I scarcely saw. The Germans don't look well dressed, but adequately enough. Strong, sturdy boots, tattered but heavy overcoats, and they have an active bearing about them. There is no loitering in the streets.

But I saw little of Hamburg. A short snack with Herr Redeker, the Hapag Lloyd man, at the Konditorei of the Zentral Omnibus Bahnhof, then I left in a small bus for the airfield where I caught a British European Airways plane to Berlin. Everything went well, except that I was rather tired and did not take much in. Berlin from the air at 5 o'clock (it gets dark early here) looked lifeless. The streets are dimly

---

[1] "Die Fahne hoch ..." are the opening words of the Nazi party song, the Horst-Wessel song.

lit if lit at all, the glitter of advertisements on the Kudamm hardly make up for it.[1] The evening streets through which we drove seemed deserted. On the Kudamm the traffic was heavier, yet one could cross this wide chaussée without much trouble. No need for traffic lights here! As in Hamburg, the shops are full of beautiful things, all apparently in plentiful supply. Leatherware, books, radios, television sets, pens, jewelry, clothing, shoes, pastry...everything. Some things are amazingly cheap by American standards. A pendulum clock for DM 47, or about $10. A cup of coffee costs 50 pfennigs and a sausage (Bockwurst) 65 pfennigs. So you can have a luncheon snack without coffee for 20 cents easily.

I walked up and down the Kudamm my first night here. Only two U.S. officers with their richly furred wives were in evidence outside the Kempinski Hotel, the most glamorous hotel in town. The rest were Germans of all walks of life, at that time of the night probably mostly the rich. The rich look elegant in their florid long hair, felt hats, suede shoes, and belted overcoats. There are also poorer people to be seen. Like the refugee couple in a little Imbiss-Stube (snack-bar) ordering soup, the man furtively taking rolls from his coat pocket to eat with it. I notice that people are looking at me but then I also still feel rather self-conscious. The doorman of the Hotel-Pension Radloff-Rumland (Kurfürstendamm 226) where I am staying, for instance, thought I came from Africa. I found two things rather strange: the empty shell of a corner house, once evidently a rather splendid building, with an illuminated wooden sign: Dieses Grundstück ist zu verkaufen. (Are there any buyers for pieces of real estate?) On another house that is being cleared of rubble, the sign says: Baustelle; Eintritt verboten, (Construction site; no entry). There is also an advertisement to be seen everywhere: Berliner Kindl— an old Berlin beer label.

The Cerfs were not at home when I tried to call them, so I went to bed very early.

27 November 1953

As in so many novels, I, the hero in this case, woke up not knowing where I was. A large double bed with eiderdown, lace curtains and double windows, a heavy, ornate white door...good, old-fashioned Germany. Outside the window workers have been hammering on a scaffolding since dawn. I rush over to the Konditorei Möring for two rolls with jam and a coffee. Old-fashioned too, straight out of an Else Ury Nesthäkchen novel with its many cakes, the tipped shelves with biscuit cans, the black-frocked, white-aproned and -hooded wait-

---

[1]Kudamm: popular abbreviation for Kurfürstendamm, West Berlin's Fifth Avenue and Broadway combined.

resses (as in all restaurants here), marble tops and white woodwork, and the many mirrors. One thing strikes me everywhere: how immensely higher the ceilings are in Europe compared to America.

I went to an optician to get my glasses mended and finally contacted the Cerfs and went to Wannsee per S-Bahn from Savigny-platz. But before that I went to two shops, one dealing in antiques and the other selling stationery, to ask about old Berlin maps. Was delighted to see an old "Mensch ärgere dich nicht" set.[1]

The ride on the S-Bahn (*Stadtbahn*, or city train) to Wannsee was quite easy. The coaches look rather poor and shabby. Wooden benches. Three categories are available: *Raucher* (smoker), *Nichtraucher* (non smoker), and *Schwerbeschädigte* (invalids); but in the last one everybody sits when it gets crowded. The S-Bahn is run by the Russian administration, hence the East sector on the map in each coach is referred to as "Demokratischer Sektor." As you approach Wannsee, the last stop before the Russian zone, you see big notices on the street running parallel to the S-Bahn, warning passengers that they are about to leave West Berlin. The notices cannot be on the S-Bahn line itself since it runs on land that belongs to the Russians. The people in the S-Bahn are incredibly polite and nice. Later I saw on a tramway at the Nollendorfplatz two youths rushing to help an old lady climb into the car and finding a seat for her.

Wannsee looks very suburban and the Cerfs live in a modern villa on the Am Sandwerder 20a (tel. 80 58 88). It is a nice flat, cosy and clean, airy and well lighted. A little like Klanovice outside Prague, where we lived in 1939. Their boy Randolph is getting golden and pink and can already sit up. I had lunch with Carol and then we all went to market. There is a wonderful little market near the S-Bahn station, up a few stone steps. A little town of wooden stands (*Bretterbuden*) lighted by kerosene lamps, resembling a country fair. Soap, cheap jewelry and toys, chocolate dolls, cakes, meat, bread, sausages— everything is to be had. The people all know Carol and are very friendly.

In the afternoon we went to RIAS— the Radio in the American Sector. There was Jay and Carol's sister Janet and her husband Daniel Calhoun, a young political analyst from Frankfurt. RIAS was worth seeing. The building looks quite modern, the street no different from so many others. It does not look like the great RIAS; ordinarily I would have taken it for some business house. There are only a couple of policemen in a little Volkswagen at the door, and the doorkeeper asks you whether you have an appointment. We were led up without much ado to the third floor, room 317, to see a Mr. Hartel. He is an American, we don't know his function but he looks and acts rather as if he had some authority. Glasses, scarred face, about thirty-five years old.

---

[1] Well-known German board game dating from before the First World War.

We began by listening to a short introductory talk. RIAS is eight years old. It began quite small but now it has expanded into branches specializing in education, a women's hour, a special service for political refugees, etc. There is only one RIAS but they have two additional broadcasting stations so they can also reach Czechoslovakia and Eastern Europe in general. They once operated on 3 million dollars per year. Now their budget has been cut to 2.78 million. All the money comes from the U.S. State Department and what profits the station makes from advertisements are turned over to the State Department. (Advertisements are useful to let East Germans know what people in the West can buy.) The effectiveness of the broadcasts must be gauged from the tales of refugees and the hundreds of letters (including some abusive ones) which the station receives regularly. The station employs about 450 people, most of them Germans, with Americans to supervise them. Half of the programs are given to entertainment, the rest to political and cultural programs. Later we saw a man and a woman listening to a tape recording of a Schubert symphony, checking for mistakes with a music score before them. In another auditorium we heard a group of boys and girls under the direction of a man at the piano, rehearsing a German translation of the American hit tune "You, You, You." We visited the newsroom and through a window saw somebody broadcasting. In another room a young man showed us the tape recordings of RIAS time signal and the newscast that people can listen to by dialing a certain telephone number. Any East Berliner can pick up the phone and get a résumé of the day's news. Apparently the Russians cannot prevent this without ripping up the entire telephone system.

Most interesting was Mr. Ossowsky, the head of the program for schools (*Schulprogramm*). He talked to us for a short while between two engagements. He tried to convince us of the effectiveness and deadliness of communist education. Free pamphlets on education are distributed to all parents and teachers. All history books (and he showed us some), physics and chemistry books, etc., are Marxist. School exams are political exams. Only mathematics has maintained a high standard in the East, he said. Refugee students must relearn most of the material if they want to take the high school diploma exam (*Abitur*) in the West, except for mathematics. The Schulprogramm tries to teach students the Western interpretation of what they have learnt at school in the East. Mr. Ossowsky appeared a very distinguished and efficient, and also a charming,man. He invited Jay and me to visit him again. There is also a *Schulparlament* here, the only one in Germany, under the direction of a Mr. Herz. We had no time to inquire into this.

On the ground floor there is a reception and interviewing center for refugees from the East. We had to wait a little to make sure no one was being interrogated just then since our visit could have upset them. In the reception center we saw a collection of underground literature, both communist and anticommunist. I picked up a copy of the *Junge Welt,* which Mr. Hartel said was communist in contrast to the *Freie Junge Welt.* But my eyes began to pop out when I began to read the supposedly communist paper and found it to be anticommunist. The leading article, "19 Jungen und Mädchen unserer Republik besuchen das Land Mao Tse-tungs," turned out to be an account of last September's attempt by communist youths to invade the Western sectors to upset the elections.

After RIAS we went to Aschinger[1] for a snack and then saw Mozart's *Figaros Hochzeit* in the Städtische Oper. Leopold Ludwig conducted and Josef Herrmann was Figaro. I most liked Lisa Otto as the pageboy Cherubino and Elfriede Troetschel as the Countess. The orchestra was quite excellent. I noticed that most of the public was British. The orchestra wore dark business suits.

28 November 1953

Early rising. Breakfast at Konditorei Möring. Optician. Then I began some house hunting. I tried a Marttel on the Kudamm and discovered that this old, dark tenement house has a telephone system from doorbell up to the apartments. I also tried to find shops which sell old maps and illustrated books and newspapers. My hunt led me to a marvelous bookshop, Wasmuth, at the Hardenbergstrasse no. 9, opposite the Technische Hochschule. It apparently deals only with art books, but a Fräulein Hagemann there was most cooperative. She told me to look up the Landesarchiv in the Archivstrasse, Berlin-Dahlem, and the Senatsbibliothek (Direktor Zopf). Also Professor Scheper, the curator at Schloss Charlottenburg, Amt für Denkmalpflege (Office for the Preservation of Historical Monuments). She was, further, anxious to get me to visit some Sino-German societies and to take a bus tour of West Berlin. She was so anxious to help (and told me to keep a diary) I had to think of Priscilla Robertson's remark in her book on the revolution of 1848, how the Parisian workers had become so sophisticated that they would resent any writer not painting their misery in the darkest and most romantic colors.

I went to the club room of the Technical University (TU), where they have lists of rooms to let. They sent me off to Steglitz which led me through the center of town. Here one really sees heaps and heaps of rubble. Steglitz is a suburb with lots of empty space and new apartment houses; somehow it reminded me of Prague's Dejvice or Střešovice. However, the room (in a beautiful apartment house) was already taken. I was sent on to Lankwitz, but the room there was too

---

[1]A popular, very cheap self-service restaurant.

Kaiser Wilhelm Memorial Church

INSIDE BERLIN'S BEER HOUSES

Conversation in a Schöneberg pub (21 Dec., 1953)

Conversation in a Kreuzberg pub (26 Aug. ,1954)

small and too poorly furnished (no proper table, no bed), so I went back into town. It was already getting late and after a snack I went to Wannsee for dinner.

Some curious characters can be seen in the streets: a man with a witch's hat and wide trousers near the Savignyplatz Bahnhof. A small boy whom I thought to be about nine years old turned out to be 15(!) and out of school, learning the trade of *Blumenbinder* (florist?). Few boys seem to wear bloomers (*Pumphosen*) any more, it must have gone out of style since the end of the war.

Throughout the day I have been quite thrilled. I am getting more self-assured. The Berliners are so friendly and courteous one always feels free to ask them questions.

Dinner with the Cerfs. After that we stopped at an international student home on Clayallee 76 (Jay had rented an Opel for the night) to see a Frau Wille and ask her whether she knew of a place I could rent. (She did not.) After that we went to the "Ewige Lampe," a "literarisches Kabarett" in the Rankestrasse. We thought it would be a political cabaret, but this was true only in the most general sense. The room was small and crowded with people. On the walls hung political cartoons. We had to share a table with a lady by the name of Vri (?), who works as the spokesman (or spokeswoman?) for industrial concerns at the Ministry of Finance. The skits were— some good, some less so. They became increasingly easier to understand as one got used to the Berlin dialect. The performers called them-selves "Die Stachelschweine" (The Porcupines), and tonight's pro-gram was called "Ach du liebe Freiheit" (Freedom, darling).

There was a very naive attack on McCarthyism in America. Two young Americans accuse one another of communism. The girl says the boy has red hair on his chest, the boy says the girl is a Communist because she wears red pants. There was a song to Princess Margaret sung by a girl in a child-like voice, clutching a teddy bear and alluding to Peter Townsend. Then a very realistic reinscenation of German traditional student meetings with caps and sashes, with the leader swearing his followers to loyalty by holding up a sword while they softly sing the German national anthem and he screams: "Deutschland! Kämpfen! Blut! Ehre! Heinrich Treitschke!"

That was not very funny. There was also a very serious poem recited by a man in prison uniform, asking on behalf of German war veterans not to glorify them in speeches, but to give them a chance to return to a normal life. (There is to be a rally of German ex-soldiers in Berlin on 30 November.) Then a Brutus-Mark Antony speech, the dead body being "der deutsche Film"; a drunkard satirizing Berlin affairs and German affairs; and a rather good skit on love in the Tier-garten as described by Malaparte and Hemingway.

Finally, a series of short scenes showing a certain Gottlob Friede (a young man resembling Mr. Everyman in David Low's cartoons) who seeks help from (1) an American capitalist, (2) a Russian war minister, (3) the secretary general of the United Nations, and (4) a German bureaucrat (*Amtsschimmel)* to promote the cause of peace (*Friede*). The American is willing to name his new margarine "Friedensmargarine" and regrets he can't do much more— he already supports so many worthy causes like the society for the protection of homeless dogs. Of course, he must first make sure that Friede is not a "commie." The war minister insists that Russians speak more about peace than anyone else (43 times in yesterday's *Pravda* compared to 28 times in yesterday's *New York Times*) and equates Friede with Russia's foreign policy. For the Soviet Union is most anxious to serve the cause of Peace: just tell us your enemies and we shall shoot them for you! As to the German bureaucrat, he is caught in a web of red tape. "Ordnung muss sein!" Alphabetically "Friede" comes only after B (*Besatzung*, or foreign occupation), E (*Entscheidung*, making decisions), and K (*Krieg*, war). The lines of the UN secretary general were weak. It all ended with a song, "Ich hab 'ne Farm in Florida." When we left it was half past 11. The Cerfs and the Calhouns went on to something called "Resi Wasserballet" and I went home.

29 November 1953

Got up early and went for a stroll in the Tiergarten. I met a couple who were going to the East Sector to attend a Quaker meeting and they took me as far as the Russian war memorial and the Brandenburger Tor. It was a grey November morning, the streets behind Bahnhof Zoo were almost deserted. The empty shells of the huge mansions of the former legation quarter (*Diplomatenviertel*) looked like the remains of a bygone civilization, a fallen empire. Among the weeds a few abandoned statues with shell holes. Near the Brandenburger Tor there was a West Berlin policeman stopping all cars for a brief inspection. A sign warns you that after another 70 meters you leave the Western sectors. I talked to the policeman on duty. He was very nice and assured me it was alright to go across the border if my papers are in order. I told him I carried a Chinese Nationalist passport, whereupon he became more doubtful. He thought I had better not go. So I just looked at the scene. The Russian war memorial with its two Russian sentries looked old and battered next to the Brandenburger Tor with its bright red flag fluttering on top against a grey November sky. Not far away stands the Reichstag building like a scuttled battleship resting on an unkempt patch of weeds and burnt grass.

On my way home I looked at the statues of von Moltke, von Bismarck, and von Roon on the Siegesplatz. They and the Siegessäule were once put up to celebrate the Prussian victories of 1864, 1866, and 1870. What contrast between them and the Russian war memorial, which has two generals' graves, two tanks, two cannons, and the strident inscription in Russian, English and German: To the Eternal Glory of the Heroes Who Fell Fighting the German Fascist Invaders for the Freedom and Independence of the Soviet Union. I am amazed the Russians could not think of a more tactful inscription. This thing will be torn down the minute they leave Berlin. But it must also have been a big satisfaction for them to put this thing up bang in the middle of the enemy's capital.

After lunch to the Cerfs'. They had Professor Flechtheim, his wife and his daughter Marian for tea. Flechtheim teaches comparative government at the Hochschule für Politik and will recommend me to some colleagues. He resembles di Gasperi.[1] There also was a Mrs. Denis and her husband (but I didn't get around to speak to him), and an old American lady who lives in Schlachtensee, is thrilled by Berlin, went to the Yale School of Music, and is a friend of Carol's mother. Then there was a young student of history from the Freie Universität, Kurt Steves, obviously a close friend of the Schencks, who in turn are the landlord and landlady of the Cerfs. I like the Schencks. The woman resembled my old landlady, Mademoiselle Pittet, in Fribourg, while Herr Schenck looks a little like the old Soviet foreign minister Vyshinsky and is very friendly. Plays the piano, paints, was formerly a Regierungsbaumeister and now still an architect. The Schencks had a touching story to tell about the arrival of the Russians in Wannsee. During the war their car was put up on blocks because there was no petrol to run it. With the garage out of use, they had planted flower beds around it. When the Russians found the car in 1945, the housekeeper vigorously protested against its removal on account of the flowers. So the Russians lifted the car over the flower beds and over the fence and not one flower was broken!

Herr Schenck also told us that there was talk about making the ruins of the Gedächtniskirche on the Kurfürstendamm a memorial against war by leaving it just as it is. Schenck himself does not like the idea; he thinks something completely new should be built there.

We listened to records. Two songs from East Berlin, "In allen Sprachen" and "Ami Go Home," had weird, almost sinister accompaniments with disharmonies and discords to go with familiar American folk tunes. Presumably they are trying to evoke the favorite communist picture of American "gangsterism" and "night-club decadence." We also listened over the radio to a political cabaret called "Die Insulaner"— Berlin being an "island" whose inhabitants look forward to the day when they would be residents of a mainland again. From one of the skits I learned that there were plans to give the victory column in the Tiergarten a new coating of gold at the cost of DM 70,000. Not only is this sum astonishingly lavish, one also

---

[1]Dr. Ossip K. Flechtheim (born 1909) was known for his book *Die Kommunistische Partei Deutschlands in der Weimarer Republik* (1948). Alcide di Gasperi was Italian prime minister right after the war.

wonders why a memorial to the defeat of France would need redecorating. I *had* noticed a fresh wreath under the statue of von Roon this morning!

After I returned to the Savignyplatz, I had a brief encounter with a Hungarian-German boy named Walpasch, a miner in the Rhineland, penniless. One feels so much at a loss when one meets a boy who is so completely on his own in the midst of Berlin, this huge sea of cobble stones and rubble.

30 November 1953

I have a room at last! I got up early this morning, arranged to hire a car for the afternoon, collected addresses from newspapers, the Technische Hochschule, and the FU, and in the afternoon Jay drove me around. By 4 o'clock we were lucky to find a very nice big room with a beautiful desk and a charming landlady at Vionvillestrasse 11. The name is Henninger, and she has relatives in America, she says. I think I'll be very comfortable in this house. There are apparently three daughters. The smallest one, Esther, I saw; she is very cute. There is also a maid.

On the way home, we passed Tempelhof airport with its monument to the airlift of 1948. The main building, now used by the U.S. Air Force, looks formidable. The giant eagle on the roof, however, looks suspiciously like the Nazi eagle with the American shield replacing the swastika. Jay also wanted to pick up some stuff at the PX. The PX is on Clayallee, a suburb where you also have the American military headquarters and the consulate general. In fact it is Berlin's Yankeetown. The PX is inside the Truman Hall and sells everything you might find in the Liggetts' drug store back in New Haven. There is also a cafeteria and a barber shop. Strangely enough, while RIAS only has a porter, the PX has a military policeman with a carbine to guard the racks of paperback novels, chewing gum, and Hershey bars. On the other hand, the name Truman Hall is only an enamel plaque attached to the door. It can be exchanged for another plaque at any time.

One thing you can't fail to notice in Berlin: servants here are still servants. The maids of the hotel where I stayed and also the maid in the Henninger home, Rena, work hard, always smile, and are extremely polite (*zuvorkommend*). They even curtsy.

I December 1953

I was very pleased to find my landlady, Frau Irmtraut Henninger, both pleasant and charming. Her husband, an Evangelical minister, divorced her recently and so she has moved here with her children.

I should find out more about living conditions in Berlin. One sees

EVERYDAY SCENES

INSIDE BERLIN'S BEER HOUSES

In the Zille Klause
(21 Jan., 1954)

In the tille Klause.

crowds outside the display windows of the pastry shops (*Konditor-eien*), looking at whole "Schlaraffenland" scenes of chocolate and cakes, yet only a few customers shopping inside. According to Frau Henninger, chocolate is too expensive for most Germans. Eighty pfennigs per bar of chocolate is too much, she says.

I watched people clearing rubble by hand in Birkbuschstrasse, around the corner from my new home. I wonder whether the workers remember the Allied bombers during the war as they pick up brick after brick, and if so, what their political sentiments are.

2 December 1953

First typed away on my overdue term paper on Emile Zola for Professor Turner at Yale. Then I went to report to the local police station in Steglitz and was amused by its bureaucracy. Interesting was a poster in the entry hall, warning German youth not to become the mercernaries of Russia. Apparently both boys and girls are given military training in the East German youth organization, the Freie Deutsche Jugend (FDJ). The posters showed boys and girls march-ing in formation, rifles slung over their shoulders. Someone had written in ink underneath: "Sachsenweiber, alles Sachsen." Why Saxons? Why this prejudice against Saxons?

Later I got my hair cut, *Fassonstil*. The whole thing cost DM 2.50, but it includes shampoo and lots of Birkenwasser hair tonic. The haircut is much more carefully done than in America. But it leaves the hair also much longer! I asked the barber about trade unions. They are not strong, he assured me, and he was not interested in them.

3 December 1953

In the morning I finished the Zola paper, then typed out letters to Professors Holborn and Turner. After lunch, back to the police station. The poor woman police official who was supposed to complete my registration nearly wept because a piece of paper was missing from her file! "How am I to process this?" (Wie soll ich denn das bearbeiten?).

Then I went to the Charlottenburger Castle, to the Office for the Preservation of Historical Monuments, or Amt für Denkmalpflege. This is not the main office, only a branch, and it consists of only two rooms with Professor Scheper in charge. Professor Scheper was out, but two women were there and they kindly talked to me. I found out that, for one thing, the Amt deals only with monuments and historic buildings. They have little on the period 1890-1914, in which I am interested, since that was not a very artistic period. Some fine buildings from this period have even been torn down, like the old post office. They showed me old books and I took down a few names, also the addresses of bookstores I might want to visit. Then we had a chat. Miss Karasek was a Berliner but dislikes Berlin. She was astonished that I should like it so much. People are no longer polite, she complained. She scoffed at my idea that Berliners were optimistic and hard-working. "Och, man muss sich ja über Wasser halten!" (Come on, we just do what we must to survive!) I asked her why Saxons seem unpopular. The Saxons are people without scruples, she explained. "Sie benützen die Ellbogen und gehen über Leichen"(They elbow their way through life and stomp on others). Saxons are opportunists who change sides without compunction— think how they behaved during the wars of Frederick the Great! At the same time, most Berliners admittedly are from Breslau. The other woman did not agree; she wanted to stay in Berlin.

Miss Karasek took me to the Wissenschaftliche Zentralbibliothek Berlin in Podbielskiallee and showed me the catalogue. The catalogue is surprisingly small, though it supposedly lists all the books available in Berlin libraries. I talked to a man in charge and asked him about using this library. To prove to him that I was a student I showed him my letter of introduction from Hartley Simpson (the dean of the Yale Graduate School). Fortunately he could not read English, for on my return home I discovered that I had given him the wrong letter, namely the routine notice sent to all graduate students approving their course program for the current year!

I had dinner in a small restaurant in the Schlosstrasse. A man was telephoning his wife, telling her he had to stay in his office for another half hour. Then he settled down again to continue drinking alone.

By the way, Miss Karasek also had spoken of Steglitz as a Nazi district since it is primarily inhabited by small civil servants. Still Nazi, I asked? Well, they can hardly have changed their Weltanschauung that quickly, can they? she replied. Then she told me about the Berlin Castle, built by Schlüter in the 18th century and which had burned in 1945. All the walls and much of the original ornamentation were left standing. Now the Communists have destroyed it with dynamite and turned it into a square for political rallies.

4 December 1953

Went to the FU, but could not see anybody because they are celebrating the fifth anniversary of the Freie Universität today. Met a 27-year-old economics student who showed me to the Mensa (a common room plus restaurant for students). He is a returned prisoner of war, had been in a Russian camp for three years, came home in 1948. He thinks the Americans should have stood up to the Russians much more firmly as early as 1944 or '45. I didn't like him too much. He asked me about anti-German feeling in England and added that there also was anti-American and anti-English feeling in

Germany— a quite pointless remark since I am neither American nor English, and it just gave me the impression that he himself shares these animosities. I was interested to find out that he belonged to a student fraternity (*Burschenschaft*) and that dueling (*Mensur*) is being reintroduced. There is voluntary Mensur (when one individual challenges another), and *Bestimmungs-Mensur*. (The latter means that one fraternity challenges another one to produce a fighter.) *Scharfe Mensur* can result in serious injuries.

After a snack I went to Martin Luther Strasse in Berlin-Schöneberg, where it crosses with Motzstrasse. The book peddler in Schlosstrasse had told me this was the center of Berlin's old-book trade. In the Matthei Antiquariat I met a bus conductor who is also collecting books and pictures of old Berlin. We may very well meet again one day in the Verein für die Geschichte Berlins, I think. I bought some books on Berlin in 1896, on Berlin dialect, and in another shop some etchings (for 75 pfennigs each) and a book of sketches by Heinrich Zille.[1] I saw a set of Eduard Bernstein's *Geschichte der Berliner Arbeiterbewegung* for DM 18.00.

Next, a visit to the Schöneberg Rathaus, which also houses the city parliament of West Berlin. It is a building designed on a grand scale, with a bust of Reichspräsident Ebert in the hall, but also dirty. The porter told me to come on an early morning and ask for Nusske, the man in charge. Outside is a market square where, so a market woman told me, on Tuesdays and Fridays vegetables, fruit, soap, cheap clothing and so forth are sold from stands.

I saw a shoe repair shop displaying a small notice: Zugelassen zur Durchführung von Sozialarbeiten; Gross-Innung Berlin (Licensed for welfare work; Grand Guild of Berlin). What does this mean?

Saturday, 5 December 1953

Early in the morning to the FU. Went to the office of the Rektorat. I was quite impressed when the secretary in the Rektorat told me she would see when I could talk with "seine Magnifizenz." (And I had only asked to speak to "Herr Hirsch"!)

My next stop was Zehlendorf (U-Bahn station Krumme Lanke) to look for the Verein für die Geschichte Berlins. This is a settlement with pine forests and new blocks of flats. The lady in charge of the historical society is in hospital and the porter, Herr Weise, did not know where the office of the society is. I must call again next week.

After a quick snack on the Kudamm, I met Jay at the corner of Gedächtniskirche and Tauentzienstrasse. We went shopping for a car (fortunately, perhaps, the one Jay wanted to buy was already

---

[1]Heinrich Zille (1858-1929), lithographer and free-lance artist, famous for his sketches of Berlin working-class people.

sold) and for a lamp. We finally ended at the Christmas fair in Tauentzienstrasse, but found it disappointing. It was a small luna-park with shooting booths and a few carousels. More interesting was an antiquarian shop in Giesebrechtstrasse, off the Kudamm, set in an old-fashioned flat: huge, old-fashioned drawing rooms filled to the ceiling with books. I bought a Berlin city map from 1900. The old man who ran the shop, Herr Rothschild, said he knew some professors at Yale and Columbia.

Jay grumbled that Germans are only clean in appearance, that's why they don't pasteurize their milk and why the Cerfs' charwoman takes the same rag to wash dishes and to wipe the toilet seat in the bathroom.

Back in Zehlendorf I picked up a copy of a veterans' journal, *Der Frontsoldat spricht.* Some of its material comes from the old military journal *Wehrwissenschaftliche Rundschau.* There was much fuss made about soldierly virtues and national destiny: we are against Hitler, but Germany's fate is not of her own making, it is being determined for her. In a future war, Germany will need good infantry tactics and therefore should learn much from the Red Army but not from the Americans, whose success in 1944-45 was only based on material superiority and on the fact that by then Germany had lost her best fighting men. The paper also boasted that Germany had designed jet planes as early as 1939 (Heinkel) and that German and Japanese submarines had met in the Indian Ocean. Well, I was not really surprised by what I read.

Evening spent with the Henningers. Around the table Frau Henninger, her daughters Marion and Esther, the son Michael, and Rena, who sat opposite Frau Henninger. There were candles on the table and Christmas decorations. The menu was potato salad and salty jelly, open-face sandwiches (*Stullen*) and tea. Afterwards there was some nice wine and home-made biscuits. It was all so *gemütlich—* there is no other word for it. Then the Henningers sang some Christmas songs (*Adventlieder*), though out of tune, I'm afraid.

6 December 1953

This morning, oh surprise! I found a Saint Nicholas parcel in front of my door. Spent the morning reading. In the afternoon, went to see Professor Harry Rudin's friends, the Schmidts.[1] They live in Dahlem, on a street, just off the Clayallee. A beautiful, cozy villa, luxuriously furnished. In the salon a charming little fireplace, thick carpets, dainty china, tasteful furniture. The son and daughter of the house received me, Carl and Sigrid. Carl is a medical doctor, Sigrid a ballet dancer. Schmidt senior came in a brown tweed sports jacket, but

---

[1]Professor Harry Rudin taught diplomatic history and African history at Yale.

Historians and Archivists in West Berlin

FU Rector Ernst Hirsch

(10 Feb., 1954)

HISTORIANS AND ARCHIVISTS IN WEST BERLIN

Fritz and Peggy Stern

Herr Schendell and Frau Engelmann (12 Dec., 1953)

Prof. Flechtheim

Heinz Siewert, Landesarchiv

Ernst Kaeber,
Berlin historian

Looking for books at the FU (8 Dec., 1953)

Otto Suhr

❑ 29 ❑

Sigrid and Frau Schmidt wore elegant cocktail dresses. The mother talked vividly and sometimes with wit, but there was a hint of vulgarity in her speech.

We talked of Paris, where Sigrid had just spent nine months, about Carl's work at the hospital, and about my thesis. The conversation for the most part was polite and pleasant, but not particularly interesting. Then, towards the end, someone mentioned the war and the atmosphere quickly became less relaxed and friendly. Dahlem, I was given to understand, is an exclusive area where personalities like Alfred Rosenberg, "Reichsführer SS" Himmler, and Foreign Minister Joachim von Ribbentrop maintained their residences. Consequently, Dahlem suffered most from the uncivilized behavior of the Russian soldiers in 1945. Villas were plundered for alcohol, the Russians were perpetually drunk. The house of the Schmidts was occupied by the Red Army for two months and most of its interior furnishing was wrecked. (One wonders where the Schmidts found the money to redecorate the whole house so lavishly.) Finally the Americans had come and things quickly improved, though the Americans also caused "some disappointments."

Suddenly the Jews were mentioned. Many rich Jews had owned houses in Dahlem, and after the war they returned to claim compensation as ODFs (*Opfer des Faschismus*— victims of fascism). Sarcastically, Sigrid remarked that all of them seemed to have survived the KZs,[1] otherwise would there be so many demands for restitution? She admitted that Jews were treated unjustly (*ungerecht*) during the Third Reich, but then went on to say they did behave differently from other people, in fact less decently, and today make themselves unpopular in Berlin once again. Herr Schmidt made a joke by referring to himself as a *verfolgter Nazi* (a persecuted Nazi.) He had been obliged to undergo denazification after the war ("filling out a form with 127 questions") and was barred from employment for several years. Yes, and former prisoners from the KZs were sitting as judges in the denazification courts, Frau Schmidt interjected querulously. Denazification should be up to the whole German nation, not just to a small segment of it, Sigrid agreed. As I listened, I thought to myself that I certainly don't want the Allied occupation of Germany to end soon.

After I left them I had a snack in Albrechtstrasse, in Steglitz. The town hall dominating the small square looked as if it were out of an old German children's book. There were public Christmas trees lighted in the street, and a band played Christmas carols. In the cafe, the radio played softly tunes that reminded me of my childhood in Czechoslovakia, and then, to my pleasant surprise, the announcer said this was Radio Bratislava. I left the cafe in a much better mood and went home.

---

[1]KZ: abbreviation for *Konzentrationslager* or concentration camp.

7 December, 1953

This morning I met a Herr Hartwig (a flabby young man, bit of a dandy) who will arrange my contacts with the FU. Then went to the Preussisches Geheimes Staatsarchiv, the old Secret Prussian State Archive, where I talked with Dr. Zimmermann, the deputy director. He promised me help, but also urged me to go to two other archives in the same building: the Archiv für Wohlfahrtspflege (specializing in municipal welfare work) and the Landesarchiv der Stadt Berlin, the city archive.

In the afternoon, went to the U.S. consulate to inquire about a visa to the United States so I can return to Yale next year. A Mr. Heyward Isham spoke with me. He thought there should be no difficulties. Went home, bought black bread, pork dripping (*Schmalz*), and some apples for supper. Today was especially cold.

8 December 1953

The whole day at the F.U. First I saw Professor Rohde, whose gentle, ascetic face I liked. He promised to write Professor Auerbach at Yale, who had recommended me to him.[1] Then came the introduction to Seine Magnifizenz Ernst Hirsch, rector of the university. The meeting was friendly, Seine Magnifizenz counseled me to attend classes as an auditor (*Gasthörer*). After that, a meeting with the dean of the Philosophical Faculty, Professor Dr. Dr. Hans Herzfeld, whom I must see again on Saturday at 11. And finally I met Dr. Lieber, professor of philosophy and sociology, who told me to explore the Stein Bibliothek, which specializes in books on socialism.

The Stein Bibliothek is at Ihnestrasse 22. An officious old maid, Fräulein Wetzstein, is in charge of the catalogue. Oddly enough, she was impressed when I told her that I had seen the rector. "What kind of man is he?" she asked. Her boss, Fräulein Stark, who runs the library, was more efficient in her advice. She told me to go to the Hochschule für Politik in the Badensche Strasse and ask to speak to Otto Suhr and a man called Keltig. The library is cramped in little rooms in the basement, books are stacked up to the low ceiling as in an old bookshop, and the card catalogue is hopelessly confused.

I was very tired when I got home. In the Hardenbergstrasse, opposite the Technische Hochschule, I saw two memorials to the victims of totalitarian rule: "Den Opfern des Stalinismus" and "Den Opfern des Nationalsozialismus." Both are no more than simple stone walls with the above inscriptions and with wreaths before them. The second one is made from stones taken from the ruins of

---

[1] Professsor Erich Auerbach at Yale was the author of *Mimesis: The Representation of Reality in Western Literature* (1946).

the synagogue in Fasanenstrasse, burned in 1938 "because of racial madness" (*aus Rassenwahn*).

Wednesday, 9 December 1953

Well, my first look behind the "Iron Curtain" since we left Prague in 1949! Of course, I went with the Cerfs. We didn't see very much, but what we saw was fascinating.

After a morning spent hunting for some suitable fountain pen ink (in the end I asked Jay to buy me a bottle of Scrip at the PX) and a visit to the Senatsbibliothek (which I think will be very useful for my work), I met the Cerfs outside the PX at half past twelve. We took the S-Bahn to Unter den Linden. The station was almost empty but it looked cheerful, tiled in light green. No stalls to buy newspapers or candy, no commercial advertisements. On the other hand, plenty of political slogans hailing the Soviet Army as the liberator and friend of the German people and calling for ever closer friendship between the German and Soviet peoples. Outside the famous boulevard looked dreary in the misty afternoon. Passersby flit by like grey shadows; they are much more poorly dressed than in West Berlin. At the Brandenburger Tor a prewar Wanderer automobile was being searched by Volkspolizei[1]; another car (an Opel) was surrounded by a silent crowd and again there were Vopos there. We didn't stop to inquire what happened.

We walked past the sturdy government buildings where last June the Berliners had demonstrated en masse, and past the Soviet embassy. To the left was the Humboldt University, decorated for the Christmas holidays. Next we came to the Haus der Kultur, also known as the Zentralhaus der sowjetisch-deutschen Freundschaft, and right after that to the Maxim Gorki Theater. Inside the theater the floors were covered with splendid red carpets and the landings with red velvet. Lots of busts of Stalin and Marx, and oil paintings of Marx, Engels, Lenin and Stalin. Appropriately enough, there were people playing chess in a special chess room next door. The ground floor also had an exhibition of textiles with loud commentary provided by a tough looking elderly woman in a blue smock. "Russische Rohstoffe werden deutsche Qualitätsware" (Russian raw materials are turned into German quality products), one poster announced. The fabrics seemed alright, the finished clothing a bit old-fashioned. Upstairs an exhibition of photos denounced Western warmongering. Vopos in great numbers walked around looking at the exhibits, and there were also many schoolchildren and youths wearing the uniform of the FDJ.

We walked along Unter den Linden towards the Berlin Castle. East

---

[1]Volkspolizei: East German people's police, colloquially called "Vopo."

Berlin looks rather like the Western idea of a communist capital: grey, forbidding public buildings and grey, subdued people silently going about their business. Lots of uniformed police dashing around in radio cars, this whole sombre picture dominated by gigantic red banners. The greater our surprise to find the Christmas fair on Marx-Engels Platz (the site of the former Berlin Castle) much more pretty than the one in Tauentzienstrasse. Fairy-tale figures, a train ride into fairyland, a "Max and Moritz" theater show[1], stands selling hot sausages and gingerbread, watches and shoes...everything much cheaper than in the West sectors. (One West mark equals four East marks.) However, whenever you buy anything other than food you must produce identification papers. Jung-Pioniere in dark brown uniforms were selling lottery tickets with the chance to win copies of communist literature. The proceeds are supposed to help pay for the construction work on Stalinallee. We walked up to a stand selling tobacco. "Haben Sie russische Zigaretten?" I asked curiously. "Haben Sie amerikanische Zigaretten?" Jay boomed out.

We left at about half past six. Carol had a swollen face from the cold. I had dinner with the Cerfs, fed Randolph, got home by 10:30 p.m.

IO December 1953

A day of hard work at the Stein Bibliothek. I drew up a long list of books and brochures on Berlin working-class life before the First World War, among them the protocols of trade union congresses around the turn of the century.

II December 1953

Finished going through the catalogue of the Stein Bibliothek. Had a plate of macaroni at the Mensa and in the afternoon visited the Hochschule für Politik in the Badensche Strasse, Berlin-Schöneberg. It was a very profitable trip. I looked up Professor Ossip L. Flechtheim in room 312. He has a very modern office, in fact the whole building is brand new. Flechtheim looked a bit embarrassed and had little to say. But he did invite me to dinner for tomorrow to meet someone who also is interested in Berlin history. Then I went and actually got to see Otto Suhr[2]. Suhr looked much younger than I remembered him from the picture in the *New York Times* when Schreiber became mayor of Berlin. His office is very large, modern and simple. He was awfully kind, asked me how I became interested in the subject of Berlin workers, racked his brain to give me advice, and finally

---

[1]"Max and Moritz" refers to Wilhelm Busch's popular cautionary tale in the 19th century about two mischievous boys.

[2]Professor Dr. Otto Suhr (1894-1957), first postwar director of the reopened Deutsche Hochschule für Politik and president of the Berlin city parliament, became governing mayor of Berlin in 1955.

referred me to a number of old people who remember the period before 1914. We talked for a quarter-hour, then he asked me to come back sometime to tell him how I am getting on. I left in high spirits. On Thursday I must go to the Berlin city parliament (*Abgeordneten-haus*) to find some of the people he wants me to talk to.

I tried to see Kettig, who runs the catalogue and who is interested in Berlin history, but he is only here on Wednesdays. Another person I am told to look up is Professor Landsberger, also at the Hochschule für Politik.

I was so elated because of this successful visit that I went into a tobacco store to buy a pipe for myself. But pipes, I found, are not very cheap. Had supper in a snackbar on Innsbrucker Platz.

12 December 1953

Paid a courtesy call on Professor Hans Herzfeld, the Dekan of the Philosophische Fakultät at the FU[1]. He is a small, elderly man who almost disappears behind his huge desk. Gigantic plants throughout the office. Herzfeld was friendly and polite, has traveled in the U.S. only last summer, and knows Hajo Holborn and Franz Neumann. Recommended me to two graduate students (*Doktoranten*) who also are writing dissertations on Berlin.

I did some reading at home in the afternoon. Then, at 8:30, I arrived at the home of the Flechtheims. They live in Zehlendorf-West, Oertzenweg 44. A small house; they have the second floor. The whole area is eery at night, a very dark highway stretches through open terrain that looks like no-man's land, and the Russian zone is only half a kilometer away.

It was a small, informal party, with punch, sandwiches, some biscuits and coffee. Dr. Lieber of the FU was there, a man with strong features who loves the opera (his wife is a singer), Dr. Walther Hofer, a Swiss historian who now lectures in Berlin (greying wavy hair, quite elegant)[2], and a young Dr. Schüler. The talk first centered on historiography. Flechtheim was telling about a new punchcard method for the study of all the members of the House of Commons in 18th-century England. There was much skepticism. Everyone thought it much more important to study the personal influence of individual political figures rather than sociological facts derived from statistics. Since Flechtheim is a specialist on communism, there was also talk of Lenin and Marx, especially on the influence of the terrorist Sergei Nechaev on Lenin. Then I met Herr Schendell, the Berlin historian whom Flechtheim had wanted me to talk with. Bushy eyebrows, very funny, given to sweeping generalizations ("Cliques are unavoidable inside all human institutions!") and cigar-

---

[1] Professor Dr. Dr. Hans Herzfeld (1892-1982) also chaired the Berlin Historical Commission.

[2] Professor Walther Hofer was then working on his study of the causes of the Second World War, *War Premeditated* (1955).

smoking. Schendell is opposed to women's emancipation even though his wife looked very emancipated with her short hair and her insistence to be called by her maiden name, Engelmann.

13 December 1953

Nothing interesting today. Had lunch at a restaurant in Birkbusch-strasse. Like so many other restaurants here in Germany, this one was practically empty. Faded lace curtains at the windows, newspapers hanging from the coat racks, carpets (even though threadbare), table cloths, flowers on each table...but no guests. All the restaurants here seem to have retained their prewar décor, only the public that used to frequent them is gone. Hotels in summer resorts out of season are like that.

Over lunch, read an article in the *Tagesspiegel*. It criticised the theory that war toys made children into future militarists. That, the author said, was the viewpoint of the generation after the 1914-18 war, but they should have known that Hindenburg had never played with tin soldiers! Ergo, concluded the author of this article, a child who never shot bibis at toy soldiers is most likely to become a *Lagerkommandant* in a concentration camp. An interesting, though not very convincing, argument, I thought. I was even more skeptical of his next thesis— that mechanical toys like motor cars and trains are dehumanizing if they carry no passengers. He forgets that the children who play with them ride in them in their imagination.

In the evening I gave in to temptation and went to the movies. An American film with Burt Lancaster, dubbed in German. Burt Lancaster played a criminal who had been brutalized by society. A scene showing him being flogged in a London jail caused someone behind me to whisper "medieval!" (*mittelalterlich!*). On the other hand, no one reacted when Lancaster was seen terrified in the London zoo at the sight of savage apes because they reminded him of his guards when he had been a prisoner of war (thus German guards?). The newsreel was good, however, better than what one sees in America. The audience gasped at scenes from the Army-Navy football game in the U.S. Curiously, when the newsreel brought a report on a laboratory in Detroit where polio germs had been discovered, boogie-woogie was used as background music. Do Europeans always associate America with night-club music, even American medical science?

Before the film began, there were some commercials. One showed an ideal family living in an ideal home being told by a friend that "Sanella Schmalz" was best for them. Now, the clothes worn by the family were obviously American, so was the interior furnishing (ranch-house style), and there was even a cowboy playing the guitar. Only: would any American family eat pork dripping on sandwiches?

14 December 1953

Went to the Friedrich Meinecke Institut, the Freie Universität's History Department, in Berlin-Dahlem, Altensteinstrasse 40. It reminded me very much of the Catholic "Foyer St. Justin" in Fribourg which I had visited so often. A low building dating from the mid-19th century, stone walls, stone floors, stone staircase, all worn by the daily traffic of boots and clogs, a dining room where the light of day scarcely penetrates through the windows, obstructed by curtains and flowerpots. Linoleum on the tables. On the first floor, a sort of concert hall, where someone played Ravel and played it beautifully. It could be heard throughout the house. Biedermeier charm, except that it does not quite fit my idea of an academic institute. The library is very small. The students I saw there worked seriously in dead silence. But of course, this being Germany, in mid-morning you hear the crackling of paper as everyone gets out his black bread with Schmalz or butter.

Had a talk with Dr. Friedrich Zipfel, who told me many useful things on Berlin history.

At lunch I met a young student from the East zone. He was very religious and very timid. He told me the recent revolt in East Germany was caused by widespread discontent, ignited by the radio broadcasts of RIAS and Radio Hamburg reporting on the strike in East Berlin's Stalinallee. And he warned that the West makes a mistake if it thinks the barracked People's Police (*kasernierte Vopo*) will not defend the communist regime. I also met a student named Hans Nowack, who invited me to his room in Offenbacherstrasse 9 after lunch. A tiny room, a real *Studentenbude*.

It occurs to me that not many American troops are to be seen in the streets. Lots of staff cars with officers near and around the FU and once a lorry full of white-helmeted, black-uniformed MPs with carbines. The Germans in the street do not look. The only armed troops on the march I have seen so far were near the sector boundary.

15 December 1953

I must be getting a little tired of my routine. Went to the FU and got Professor Hofer's signature so I can be an auditor in his seminar. In the afternoon, looked up Helmuth Weidmüller, one of the two doctoral students writing on Berlin who had been mentioned to me by Herzfeld. He had little to say, alas, though he looked quite friendly. His landlord was more interested in talking with me than Weidmüller, because "so'n Ausländer schneit nicht alle Tage ins Haus" (foreigners don't show up in your home every day). I went over to the public library (*Volksbibliothek*) of Zehlendorf, and though I didn't find anything useful for my research, I was pleased by its modern, clean look (like the passport control station in an airport) and the dozens of children asking for books. Went home in the late afternoon and bought a Christmas tree with Esther, the landlady's little daughter.

16 December 1953

Morning seminar with Walther Hofer, Ernst Fraenkel and Eugen Fischer-Baling.[1] Fraenkel looks like Professor Bemis, the diplomatic historian at Yale, and has personally been to Korea. Fischer-Baling, in turn, resembles the Cambridge philosopher Bertrand Russell. He was once the librarian of the Reichstag. Some 30 to 40 students were sitting around a large seminar table, among them a number of Indians. There was a surprising amount of come and go. Some students arrived as much as 30 minutes late. Some of them stood when they spoke, others remained sitting. Everyone rapped the table when a report was finished or someone scored a point. I was asked for my opinion on Communist China and afterwards people also knocked the table. One student talked for about 20 minutes on the political situation in the Soviet satellite countries since Stalin's death. He had a manuscript before him but mostly talked freely. I thought he was very competent, but the criticism he received from fellow students afterwards was quite harsh, harsher than the student criticism in a seminar at the Yale Graduate School. Helmuth Weidmüller was there too. He thought the FU's Meinecke Institut had a much higher intellectual niveau than the Hochschule für Politik. But if this session was representative of the Meinecke Institut's level of competence, it was no better than Yale's. Of course, students here know much more than we do in New Haven about the political situation in East Germany.

Lunch in the Mensa with Weidmüller, then an unsuccessful trip to the Hochschule für Politik. Landsberg was not there. Dr. Kettig turned out to be useless as a source of information and uninterested. I met Dr. Schulz, a very young Assistent, who asked me to see him at his house tomorrow at 4 p.m. I thought for a while that I might go to Charlottenburg, but it was too cold so I stopped somewhere for a cup of hot coffee and went home. A hot bath, some reading, and then to bed. The weather is really getting very cold.

17 December 1953

A busy day. In the morning I was at the Landesarchiv Berlin, where I spoke to Dr. Lachmann and a younger archivist, Herr Köhler.

---

[1] Professor Ernst Fraenkel (born 1898) was the author of *Military Occupation and the Rule of Law* (1944). Professor Fischer-Baling subsequently published his lectures in Berlin under the title *Besinnung auf uns Deutsche* (1957).

Both men are enormously well informed about Berlin. They said that much of what I want to learn about life among the working people at the turn of the century is located in East Berlin libraries. But they will try to get me as much as they have here, especially original materials.

After lunch, to the Rathaus Schöneberg, where I wanted to attend a session of the city parliament. I had no trouble getting into the session since I mentioned the magic name Otto Suhr to the Ordner (supervisor) of the Sitzungssaal. (The porter had told me I had no chance of getting inside.) I was given a slip of paper on which I had to write down my name and address, and the names of the two delegates (*Abgeordnete*) to whom I wanted to speak: Adolf Wuschig and Anna Nemitz, both SPD deputies from East Berlin.[1]

The Sitzunssaal is not very impressive. Not very large, dark, more like a courtroom. Through the windows (quite fine windows with small panes of yellow and white glass) you see the ruins of destroyed buildings. (This area was badly damaged in the war.) Suhr spoke, but not very well. His voice is monotoneous and he pronounces his s in the North German manner, with a hissing sound. "Wir schreiten jetzt zur Abs-timmung." He is not very patient either, and repeatedly asked for silence. "Meine Damen und Herren, ich muss doch freund-lichst um Ruhe bitten!" he shouted several times, annoyed. Voting was by show of hands, and Suhr decided whether or not a motion had passed rather arbitrarily, I thought, for he always would pronounce his verdict only a second later. I listened to a youngish SPD Abgeordneter who proposed that the Senate should be instructed to ask the Allied and the Soviet commanders in Berlin to remove all obstacles to freedom of communication between the East and West sectors (post, telephone, tramway and bus lines.) I had to go, but the session, I am told, got quite lively later.

I went to the office of the SPD Fraktion[2] to ask where Wuschig was. There I met Landsberg and his assistant, Mateid. Landsberg was rather impatient at my intrusion and I didn't like the looks of his assistant, who reminded me of the bodyguard-chauffeur our defect-ing secretary Tseng had back in Prague, in 1949.[3] But then Anna Nemitz came, a very old, fine lady, white haired and bent with age—50 years in the service of the SPD. She said she would arrange to see me after New Year at her daughter's flat in Charlottenburg. Wuschig came later. He also looked very old, but, unlike Nemitz, he seemed embittered. He referred to himself as "once the most powerful man in Berlin." That was before the First World War, when he managed

[1]Anna Nemitz (1873-1962) and Adolf Wuschig (1870-1955) were both granted the title of city elders of Berlin.
[2]Fraktion: parliamentary group of a political party.
[3]At the Chinese embassy in Prague, as in many Chinese missions in 1949, there were staff who secretly went over to the new communist regime in China.

the SPD election campaigns in this city. He told me to bring him a German translation of my thesis when it is written and he would then correct it for me. When I left him he hardly noticed that I shook his hand. Looking back as I walked away, I saw him gazing vacantly into the distance, very lonely.

My final achievement today was meeting Dr. Schulz-Popisch in Lichterfelde. A thin man, still quite young, the picture of a bookworm. A walking bibliography.

At home, found a Christmas card from the Cerfs and a letter from Fräulein Hagemann of the Wasmuth bookstore.

18 December 1953

Spent all day in the Landesarchiv. Had a few old city maps photocopied for me. Herr Siewert, one of the low-level archivists, always politely stands at attention when you speak to him. This can be quite embarrassing.

Telephoned the Cerfs. Jay is in bed with a boil. I'll visit them on Sunday. Went to the Amt für Denkmalpflege but got there too late. On the way home the U-Bahn was crowded. An officer of the British Royal Engineers was standing, holding on to a strap. A German sitting on a bench was loudly cracking jokes at his expense. "You can't sit down unless you are a war cripple (*Schwerbeschädigter*) like me," he cried, and, "All of us are now NATO soldiers!" The other passengers laughed heartily. The Englishman grinned but said nothing and remained aloof.

19 December 1953

Went to the Landesarchiv in the morning but got little studying done. Dr. Lachmann introduced me to Dr. Ernst Kaeber, the director and well-known city historian.[1] His specialty, however, is premodern Berlin, from the earliest settlements to the 16th century, and administrative history. He sent me to the Senatsbibliothek, where he already had ordered that some books be laid out for me. At the Senatsbibliothek a Herr Parzefal received me and recommended that I consult the reports they had by factory inspectors (*Gewerbeinspektoren*) and school inspectors.

In the afternoon, ate pea soup and sausage (*Erbsensuppe mit Bockwurst*) at Aschinger's for 85 pfennigs, or about 11 cents! Walked along the Kurfürstendamm, window shopping. At 5:30, just before going home, decided to have supper in a proletarian bistro near the Schlosstrasse. Pictures of prize fighters on the wall, an American

---

[1] Ernst Kaeber (1882-1961), archivist and city historian, was the editor of *Der Bär von Berlin*, the yearbook of the Verein für die Geschichte Berlins.

Coca-Cola calendar. Tables covered with linoleum. In the corner some people playing cards. At my table, two workers, furniture movers by trade, but without steady jobs (*Gelegenheitsarbeiter*). By good chance they began talking to me about the good old days under Kaiser Wilhelm II! Unfortunately it was difficult to follow them because they did not speak clearly. (In fact, they themselves said that they did not know how to talk and kept shoving each other to make their points.) But I got the gist, which was that everything had been much better before the First World War. They ate their cold cutlets with knife and fingers and the proprietress wrapped the bones in newspaper for them to take home for their dog. There was American swing music coming from the radio. On the wall hung one of the gambling machines that are so popular in Germany. The walls were dark brown, the color of strong tea. Thick lace curtains before the windows. For only DM 1.50 I got a huge plate of lentils with bacon plus a hard roll and a boiled sausage, followed by a cup of coffee.

20 December 1953

Read half of Hans Modrow's *Berlin 1900*. Quite good. But also found that I am no longer used to reading steadily for hours on end. Went to visit the Cerfs' for tea. Colonel and Mrs. Denis were there, whom I had met once before. It was quite informal because we were sitting around Jay's bed. Jay is still recovering from a small, painful operation for his abcess. He told us that the doctor at the American military hospital, a German, had been a sadist, reprimanding him for showing pain. While we were chatting, the neighbors complained about the car which the Denises had left parked outside their house. No, not because it blocked their driveway, but because it had a license plate with U.S. Forces in Germany on it. They didn't like that.

There are all kinds of license plates on cars in Berlin. "KB" stands for Kommandatura Berlin and is on all German license plates. Black plates with white letters and "BZ" are vehicles of the British occupation forces. Red plates with white letters reading "FFA" are French. The Americans have yellow plates reading "U.S. Army," green ones reading "U.S. Forces in Germany," white ones for "U.S. Mission in Germany," and again white ones for "U.S. State Department." The State Department cars which one sees around Dahlem are invariably black; sometimes they are black Volkswagen vans with a German driver and a passenger in trilby and black overcoat— looking like Dick Tracy escorting top secret documents for shipment back to Washington.

Winter 1953-54

Berlin — Neuköllu, 1st Sept 1154

Working at A ... S-Bahn ...
S-Bahn ...

21 December 1953

Went to the archives. Dr. Kaeber was very nice and invited me to his home for supper on 26 December. He also talked about his youth. He had studied in Königsberg under a Professor Krauske, and later under the famous Prussian historian Otto Hintze. After I left his office, in the reading room, Herr Köhler showed me a picture book of Berlin in 1928 and took the time to comment in detail on each photograph.

Lunch at the FU Mensa, and to pick up my auditor's card (DM 30.), then went home. In the late afternoon, Frau Henninger and her children took me to the Funkturm, Berlin's radio tower which looks like a mini-Eiffel Tower and is near Witzleben. The Christmas fair was already closed and the view from the Funkturm restaurant not particularly exciting. We had coffee at about double the normal price. Frau Henninger tried very hard to make the afternoon "gemütlich," but I was bothered no end by her German nationalist mentality, a mixture of pride and self-pity. Clearly, the Henningers believe Germany should have won the war. But for the intervention of America, they said, Germany's soldiers would have defeated England and Russia. Frau Henninger wanted to know how Americans felt about the total destruction of Germany. I brought up Warsaw, Rotterdam, Coventry, and Lidice, but was told these were only a few towns. "Think of the whole of Germany in ruins!" At the same time Frau Henninger never fails to remind me that she has some American relatives, has once been to New York, and knows some English. She told me she could never really "hate" Americans because she does have some American blood in her veins.

I found a way to leave the Henningers at the Schöneberg S-Bahn station. It was snowing a bit and I strolled around in the empty dark streets. Around 8:30 I dropped into a bistro to order sausage and a hard roll and some hot soup. An old man motioned to me to sit down with him near the oven and soon began talking to me. His name was Max. He had lived in Berlin for 47 years, he told me. Learned the trade of *Eisendreher* (iron turner?) in Silesia. At age 17, comrades had advised him to go to the great city, to Berlin, where working conditions were better, the trade unions stronger, and the workmen more united. So he had come to Berlin and joined the Metal Workers' Union. The first two weeks he had been unemployed, then the municipal employment agency had found him a job. Outsiders were often preferred to native Berliners because they accepted lower wages. But while he was a good unionist, he was still critical of the Social Democratic Party. In both world wars, he said, the Social Democratic politicians betrayed the people to the capitalists, and today Ollenhauer, Schumacher, and Neumann are doing the same again. By contrast, the SPD under the old leaders Bebel and Wilhelm Liebknecht before 1914 had really united the working people against their exploiters.

Our conversation was constantly interrupted by a young tramway worker, Gerhard, 33 years old and slightly drunk. Gerhard called himself an idealist: "Let all men be friends!" he shouted. On the other hand, he also wanted the Germans to stand united against the outside world. Every nation on earth stands united when the fatherland is in danger, he said, only the German nation does not. Consequently, Germany has lost two world wars. The Germans have not yet learned to be united, they must learn it now! His opinion of Hitler: Hitler had his good points. Gerhard had been an airplane mechanic for the Luftwaffe during the war, earning 68 marks a week. Hitler's nationalism had been alright. His only mistakes had been the Jews and the war. And why had he, Gerhard, fought for Hitler? "Befehl!" he answered. In Germany you don't go against orders.

In the meantime Max grew quite agitated. He also began to shout: "Hitler? Hitler was a Lump (scoundrel)!" The Führer was evil incarnate. His rise to power had meant there would be world war. But then Max suddenly switched and attacked the Americans too. The Americans? They have destroyed our homes, killed our women and children. Never shall Germany join forces with the U.S.A. "Deutschland mach dich frei! Mach dich frei!" (Germany, be independent!), he cried over and over again. He insisted on paying for my coffee. This is the first time a poor, simple workman has invited me to something.

P.S.: I was astonished by the knowledge of both men. Gerhard mentioned Queen Victoria in passing, and when Max said something about the Russo-Japanese War, he immediately knew: "Yes, Port Arthur, 1907 [sic]." Max, in turn, proudly brought up some names of Chinese rivers and towns, tapping his forehead with his finger, "ich weiss! ich weiss!" (I know, I know!). And then I remembered how the old worker in Schlosstrasse two nights ago had spoken a few words of Danish and promptly claimed that he was bilingual.

23 to 26 December1953

I was too busy to write these last few days. I worked in the archive up till Christmas Eve at noon. There is a Frau Dr. Täuber compiling a catalogue of Berlin pictures in Herr Siewert's room. She is an old

Estonian who rolls her r's very much and hotly argues the thesis that all the minority nationalities in the USSR want to break away from Greater Russia. She thinks it shameful how the West persists in identifying these nationalities as "Russians." She lent me three samples of a paper published by ABN (Antibolschewistischer Block der Nationen). All trains arriving in East Berlin from Poland are riddled with Polish partisan bullets, she claimed. The UPA (the nationalist Ukrainian army, or "Bandera") is very active and an underground Ukrainian government is in telegraphic contact with the West.

Herr Köhler reveals himself as a very knowledgeable man. But I don't understand why he says Germans are not militaristic at all, and that they are individualists. According to him, the Germans have a hard time explaining themselves to foreigners; such are the circumstances since the "Zusammenbruch" of 1945. But he concedes the Germans overdo their zealousness for work. We also talked about Christmas, which Koehler described as the one occasion in Germany when grownups and children join to form one community.

I spent the afternoon and evening of the 24th walking around the Kurfürstendamm and Joachimstaler Strasse. Not much to see. A vast field of rubble (*Schrottgelände*) around Nollendorfplatz shows the devastating effect of Allied bombing in all its grimness. Few people were on the streets, probably out for some last-minute purchases. Something I never saw anywhere before struck me as very nice: candles in all the windows in remembrance of those who have not yet returned from war captivity. "To show them the way home," someone explained to me.

I was home by about half past nine. Sat up with the Henningers in their living room, playing Halma. They gave me as Christmas presents a Christmas cake (*Stollen*), a *bunter Teller* (plate full of cookies), and a book, Paul Weiglin's *Bilderbuch von Alt-Berlin*, which was very nice of them.

The next day, Christmas Day, I worked in my room in the morning. For lunch I was invited by the Henningers, and again for cocoa in the afternoon. Later in the evening I invited them to the movies to see Walt Disney's *Peter Pan*, and when we came back we still had supper and played rummy till midnight.

Saturday, the 26th, was a rewarding if exhausting day. In the morning I rode the S-Bahn to Wedding, the classical working-class district. The streets looked indeed shabby, especially the famous Ackerstrasse, which, although quite wide, is flanked by dingy tenement houses three to four stories high, with dirty doorways, rickety staircases, shabby front walls. I saw children with curiously high cheekbones and slant eyes. I also noted the large number of funeral agents, hospitals and old people's homes, the big crematorium, and lots of shops selling coffins. Other stores looked well stocked, though the wares were unsophisticated. The last time I had seen a European industrial town was five years earlier in Czechoslovakia: Plzeň looked like this. I visited some of the hospitals which lay already outside of town, the Jewish Hospital (founded 1914) and the Lange-Schucke Stiftung at the corner of Reinickendorfer Strasse and Iranische Strasse. The latter is really an old people's home. Notices tell people they must *carry* their bicycles indoors, not wheel them, so as to keep the floors clean. Long corridors with lots of doors, like a boardinghouse. It was dark, very quiet, and smelled of dampness.

Before I forget, I should write down that I also went to see the newly reopened "Schrippenkirche" (bread-roll church) in the Ackerstrasse. The church was already closed. It looks fairly new, of red brick, with green doors, away from the street and hidden by a wooden fence. An old woman took me up to see a nun. I discovered I had landed in a home for young girls (*Mädchenpensionat*) and exactly at lunchtime to boot, which explains why Mother Superior was anxious to get rid of me as quickly as possible by simply thrusting a newspaper clipping into my hand: all I needed to know about this institution was in that article, she told me. The Mädchenpensionat belongs to the Innere Mission, an Evangelical organization dedicated to missionary work among the poor, whose chief offices are in Dahlem.

Speaking of nuns, I wanted to look for the Dankeskirche (Thanksgiving Church, dating from the 1890s) on the Wedding Platz and asked the way in a bistro. The innkeeper was 75 years old and an old Weddinger. He said there was no use my looking— the church and the famous restaurant Fürst Blücher were destroyed in the war. His wife, though she knew much less about the local history of Wedding, was distressed to see that I got so little help from her husband. When I offered to buy him a glass of beer, she said no, he shouldn't drink, and then suggested that I might buy her a schnaps instead. I did.

I walked around the place where the Gasthof Fürst Blücher once stood and discovered in a nearby building a kind of nursing service run by a religious order, the Schwesternstation der Dankeskirchengemeinde, Fennstrasse, just off Wedding Platz. I simply climbed the three flights of stairs— old and creaky— and found myself in the Konfirmandenzimmer, a large, empty room with stacks of chairs on both sides and a large painting of Jesus Christ, the only picture saved from the destroyed Dankeskirche. Two nuns sat down to talk to me. They were very kind but I think also afraid of me, and they wouldn't tell me their names. As I looked around in the dim light coming through the windows, I saw in a far corner a stand with a wash bowl and a large pitcher. Was this the first aid station, I wondered? The sisters gave me the names and addresses of a few people who may tell me more about Wedding workers and religion. They suggested a visit to their chapel in Grenzstrasse.

However, I landed in the Reinickendorfer Strasse. I was curious to see whether I would still find the remains of the Arbeiterkolonie at number 66, an old workhouse that the church ran before the First World War. I got into a dark but expansive courtyard, asphalted, with grey houses in front and a reddish brick building in the rear. Trashcans, a burnt-out petrol pump, a few sheds. It all looked abandoned except that a notice pointed to the existence inside of some municipal office (*Ausgleichungsamt*), and a factory making work clothes. A few noisy youths hung around near the two archways leading to the street. And here I met an old man, Wilhelm Küpper, 71 years old, who said he is the only surviving member of the former workers' colony (it closed in 1922). When the Arbeiterkolonie flourished, its inmates produced brushes. Küpper still is a brushmaker. He was glad to talk to me and pointed out the windows where the workrooms had been, the dormitory, and where in the yard there had stood green trees before the war.

So it was altogether a successful trip. Only I nearly landed in the Soviet sector on my way back to the center of town. I walked up a wrong street and suddenly saw myself facing a parked dark red Vopo car. I went and stood at the next tram stop, pretending to wait. After a while I made as if I were impatient because no streetcar came and walked back from where I had come.

At 4 it got dark. There was no point in returning to Steglitz since I was invited to supper at Dr. Kaeber's in Moabit. So I went to see a German movie, *Aus dem Tagebuch einer Verliebten* (Diary of a woman in love), which had gotten quite good reviews in the *Neue Zeitung*. The film was very good, too. The story was set in the present, briefly touched on the end of the war (a scene of American soldiers arriving in a German town) and was remarkable for its overall restraint. Sometimes funny, more serious towards the end, it avoided extreme passion or melodrama. The hero in the story had won a Toto prize and started to spend the money before cashing his ticket. But it did not turn out that he had misread the number and won nothing after all, or lost his ticket, or some such cheap movie trick.

I arrived at Dr. Kaeber's home at exactly 7:30. He lives with his wife on the third floor of a tenement house in Dortmunder Strasse number 6— the only house in this street without bomb damage. We were six at table. Besides Kaeber and his wife (a very delicate, handsome old lady) there was a middle-aged woman who boards with them, and Dr. Graber, an archivist from Kiel, and his wife. We had a mayonnaise salad, sandwiches, and tea with rum. Later I was introduced to poppyseed cake (Mohnkuchen*).* Very agreeable evening. What was most interesting is that these are the first Germans I have met who have said that the German people, at least in the West, live in too much comfort considering their responsibility for the war. Dr. Kaeber was dismissed from the archive when Hitler came to power and his books were not published. I assume Dr. Graber shares Kaeber's political views. They are close friends. I went home at ten o'clock.

Sunday to Tuesday, 27 to 29 December 1953

Had a hangover. Couldn't do much work. Bad weather. Heard that both Mrs. Denis and Dr. Lachmann had tried to invite me on the 26th, which was very kind of them. Was so bored I went to see the movie *Der Feldherrnhügel* in the Schlosstrasse for 1 mark (cheap by American standards). It was quite a good comedy, satirizing the Austro-Hungarian army before 1914 and Prussian militarism. Monday and Tuesday were better. Lots of mail from Professors Rudin and Turner, from Yale friends and the Yale Alumni report of Griswold. I went to Charlottenburg on Tuesday to get more information from the Amt für Denkmalpflege, but there was little to find. On the way home (it was nearly 4 o'clock) I decided to get lunch and an innkeeper sent me to a butcher shop where, he told me, they had a *Mittagstisch*. Curious, I followed his advice and made a great discovery. The place is Ferdinand Erlebach, Wilmersdorfer Strasse 152a, Charlottenburg. I have long wondered where the workers of Berlin eat when they don't eat at home, since bistros usually only have hot sausage and rolls, and restaurants are too expensive. (I never see workers in restaurants.) Now, this Mittagstisch was above a butcher's shop. Outside the shop, at the window on the first floor, you see a sign reading "Mittagstisch." You go through the (smelly) shop, up a dark, rickety wooden staircase, and come to a big room. The ceiling is low, the walls are thin wooden boards with the upper half painted white, the lower part with a pattern of green leaves to create the illusion of wall paper. Iron hooks on the wall for overcoats. Linoleum on the floor. Lots of elderly spinsters and widowers quietly sitting at simple tables eating soup out of huge bowls and plates, with lots of potatoes and sauerkraut. The submissiveness of the guests, the poverty of the surroundings (some preposterous plants on impossible flower stands in front of a dirty window through which one sees the rears of houses) all give you the feeling of being in a charitable institution. No drinks are served. You get a free plate of hot soup (quite good) and a tin spoon. Today it was *Graupensuppe*. I ordered a *Hausmacherblutwurst* and got a big blood sausage with lots of potatoes and sauerkraut and the whole meal cost only 1 mark, or 25 American cents. In the U.S. it would have cost 75 or 95 cents. I tried to ask the waitress whether such Mittagstische were a common institution in Berlin, but she had no time for conversation.

30 to 31 December 1953

Long conversation with Köhler. He was a soldier with the Wehrmacht in Italy, taken prisoner by the British. Has some anti-British prejudices ("Englishmen are disdainful of other nations") and thinks the German people are misunderstood abroad. The Germans were never as tightly controlled under the Nazis as are the Russians under Soviet rule, he said, and the inmates in the German concentration camps were for the most part the rotten elements which surface in any society following a revolution.

Silvester (New Year's Eve) I spent mostly at home, reading. Then in the evening I went to the Titania Palast to listen to Beethoven's Ninth. The RIAS orchestra and the choir of St. Hedwig's Church were conducted by Ferenc Fricsay. The audience seemed primarily from the lower- and middle-middle class; no workers. The performance was quite excellent; I have never heard it so distinctly and clearly before, sitting only four rows from the orchestra pit and able to observe the fingering and bowing of the first violins very closely. The timpani seemed overly loud from so near, however. The cello players reminded me of a group of submissive hounds as they looked up to the conductor.

I went into a Gaststube for a coffee on my way home. It was in Schützenstrasse, a working-class street. There was accordion music and dancing, the public and the waitresses wore paper hats, it was mildly hilarious. I sat at a table with an old worker who was very polite to me, and was accosted by a man who was drunk but also of a friendly disposition. Home by ten past 9, I found the Henninger children trying to throw a party without much success, so I bought a bottle of red wine and after that it was quite good fun till 1 a.m., when we all went to bed.

6 January 1954

Little has happened, and so I haven't written for nearly a week. Visited the archives, had a snowball fight with the Henningers, the weather was beastly cold.

But today was exciting. Jay, Carol, and I finally took the tour through the Soviet sector with the American military bus. The bus left Truman Hall (the PX store) at 12:30. So that I could travel as an American, Carol produced litle Randolph's American passport for me to hold in my hand. Fortunately, no one askcd to see the inside of the passport. First the tour took us through the Western sectors: Steglitz, Tempelhof, Schöneberg, Neukölln. Then we crossed the river Spree and entered Treptow, which is already the Russian sector. One is allowed to take pictures as long as they do not include military and semi-military installations, Vopos and Russian soldiers. We stopped 20 minutes at the Russian "Garden of Remembrance" in Treptow, a park where 26,000 Russian soldiers lie buried. There is a stone figure of a Russian mother in mourning, the entrance to the graves is flanked by two huge Soviet flags carved in red marble and two figures of Russian soldiers with bowed heads, kneeling, helmets in arms. At the end stands a mausoleum topped by a figure of a Russian soldier holding a child in one arm and a sword in the other. Lots of inscriptions ("glory, glory, glory") carvings of Stalin's sayings in stone obelisks (references to "faschistische Schurken" (fascistic scoundrels). Inside the mausoleum is a fresco, on the ceiling a huge model of the "order of victory," and a book containing the names of 26 great heroes. Vopos were guarding the mausoleum, uncouth youths with long hair.

We went through other parts of East Berlin. Everywhere evidence of destruction. A huge bunker full of shell holes, the Ost-Bahnhof (renovated), Alexanderplatz, HO[1] stores and, finally, Stalin Allee. The contrast between this showcase boulevard and the rest of the city is stupendous. Huge yellow stone edifices with elaborately decorated windows and balconies, looking like Moscow or a resort hotel on the Crimea. Behind the Allee, ruined houses. We passed the Museums-Insel, saw the remains of the Reich chancellory and Hitler's bunker.

Then we stopped at the Russian war memorial in Tiergarten. The two Russian soldiers challenged a GI trying to photograph them. There was also a Herr Paul Erdmann, 77 years old, who introduced himself to us as tour guide. To Wannsee for dinner, and then home.

7 to 8 January 1954

So little is happening that I am slipping behind with my diary again. Work in the archives. Herr Siewert and Herr Köhler warned me against being too careless regarding safety in Berlin. They think I could be kidnapped in the Wedding if I go too near the Soviet sector, and that if I ran into an identity control in the East sector I would have no chance of returning to the West sector. I would not be held by the Vopo long, they said, but handed to the Russians in Karlshorst immediately. "Dann ist's aus!" said Siewert, "die erschiessen Sie noch am selben Tag."[2] Both think that since foreigners are all watched in East Berlin, my presence would be noted. And if whoever observes me sees that I am not being followed, he will ask the Vopo to stop me and demand my papers. They almost frightened me with their talk.

Lots of snow. Snow fight with Esther and her little girlfriend, Helga. Talked to Rena, the maid. She thinks working is fun: "Arbeit macht das Leben süss." I think she is being exploited here.

IO January 1954

Have caught a cold, with lots of tummy ache. Went to the Cerfs' for tea. Lots of guests: the *New York Times* correspondent Walter

---

[1]HO: Handels-Organisation is the communist trade organization.
[2]"That's the end. They'll shoot you the same day!"

Sullivan and his wife, both of whom are fond of China and were very charming. Walter has traveled through Hunan and Sinkiang provinces, and lived in Shanghai under the Communists in 1949. There were a number of half-German, half-American couples, among them Mr. Isham, whose wife is German. Isham told me the head of the visa section at the U.S. consulate, a Miss Ellis, is skeptical about my chance of obtaining an American visa ("Where would he go after he finishes his studies at Yale?"), and consequently that I should go and see a Mr. Bradford at the consulate and tell him Isham sent me. Bradford would be more sympathetic. A German by the name of Gabriel (*sic?*) said he would help me get in touch with Rudolf Stammer, the socialist, and another couple gave me a ride in their jeep to the S-Bahn station. Late at night, Jay rang up twice, very kind of him, first to ask how I felt, second to invite me to come along on a visit to the Siemens Schuckert Works, makers of electrical appliances, on Wednesday. Hooray.

II January 1954

Worked well in the archives. Found lots of material on the history of the Siemens Works. Later went to the offices of Berlin's most important paper, *Die Neue Zeitung*, to ask for more information on puppet theaters because they had brought an article on *Puppenspiele* two days ago, which I had found delightful. I was disappointed to find out that puppet shows are not given by old professionals but by the art institute (Hochschule für Bildende Künste) in Schöneberg. There is to be a performance next week; maybe I can go and see it.

The *Neue Zeitung* has its offices near Breitenbachplatz. Parked in front of this modern but cheap building were only American cars with green plates, "U.S. Forces in Germany," and a black "U.S. State Department" van. The paper represents the American viewpoint to the German public.

While I was there I also asked in the newspaper archives about materials on Berlin around the turn of the century but was told to try the Ullstein publishing house in Tempelhof. On the way home I bought the novel which Köhler had recommended, Erich Wildberger's *Ring über Ostkreuz*, a Rowohlt book (1.50 marks), which deals with today's Berlin.

At the tram station Dahlem-Dorf waiting for number 40 to Birkbuschstrasse, I overheard two girls talking. One said: "Yesterday two civilians were arrested in front of our house. There were some ten cars and these two odd-looking civilians. And then they were arrested..." I wondered whether they were East Berlin residents.

After dinner in Schlosstrasse I visited Herr Kadzig and his wife in Vionvillestrasse 11/12. They live in one room about one-third the size of the room I have at the Henningers', yet three people sleep here!

Herr and Frau Kadzig and their 16-year-old granddaughter. Under the sideboard is a collapsible bed, presumably for the old couple; the girl sleeps on the couch. There was a dressing table with some eau de cologne and a cupboard. On the table was a glass bowl with old letters. Under the table at which we sat they keep their kitchen utensils. At the window, a plate with liverwurst. The clock on the wall didn't work. Frau Kadzig had no chair to sit on; she sat on a wooden box near the stove. The granddaughter, who has a job at the bakery around the corner, had very red hands. She went out after promising to be home no later than 10:30.

The conversation did not turn around old Berlin as much as I had hoped, because Kadzig only lived in Berlin for a short time before the First World War. He had been a journeyman baker (*Konditorgeselle*) in Berlin in 1905. But he presented me with a copy of the *Berliner Illustrirte* of 1937, the special number commemorating Berlin's 700th anniversary. He also gave me a postcard dating from the great inflation of 1923, with postage stamps on it costing millions of marks. His wife is quite a sweet old lady, a pensioner in her own right since she also worked throughout her life. She knows shorthand and read me a poem that she had taken down in shorthand. It dealt with the game of chess and how its rules resemble the rules in real life. She also wanted to lend me a book on Siemens, because her son worked there as a draftsman some years ago; he is now drawing for an illustrated paper in Düsseldorf.

According to Herr Kadzig, there is still much unemployment in Berlin, though older people are being retired early to make room for the youngsters coming out of school. The other day he had gone to the Kudamm to apply for a job as packer ("Rentner gesucht"). But at 7:30 a.m. the staircase was already filled with people.

I was touched by the generosity and contentment of these "little people," as they call themselves. They treated me to cider and rolls with liverwurst. The woman enjoys the view of the courtyard from her window and her freedom to take a nap or walk the streets at a time when formerly she had to be at her job. They asked me to come with them to the Titania Palast sometime. American cultural films are shown there daily free of charge.

When I got home I told Frau Henninger that I had been with the Kadzigs. "What," she exclaimed in horror, "you already know the neighbors?" (Kennen Sie schon die Nachbarn?). That reminded me of Carol's story that Frau Schenck does not consider it "fein" to associate with one's neighbors.

13 January 1954

Very crowded day. I left earlier than usual to take a train to S-Bahnhof Heerstrasse in Spandau. There I met Jay. We took the tram number 75 down Heerstrasse to Pichelsdorferstrasse and down Adam Strasse towards the prison. (This happened to be a very modern tramway with conductors seated inside a booth that has a loudspeaker.) As we passed a school, Jay suddenly said he'd like to visit it, and so we got off the car and walked in. It happened to be the Oberschule for girls, Praktischer Zweig, in Adam Strasse. We got to see the Schulrat, who sent us to the 9th grade where a lesson in *Berufskunde* (career choices) was in progress. There were about fifty girls in the class, aged about 15. Discipline was not very strict. We were introduced as two "Herren aus Amerika" who wanted to know about schools in Berlin. We were shown report books by the girls and listened to some girls reading out their essays. A young schoolmistress sat with us to explain. The girls are in their last grade, she told us; next year most of them will go to work unless they go on to middle school. In this course they discussed careers in the textile industry, in social welfare, etc., and combined their studies with visits to factories and institutions, while collecting pictures and samples to paste into their report books. Many of the girls, we were told, wanted to become salesgirls (some of them already worked after school), others wanted to become dressmakers, one a laboratory assistant in a photo shop, others kindergarten nurses or hospital nurses. None wanted to become a teacher. One of the reports we listened to dealt with the history of the International Red Cross. It was quite well done, except that the battle of Solferino (1859) was placed in the First World War. Finally the Schulrat came to see how we were doing and we left, each of us politely escorted to the main door by a little girl. Two more came running after us with a notebook that Jay had forgotten.

We went on to Spandau Prison. A red brick building surrounded by a high brick wall, close to a street. Barbed wire on the wall, barbed wire before the wall. A large sign read: Do Not Enter Fence; Guards Have Orders to Shoot. Den Zaun nicht berühren; Wachen haben Befehl zu schiessen. British soldiers armed with rifles stood on watchtowers along the wall, but there was no sentinel at the gate itself. We spoke to an American jailkeeper for a few minutes. He told us we were lucky it was not the Russians' turn to mount guard, for in the past they have seized American visitors and beaten them up. As to getting inside the prison, that was quite impossible: there was nothing to see, nothing to hear, no one to talk to. The British, too, try to keep the Spandau issue quiet and don't want to deal with anyone who might be a reporter. We left, not without first sticking our noses into a side courtyard and promptly being evicted by a German guard.

So we continued our way into Spandau itself. Past the Rathaus (which straddles part of the old moat) to roam through the narrow, provincial-looking streets of the town. There was a small open-air market where we bought hot Krakauer sausages and doughnuts (*Pfannkuchen*). We visited the local Heimatmuseum, where a Herr Müller gave us a private tour. Old chests, old swords from the 13th century, Stone Age tools, flags and emblems of medieval guilds. Many of these historical discoveries are of recent date, Müller told us, because Spandau today no longer gets the gravel it needs from the East and has to dig its own, which is a boon to anthropologists and local historians.

Unfortunately the old Nikolaikirche (built 1398) was closed, but we visited the old Spandau fortress with the famous Juliusturm, which now shelters a *Baugewerbeschule* (trade school for construction workers). Herr Siewert's acquaintance, Panin, was not there.

After a coffee we took a taxi to Siemensstadt. The car was a delightful postwar Mercedes four seater with a diesel engine, cheap and good, only rather noisy. When we arrived at the Siemens Works we were ushered into the hall of the administrative building on Nonnendamm Allee. Several hundred people were assembled there: foreign students, professors and diplomats. In groups of 10 to 15, we were led by guides through the *Schaltwerk* and the *Dynamowerk* of Siemens Schuckert. Huge workshops, lots of noise, but everywhere very clean, brightly lit, some with cheerful walls painted cream-color or pink. Most of the explanations were too technical for me. I did note, though, that the workday was $8\,^1/2$ hours long and the average pay 1.25 marks per hour. Siemens is not as highly mechanized as are American plants, we were told, since its customers are less interested in standardized products and more in equipment specially made for specific purposes.

The tour was followed by a reception in an ornate dining hall where, the waitress told me, workers and employers take their lunch together. There was good coffee, biscuits, cigars (I tried one), and horrible cigarettes. Two speeches: one by Herr Vockel, the official representative of the Bundesrepublik in Berlin, who wore a black eyepatch, and the other by Herr Besold, manager of the *Schaltwerk*. Besold talked about the reconstruction of this plant after 1945 and praised the British troops who had given much help. There was no discussion afterwards. By chance I talked to the head of the Indian military mission in Berlin, Mr. Mennon, who told me his cousin was on a visit in Berlin. And who was that cousin? No one else but Joy Raghavan, last seen in Prague when his father was the Indian ambassador there! So I'm invited to tea at the Indian mission tomorrow. I also made contact with the Siemens archive, where I may find some materials for my thesis.

To Wannsee with Jay to have a curry dinner with him and Carol, then home to Steglitz.

14 January 1954

Since I had to be at Charlottenburg for tea, I left in the morning to go into town. On the train I met a man who told me that, technically, the Vopo could arrest anyone they wanted on the S-Bahn even when the train traveled through the Western sectors, because the carriages and the tracks fall under East Berlin's jurisdiction. Only the Vopos wouldn't dare, for the passengers would surely interfere.

I got out at the Soviet war memorial in Tiergarten to look up Herr Erdmann, the old guide, on the chance that he had something interesting to tell me. He asked for 3 marks, but the poor man had little to say. Born in 1886, now still living in Charlottenburg, Ilsenburger Strasse 36, he stood with me in the slush just behind the barracks for Soviet officers, whispering to me while I took notes. We must have looked suspicious to any Russian looking out of the barracks window since no one could have guessed that Erdmann was feeding me nothing but standard clichés about Berlin history during the Bismarck period.

From Lehrter Bahnhof I went to Westend in Charlottenburg, and soon found the "Heinrich Zille Klause," in Sophie-Charlotte Strasse 88, so named in memory of that popular artist of the Berlin poor who died in 1929. There was a waitress there who showed me the collection of over 100 Zille drawings hanging on the walls. She told me that a few days earlier, a "Zille Cabaret" had taken place here to celebrate Heinrich's 96th birthday. Only local people had come— this is a working-class region— but there will be a repeat performance this weekend. The "Zille Freunde" (friends of Zille, originally over 100, now shrunk to 5 or 6) still gather in this pub every other Thursday after 5 p.m. to sit and talk around their Stammtisch. They keep a book. I said I would try to meet them next Thursday.

The inn was originally called "Zum Alten Dessauer," but became the "Zille Klause" in 1948. Outside there is a memorial plaque donated by the city of Berlin in 1931. The Hitler people tried to take it down for scrap metal, but it was hidden and so saved for posterity by workers ("von Arbeiterhand"). Also saved and now hung on the wall inside the pub is Zille's favorite verse: Am Tage Arbeit, ernster Wille,/ Abends einen Schluck in der Destille,/ Dazu ein bischen kille-kille,/ Das hält munter Heinrich Zille.[1]

I was told Zille's son lived upstairs, so I climbed up but he was busy and I was told to come back at 3:30 p.m.

I went for a walk through Charlottenburg, had a coffee at a cafe in Wilmersdorfer Strasse, had a look at the Zillestrasse, and finally landed at the Bezirksamt Charlottenburg der Stadt Berlin, Abteilung Gesundheitswesen (Department of Public Health), in Gierkezeile. I went up and was introduced to a Frau Dr. Thiele, who seemed to be the chief of the institute. We had a pleasant talk for about half an hour. No, there were no records on the standard of health among

---

[1]Roughly translated: "In the day time honest labor,/ In the evening a glas in the pub./ Add a little innocent frill(e)/ And you'll make happy Heinrich Zill(e)."

workers left from the years before the First World War, Frau Thiele told me, and suggested I should try the Health Department (Landesgesundheitsamt) in Invalidenstrasse 52, near the Lehrter Bahnhof. Then we talked about Berlin. Frau Thiele likes Berlin and wouldn't want to leave here. (Outside the window one could see ruins, a grey sky, slush, drizzly rain.) Like so many people I've met, she thought the Berliners have "'ne grosse Schnauze und ein gutes Herz" (Berliners are brash but they mean well). During the war she lived in the western part of Germany and was homesick for Berlin all the time. West Germans, in her opinion, are narrow-minded, and their cultural ties are with France rather than with Germans to the east of the Elbe. The role which Berlin has played since the end of the war has deepened her attachment to the city. Charlottenburg, in particular, has gone through difficult times: its population has become more mixed in recent years and though the number of deaths from tuberculosis is declining (the worst years were 1945-47), the absolute number of TB cases is increasing.

Frau Dr. Thiele's office is funded by the city of Berlin. It caters to the elderly and subsidizes needy pensioners and refugees from the East. (One really ought to study the many provisions available in West Berlin for people coming from across the frontier, from the refugee camps to the special rates offered by movie houses to Ostbewohner.)

After I left Frau Thiele, I went back to Sophie-Charlotte Strasse to visit Walter Zille and his wife. Fourth floor. We sat down in an old-fashioned dining room stuffed with furniture and nicely heated by a big tile stove. There was a large buffet and, of course, lots of Zille drawings on the walls. The waitress in the "Zille Klause" had said Walter had no job and just lived on the sale of his father's pictures. Walter said that his father had died a poor man ("down to his last shirt"), but he himself obviously is comfortably off. I took shorthand notes as he talked. Then he sold me two small pencil sketches for 10 marks. Originally, he had demanded 20, adding that they were really worth 150 marks each, not counting 50 marks reproduction fee. I don't know why in the end he asked only 10 marks. If all he says is true, I made the best bargain of my life. But probably it is not true.

I had to hurry to make it to the Mennons' in time and took a taxi. They live in the big villa belonging to the Indian mission in Berlin, which also is accredited to the Bonn government. The party consisted of an Indian army officer just arrived from London and now touring Germany, Mrs. Mennon (very youthful and charming), her two little boys, aged 5 and 2 (their eyes were rimmed in black apparently to keep them cool), Joy Raghavan, and a German woman who is married to an Indian and now works at the Indian legation in Berne. Very pleasant tea with some Indian dishes and English cigarettes kept in a sandalwood box which lent them a particular aroma (quite unintentionally, I believe). The conversation was polite and pleasant, not profound, but then it would have been impolite to ask searching questions and in any case I was dog-tired. Since the Mennons are close friends of the Sullivans I hope I shall see more of them. They have a Volkswagen painted like a British military vehicle.

15 January 1954

Got up early and waited for Jay at Steglitz S-bahnhof to go to Tempelhof. From there by no. 98 tram to Marienfelder Strasse where the Central Refugee Organization for all Berlin has its headquarters: the Zentrale Notaufnahme. It is in a suburban area. You see factories, open unbuilt land, housing blocks dating from the 1930s, and you can even see some open fields. The tram does not go so far, the road is bad, there are few shops. Berliners call this "j.w.d." (*janz weit draussen*, or far out of town).

The Refugee Center is a newly constructed housing settlement, meant for private families as soon as German reunification has put an end to the refugee problem. We saw a Mr. Ganzhow (?) who connected us with a Herr Exner. Exner answers his telephone by saying, "Fürsorger Exner, Marienfelder Strasse!" When we came he was just talking to a twenty-four year-old refugee, Ernst Gries, whose admission process as a refugee had begun on 15 October last. As far as I can gather, he wanted to leave this camp so he can move to another one in Wannsee, Am Sandwerder no. 33, for which he had become eligible on reaching age twenty-four. (His birthday was yesterday.) He wants to be moved, he said, to avoid being disturbed. He is a member of an underground movement and has important papers to protect.

His readiness to talk about his secret work seemed to me to point to some immaturity on his part, a wish to impress. He showed Jay and me his membership card from the Association of the Victims of Stalinism (Vereinigung der Opfer des Stalinismus), which he obtained for having been in a Soviet concentration camp. Last October he fled from the island of Rügen. Herr Exner also thinks Gries is exaggerating his importance in the resistance group. However, Gries assured us the group could not function without him.

After we left we had a long talk and a guided tour with Exner. There was a block for boys (Haus M), one for girls, and one for grownups. There was a block where the Americans put refugees they wanted to interrogate more, a quarantine for people infested with vermin, a quarter for the sick (the seriously ill are sent to hospitals), a communal kitchen and dining hall (very nice), a kindergarten (only for daytime but very beautiful, for 100 to 150 children, built by the Reuter-Stiftung) and a security office (Block "P," see later). Exner told us these curious statistics: 20% of the refugee youths want to marry: 14% of these have brides when they arrive, the rest of them quickly find someone to get engaged to in the waiting room.

The place is very new. It was first opened 10 weeks ago. The greatest number of refugees (ca. 1,000 a day) came during the 12 months before the uprising of 17 June, 1953. After 17 June and with the four-power conference now approaching, the number of fugitives has greatly fallen off. People in the East are once more hopeful about the future.

There are spies among the refugees. Posters in every building warn you not to reveal your name, your former home address, and your future destination to strangers. *Spitzels* are seldom caught and difficult to convict— mere suspicion will not do. Spies also usually have the best credentials.

Most people come across the border for economic reasons; few are moved by political principles, though economic difficulties are often the result of political circumstances. For example, economic sabo- teurs. There was one here recently who had stolen food worth about 250 East marks from a HO store. Young people often come to escape the "Dienst für Deutschland," a compulsory labor service demanded of young men betwen 16 and 18. It is a convenience to the state: it gets cheap labor and can indoctrinate its youth at the same time.

Consequently, all refugees are classified as either A or B. Class A is for genuine political refugees who have come because of "danger to life and limb" (*drohende Gefahr für Leib und Leben*). They get better treatment and have some legal claims to compensation for losses sustained by coming to the West. Class B refugees, by contrast, only get assistance to settle in West Germany. There are also refugees who are refused recognition as either A or B. These are sent to a permanent camp (*Stammlager*) here in Berlin. "Refused" means none of the West German *länder* is willing to receive this particular individual. But no refugee is ever sent back to the East, not even a criminal on the run from the police, though the Western police may prosecute such an individual.

The camps are financed by the Bundesrepublik (80%), and by Berlin (20%). Donations are received from other sources as well. The buildings were subsidized by American Marshall aid.

When refugees arrive in West Berlin, the police first take them to Marienfelder Strasse. Here they receive their *Laufzettel* which tells them where to report to for medical checkup, X-rays, the *Sichtungsstelle* (Allied intelligence), and for their *Zuständigkeit* (their claim to the right of residence somewhere in Germany). The Laufzettel includes visits to welfare agencies, the German police, and finally representatives of one or more of the *länder* in West Germany where they might setttle. If everythings goes well they will find themselves, two weeks later, at the airport (*Flugstelle*) boarding a plane to West Germany. During these 14 days they are housed in barracks outside Marienfelde, usually not as good quarters as these here.

Block "P" is the block where the French, British, and Americans screen the fugitives. The Allies can stop the processing for any refugee before he even reaches the German authorities. There was quite a "cloak and dagger" atmosphere in Block "P." We got in and spoke to a Mr. Mertens (the chief American officer, Storm, was not in) and he allowed us to move freely in the camp and to question people if they wanted to talk. "Only don't come near *our* block!" he asked us, and locked the door after we left.

On the way home from Marienfelde Jay and I went to the Ullstein Haus to look into the situation of the archives there. The Archivleiter is called Herr Ellendt. Jay found more for his thesis on the FDJ than I for mine, but I was told to come back next week. We did some shopping on Tempelhoferdamm, then stopped in Steglitz, where Jay bought himself a black Loden overcoat.

16 January 1954

Called Joy Raghavan but he said he had to stay at home to look after Mrs. Mennon who was not feeling well. Worked at home. In the afternoon, decided to go to the Wedding to join the tour through the main street car depot (*Hauptbetriebsbahnhof*) of the Berlin transport corporation (BVG) in the Müllerstrasse. Disappointing, since it was a rather superficial guided tour. But there were some interesting observations I could make. The tour was organized by an Arthur Fleischer, a folksy local historian (*Heimatforscher*). He has a regular program on the radio in which he always talks on some Berlin topic. Last time, he spoke about Berlin's oldest quarters (Alt-Berlin). Fleischer looked crude and vulgar, and actually had nothing to contribute to this tour of Berlin's tramways, except that he collected the fee of 50 pfennigs. He nevertheless was immensely popular among the older ladies, who craned their necks to get a good look of him. Most people seemed lower-class, many with children, families of BVG employees, lonely spinsters. Fleischer told some jokes but I did not care to get to know him.

We climbed into trams and were given a very elementary lecture about them, but the audience liked it. Old women were competing like schoolchildren to be the first with the right answer to some easy questions. I paid more attention to the coming and going of the BVG crews. Male and female conductors were checking in at the big entrance hall, counting the money in their big leather purses, drawing their next day's assignments. One of the engineers told me it takes several weeks of instruction and two examinations to become a tramway driver, but that otherwise no previous training was needed.

My ride home by streetcar took two hours. I went via Ernst-Reuter Platz, which I hadn't seen as yet. Ate at the "Berliner Kindl" in the Schlosstrasse and got home around 8:30, dead tired.

Sunday, 17 January 1954

Read most of the day, got rather bored. Marvelous weather outside: mild, with pieces of blue sky now and again, the streets grey and brown, and the air very pure. Everything is seen in sharp outline. I had a stroll in the Stadtpark not far from my digs in the afternoon, and coffee at a Konditorei. In the evening, Mrs. Henninger asked me to come and listen to Wagner's *Flying Dutchman* over radio RIAS and gave me a cup of tea plus a *Stulle*. We also heard the news. The foreign ministers of the four powers are going to meet in the American sector and the Soviet sector here in Berlin, alternating every week. And Djilas in Yugoslavia has been kicked out of the Communist party for advocating more lenient party discipline.

19 January 1954

Yesterday I was at the archives, where I learnt that Köhler is not coming back and that he will be replaced by Frau Dr. Täuber. Köhler had been engaged for only six months under the emergency program (*Notstandsprogramm*) financed by the European Recovery Program (ERP). This is a program that offers unemployed Berliners a job for half a year every year. The money comes from America. Koehler will probably have a hard time maintaining himself during the coming months. Poor man. Berlin looks so prosperous on the outside. Sometimes one forgets how many of its inhabitants are in distress.

Today I went to Siemensstadt to look up Herr Dipl. Ing. Eisele. Eisele is a charming man, director of public relations (*Werbeleiter*) of Siemens Schuckert, also chief of protocol. (He advised me that, whenever I wanted to look up a firm in Berlin, I should ask for the *Werbeleitung*.) Eisele was talking to a distinguished-looking elderly gentleman in black, who designs advertisements for Siemens. The two men were drinking coffee and offered me some too. Then we went upstairs to the fourth floor, the Archiv-Bücherei, where a Fräulein Lade took charge of me and showed me brochures and books about the history of Siemens and of the Berlin metal industry. Then we went to another archive on the second floor, where a Herr Dr. Heintzenberg showed me rows and rows of empty book shelves because the archive is in the process of being moved to Munich where a Siemens museum will be opened in May. But he still has manuscripts on the family history of Siemens and of prominent staff members who had made notable contributions to the firm's development. For questions about welfare provisions and work conditions, he said, I must talk to a Frau Doktor Weber, who today was attending a session of the labor arbitration court (*Arbeitsgericht*). I went to speak to the *Werkschutzleiter* (head of the factory police), and he also recommended that I talk with Weber.

At the Maison de France (3 Feb., 1954)

THE ALLIES IN BERLIN

Allied Control Council, Kathreinerhaus (1 Feb., 1954)

Sargent Lamb of
the Anchor Service Club.

US Military buses have
their own stops.

Herr Eisele had reserved two seats at the Siemens restaurant and invited me to lunch. He called it a snack (*Imbiss*), but it was a banquet. There were 3 kinds of wine and sherry, soup, Sauerbraten, dessert, coffee and cakes, followed by cigars and cigarettes. It rather overwhelmed me. Eisele was the perfect host, chatting about the Chinese poet Li Tai Po and about his relations with the Vopos when he drives his car through the Eastern zone. He seemed to have all the time in the world. We were alone in a small dining room reserved for guests.

After lunch I worked at the Archiv-Bücherei. At 5 p.m. I went back to Eisele who introduced me to Dr. Kurt Busse, editor of the factory magazine. Busse promised to draw up a 20-point questionnaire with which I could interview old workers of Siemens. He even said he would pay me for a good report on their reminiscences. I left very happy after promising to be back soon to see Frau Dr. Weber and also a Fräulein Thomas, who is in charge of welfare work.

I left with two books that were given to me: Werner von Siemens's *Lebenserinnerungen*, and Karl Burhenne's, *Werner Siemens als Sozialpolitiker*. I also borrowed a few books from Fräulein Lade. She was on the same train as I. To my astonishment, as soon as we were outside Siemens, she told me that she didn't like working at Siemens at all ("I'd rather bite off all my fingers than stay there any longer!") and that she was planning to emigrate to Brazil. I made my way to the Hochschule für Politik to meet Jay and Carol. I had told them about a puppet show that was to take place there. Alas, they made the mistake of going to the Hochschule für Bildende Künste instead, so we missed one another.

Everyday I meet people who discuss Berlin's outlook for the future. Today I had heard Eisele remark to Busse, that Berliners have developed a sense of inferiority towards West Germans. The West Germans show so little concern for the Berliners' struggle to remain free. To me he said that he had faith in Berlin's future "even if I have to force myself to believe in it!" Yet he knows that Siemens is quietly shifting its assets from Berlin to West Germany. Whenever the Vopos stop his car for border inspection they ask him how soon Siemens will abandon Berlin, and Eisele always denies that Siemens will move. "But then, Herr Doktor, why do you travel so often to Erlangen?" the communist policemen will ask. "Don't forget," Eisele then answers, "I drive just as often from Erlangen to Berlin!"

20 January 1954

Worked at home, then went to the colloquium at the FU. Met Klaus Androwsky there, a young man who got his B.A. from the University of Kentucky and teaches English at the German-American Library in Zehlendorf. He invited me to come and talk to a conversation group that he leads on Mondays.

For dinner I went to Jay and Carol. Splendid meal. Randolph can already crawl around and take cans of baby food from the bottom shelves.

At 8:15, our friend Ernst Gries arrived. He came in a raincoat made in East Germany and wore a small silver badge on his lapel, apparently the insignia of some anticommunist organisation. He brought a wad of anticommunist materials: an envelope full of leaflets, an illustrated paper with the photo of some film star on the cover and political diatribes inside, and a fake letter signed Wilhelm Pieck, president of the German Democratic Republic, in which Pieck says such things as "I am glad to see the exploitation of the German people for the good of my Soviet fatherland." In this letter butter is referred to as "Butter: check your dictionary (*siehe Lexikon*)." Also he brought a comic strip history of the KPdSU(B) "not written by I. W. Stalin" with some very good cartoons. One showed Pieck, Grotewohl, and Ulbricht in a boxcar being sent to the Soviet Union: "The last of the reparation payments." Ernst said he himself had thought up the text of some of the leaflets.

Ernst next filled us in about the many independent anticommunist organizations in Berlin. There is the VPO, or Association of Political Refugees from the East (Vereinigung Politischer Ostflücht-linge), to which he himself belongs. The VPO operates openly as a public assistance and information service, only its anticommunist propaganda work is underground. Gries, who belongs to the propaganda group, is leader of a team of 10 men aged between 23 and 43. He only knows his immediate superior. His cover name is "Danzig," hence his group is called Gruppe Danzig. Every man is known by the name of a river: Garonne, Ems, etc. They know little about each other, particularly because they come from very different walks of life: one is a commercial employee, another an electrician, one a driver, and several are working for the East German government. Gries is not sure where the organization gets its money, but he assumes it comes from the intelligence service (*Nachrichtendienst*) in Bonn, the American CIA, big industrial concerns like Krupp, and from the Association to Fight against Inhumanity (Kampfgruppe gegen Unmenschlichkeit).

The current mission of the Gruppe Danzig is to disseminate propaganda material and to collect information about the East sector and the Soviet zone. Bonn has a file on each member (name, cover name, age, profession, etc.) which it will check against lists of the VPO underground after Germany's reunification. All military information obtained by Danzig is directly given to the American intelligence in Fabeckstrasse, Berlin-Dahlem. Gries himself is supposed to gather information on Soviet fortifications on the island of Rügen. Only recently he was able to supply the Americans with a detailed description of one Russian barracks on that island, complete with the layout of underground tunnels and the organization of its guard.

When they do dangerous work, some of the men carry firearms. For propaganda work such precaution is not needed, of course. Indeed, sometimes outsiders can even be asked to help out. A few days ago Danzig asked ten boys from the Soziales Jugendwerk in Wannsee to help him drop leaflets. For any risky expedition you may later be asked to show proof that you actually carried out your mission. To prove that he had been to Rügen he brought back photographs of Russian posters.

One propaganda action consists of sticking leaflets on trains bound for the Eastern zone, dropping fake railway tickets with political jokes on the seats in the compartments, tossing firecrackers filled with political leaflets on passing Red Army trucks. They have rockets with 15 minute time fuses that can scatter handbills on the other side of the sector boundary (these rockets have a range of 400 meters and can also be fired from Wannsee to Potsdam). According to Gries, thousands of letters received by his group testify to the effectiveness of their propaganda. Only one person so far has been lost.

There are other organizations in Berlin. An Investigating Committee of Liberal Jurists (Untersuchungsausschuss freiheitlicher Juristen) studies every court sentence passed by an East German judge and files it away for the future day of reckoning. The same committee also provides advice to people's judges (*Volksrichter*) in the zone who are troubled by their work. Blacklists are regularly published by the Freiheitliche Juristen with the names of suspected agents of the SSD (Staatssicherheitsdienst, the East German state security service). Gries had one such black list in his wallet.

The Vereinigung der Opfer des Stalinismus have offices in Charlottenburg. Their chief mission is to collect information about missing people who are presumed being held in the East.

A Free Association of Volkspolizisten helps escaped Vopos to make their way in the West and counsels would-be defectors on the safest way to come over to the "free world."

There is even a Free Association of German-Russian Friendship in Nikolassee to help repentant members of the communist Association of German-Russian Friendship.

One curious piece of information concerned counterfeit American cigarettes made in East Germany: Camels, Chesterfields, and Pall Malls. They are superior to ordinary East German cigarettes, but not as good as the original products. Gries said the Communists first hoped to sell these cigarettes on the West German market in order to earn hard currency. When that didn't work, they decided to sell them in East Germany (1) because many people bought them, (2) because shopkeepers who sold them could be accused of black marketeering in "Amizigaretten" and nationalized.

This has been such a long entry, I might as well make it very long.

Here, finally, is Ernst Gries's vita, as told to us by himself this evening.

He was born in Berlin on 14 January 1930. During the war he received some pilot training in anticipation of serving in the Luftwaffe and later employment with Lufthansa. The war ended when he was fifteen. Together with other Hitler Youths of about his age he defended the Horst-Wessel Haus in Berlin against the Red Army during 8 days of fighting. The Russians finally blew up the house with a land mine. Gries managed to evade capture, but someone recognized him during the retreat.

After the war Gries first worked for the American Military Police. In 1947 he was arrested by the communist police on a Berlin railway station platform. During eleven weeks of interrogation they tried to make him confess he was an American spy. Because he would not confess he was finally charged with having blown up the Horst-Wessel Haus in 1945 and was sentenced to 25 years in a penal camp on the island of Rügen. There his task as a forced laborer had been to help dig a canal for the Russians (which never got finished) side by side with civilian laborers from Rügen. With some of these civilians he organized a resistance cell. In October 1953 he escaped inside the water tank of a small gauge railway. Two fellow prisoners and one of their guards, a Vopo, escaped with him. They reached the mainland and walked south into Brandenburg towards Berlin. There they ran into a large-scale manhunt by the military People's Police (kasernierte Vopo). No, this manhunt was not organized to catch them; five Czechs had just made a spectacular break across the Bohemian mountains and were also heading for the free West. Gries and his comrades had to hide near a lake. Gries alone swam across, the others tried to walk around it and have been missing since. One, Gries is sure, was shot to death.

Gries had a fiancée in 1947. (Presumably he became engaged just before his arrest.) After he had escaped, he heard that she had gone to Rügen to look for him and had been told there that he had been shot "trying to escape." Margot returned to her home (where?), was arrested, and died in prison. (He showed us a letter from Margot's sister-in-law, but this letter only mentioned Margot's death in a hospital while undergoing surgery. It said nothing about arrest and prison.) The point of telling us the story, however, was so we would understand why Gries today is such a "fanatic fighter against communism." His family lives in Australia, he says. (True? Or is this conveniently far away to make checkups more difficult?)

Gries wants us to meet some people he knows in Berlin. One is called Günther Heinrichs, a member of the FDJ Zentralrat (Central Council) and an illegal Communist party representative in West Berlin. Heinrichs and some other communists trust Gries because they don't know that he was a prisoner in Rügen. Heinrichs and he have known each other since 1947.

Finally, here is an account of a recent action carried out by the Gruppe Danzig: On 11 January 1954 they were riding the S-Bahn between Schlachtensee, Nikolassee, and Wannsee (in the Western sector), sticking leaflets on the walls of the train compartments. Because the leaflets are backed by very good glue the communist railway administration is forced to take carriages that have been "treated" like this out of circulation until the leaflets can be removed in workshops. Then two railway policemen (Trapos, or *Transportpolizei*) appeared. Gruppe Danzig retreated to the railway platform, which is still under communist jurisdiction but inside the Western sector. The Danzig men surrounded the Trapos and demanded their arms. Two West Berlin policemen watched nearby but did not intervene. They told Gries that they could do nothing unless the Trapos opened fire, in which case they would shoot them. The Trapos lost their nerve and fled into the street. There they were immediately arrested by the West Berlin police for carrying arms without a permit.

Something similar supposedly also happened today. Gries had a written report about it in his pocket that he had just finished writing before coming to the Cerfs'.

(Gries left us more bewildered than before. I wish we could talk again with Fürsorger Exner. Does *he* trust Gries??)

21 January 1954

Went to the archives. Frau Dr. Täuber showed me some local chronicles of Berlin districts. At another table sat a novelist with a small portable typewriter, copying an article he himself had written for the Lokal-Anzeiger in 1936 but had lost in the war. He was from the island of Rügen, which he had fled after refusing to write books for the communist FDJ even though the pay had been good. Of course, I immediately asked him about conditions on that island. He confirmed in general what Gries told us yesterday. The former Nazi Kraft-durch-Freude installations have been turned into impregnable fortifications, he said, and on Peenemünde the Soviets are ready to launch rockets again. It is a pity I didn't get the novelist's name; it began with L. He said he did not want to write a novel about West Berlin because today all that the West Berliners want to read is American-style detective stories.

At 11 a.m. I was taken upstairs to see Frau Dr. Quast, who heads the archive for social work (Archiv für Wohlfahrtspflege). Dr. Lachmann himself introduced me to her. On the way upstairs he told me that he had studied together with Hajo Holborn in Berlin many years ago, once taking a seminar on ancient German, another time a seminar under Friedrich Meinecke. Frau Dr. Quast also began our conversation with references to American acquaintances. "Do you know Professor Evelyn Burns at Columbia? You must greet her for me when you return to New York." She was very helpful and practically proposed herself as my research director. Her archive may be the biggest of its kind in Europe, she said. Nearly everything has been saved because the Russians were never here, but unfortunately some holdings were evacuated to East Germany during the war and these were never returned. Today the archive maintains contacts to every social welfare organization in the world.

I also visited the Meteorologisches Institut in Podbielskiallee, a branch of the Freie Universität. A rather pleasant official talked with me but, as expected, there was nothing extraordinary to learn about the Berlin climate around the turn of the century.

Mrs. Henninger's birthday party was in the afternoon. Two priests were invited to coffee and cakes. A Dr. von Arnim gave me the titles of books I should read on Adolf Stoecker, the court preacher in Berlin half a century ago; and another clergyman grumbled that the Berlin workers disliked the Christian religion because the Social Democratic party was led by Jews. Only the Catholic church had to some extent kept the workers' sympathy because the Catholic church had also been persecuted by Bismarck.

After the Kaffeeklatsch, I went off to see the Zillefreunde in the Zilleklause. Talked with them for an hour. There were four of them there and they seemed glad to have a stranger visiting them. I was treated to an orangeade. Then Heinz, a drunkard, 29 years old, started to molest me. He said that he was a Nazi and still believed in Nazi ideas. He sat down next to me and clutched my coat. He held to the strange theory that democracy was incompatible with economic prosperity. America and Britain owed their democracy to their poverty (??), while Germany, owing to her prosperity, didn't need it. The Zillefreunde saw that I found him a nuisance and tried to protect me from him. Heinz's bride also did her best to get him to come home. A workman, who had watched the scene from the other side of the room, walked over to apologize for Heinz and to congratulate me on my German. I told him there was nothing to it, I was born in Charlottenburg. Then he laughed and seemed more at ease. The Zillefreunde assured me there were not many Nazis like Heinz left in Berlin. At the same time they thought, yes, English workmen were really much worse off than German ones. They made me sign the guest book in Chinese. The fat proprietress kept stroking my back and lamenting loudly that she had not met me when I had first called a few days ago. I left hurriedly when the coast seemed clear.

26 January 1954

Haven't written for a few days. I must try to recapitulate. On Friday, I met Jay for lunch at the Mensa, where I showed him this diary because he wanted to read what I had written on Ernst Gries. He decided to borrow the whole diary. (When he returned it on Monday, he said I wasn't critical enough about the people I meet.

Well, of all the...!) We went to the FU immatriculation office, where Jay had something to do, and there met a Mr. Samuel J. Cobie, the only American lawyer with a practice in Berlin. Poker face, perpetual smile. We told him that we were looking for jobs as interpreters so we could see the four-power-conference from the inside, and Cobie sent us to see a Mr. Jules Bernard at HICOG in the Clayallee. After a stop at the Landesarchiv, where Siewert was delighted to meet Jay and showed him some newspaper clippings about the FDJ, we went to find Jules Bernard. It was the first time I had been inside the HICOG building. Dulles was expected that afternoon, his limousine was already waiting for him in the courtyard. (Big black Cadillac, flags on both fenders, blue lights and siren.) Inside HICOG much hustle and bustle in all the corridors. Jules Bernard was a slight man with a crew cut and relaxed manner. He was slumped in his chair, exhausted, while hectic conferences went on in adjoining rooms. When he heard what we wanted he sent us on to see a Mr. Cox at the Information Department. Cox was a fat, undersized man in a bright blue suit. He was kind enough— he said we should come and see him after the conference, he'd like to get to know us— and took down our names, but we doubt that he'll be able to get us into the conference. There were MP sentries standing rigidly in the corridors, the doors had fresh name tags in vivid red color, one for John Foster Dulles, one for Douglas MacArthur, Jr.

I did little over the weekend. Went over my notes and tried to sketch out my future thesis. Monday was bad: I lost my traveler's checks. All of them. On the way to the Tiergarten to return some books to the Senatsbibliothek I had noticed a clothing store that had a sale and bought a much needed coat. But when I got home I couldn't find the rest of my money! Telephoned all the places I had been to; finally went to the American Express company in Dahlem to report my loss. I was sent upstairs to the office of the "Amerikanische Kriminalpolizei," where I had to sign my written statement in the presence of an officer named Campbell. While Campbell was out for a moment I peeked at the papers on his desk. They concerned someone who had been observed climbing into a building through a window.

I walked around in the bitter cold. It was 5 p.m. and at 8 o'clock I was supposed to talk to Androwsky's English-language group in the Amerikanische Bibliothek, Goethe Strasse 35. But I didn't think I could hold out in the cold streets for three hours, so I found Androwsky to make a new date for next week.

Today things looked up again. Worked a little at the archives. Frau Dr. Täuber had some pamphlet material for Jay and two brochures for me dealing with the Ukrainian underground. She is determined to enlist me for her good cause. And when I got home I was told that my checks had been found at Leineweber, the clothing store, and were at the police station.

Called Eisele. Have to be at Siemensstadt tomorrow by 10 a.m.

27-28 January 1954

I am finding that thumbing through the *Vossische Zeitung* day after day is a real chore. After one week I still have covered only one month in 1913! I want to read every number from August 1913 to August 1914 to give me an idea of life in Berlin on the eve of the First World War.

Yesterday, however, I did not read the *Vossische Zeitung*. First I went to Siemensstadt. Eisele was as polite as always. I got to see Frau Dr. Neumann of the Archiv-Bücherei, who was not of much help, and Fräulein Dr. Weber, who reminds me very much of Frau Dr. Quast and all the other welfare ladies that I have met in Berlin. That is, she is small, thin, bespectacled, and aggressively cheerful. I have to come back early next week, by which time she will have collected some materials for me and also the names of retired Siemens workers whom I can interview.

After that I rushed over to Columbiadamm police headquarters. Several spacious, cobbled courtyards and what looks like former riding stables. Red brick buildings. Lots of blue police lorries and riot cars. It was bitter cold and at the gates the police sentries wore huge felt boots and ear muffs. When I went in to ask for my travelers' checks there was a silly bureaucratic problem first. I could not get the checks until I paid 12 marks reward to the finder plus an office fee (*Verwaltungsgebühr*), but without the checks I had no money to pay. Finally, they let me tear out one ten-dollar check, run for 30 minutes through the bitter cold to a bank to change it into German marks and then run the 30 minutes back to the office. Whereupon the German policeman said to me, smiling: "We don't like to be so bureaucratic here in Berlin, but what can you do? We must obey regulations. Don't put this down in your memoirs when you write about us."

When I left Columbiadamm it was already 3 p.m. There was no point riding home since that would take one hour and by 5 p.m. I would have had to leave again to have dinner with the Cerfs in Wannsee. So I decided to indulge myself. After two days of living on bread and apples I gorged myself on a lunch for 1.50 marks and then went to see the film *Pünktchen und Anton* based on Erich Kästner's famous children's story.[1] Quite charming, though it was set not in the 1920s but in the 1950s. Direktor Pogge owned a factory making stockings instead of walking sticks and he owned a Cadillac convertible. The acting was marvelous, especially the scene in which the thieving maid, Fräulein Andacht, is dancing with Robert der Teufel.

There were lots of children at the movie, mostly working-class. I

---

[1] Erich Kästner (1899-1974) is best known for his children's book, *Emil und die Detektive* (1929)."

started to talk with a little boy named Bernd. His father is a toolmaker by trade, but now has to work as a coal carrier. Mother wants Bernd to become a doctor, but Bernd says he is not sure he would not rather become an artist. He seems too small for his 7 years, but exceedingly bright and serious. He said he often sees cowboy films but they are really bad, because the cruelty they show leads to wars. About the Russians: they look so nice and yet are such swine (*Schweinehunde*). We talked about *Pünktchen und Anton*. To my bewilderment he told me he was sure Anton at one point had wanted to commit suicide. Children in a Kästner story committing suicide? Impossible! Or do children commit suicide in the world little Bernd lives in...?

Arrived late in Wannsee. Had a nice evening with lots of pilaf cooked by Carol. But no Ernst Gries turned up and no FDJ girl, as promised. We talked about Germany. Jay thinks Russia doesn't want Germany reunified because her hold on East Germany is so secure— why jeopardize that?

In the S-Bahn on the way home to Steglitz, three loudly laughing women were sitting across the aisle from me. One of them was putting on two overcoats because she did not want to be seen carrying a spare coat over her arm as she enters the Soviet sector. An old man at the other end of the carriage seemed to enjoy her cracks at the Communists very much. He finally came over and gallantly helped her into her second coat.

Today was spent dutifully reading the *Vossische Zeitung*. Over lunch break Siewert told me that he is against all political commitments. He will not go and see the new film about Hitler, *Until 5 Minutes after 12*. He thinks we should put the last war completely out of our minds. He was a ground radio man (*Bodenfunker*) for the Luftwaffe in Finland during the war.

After a lunch in Schöneberg, met Jay and Carol in the Rathaus. But there was no session of the Berlin Parliament for us to attend. My fault, I ought to have checked. So, since the babysitter for Randolph was already engaged, we went to the Kurfürstendamm, which Carol has not seen yet. But it was too cold to stroll about and we ended in the Marmorhaus seeing the movie *Ein Leben für Do*. The film had been praised in the papers as one of the best postwar movies of Germany. Filmed partly in Africa, partly in Switzerland, the story was sentimental; Carol cried. The final scene showed Do, by then a grown-up girl, reunited with her "Daddy" in Africa. She rushes up to him and embraces him in the middle of a field, surrounded by his African workers. A Berlin woman in the row behind us whispered: "In front of all those blacks!" (Vor all den Schwarzen!). We ended the evening at Aschinger's, eating hot soup, and Jay stole dozens of rolls and stuffed them inside my coat pocket while the guests around us stared, scandalized.

Got to Schöneberg in time for the lecture on the future layout of the

Kurfürstendamm and the Memorial Church. The lecturer was an architect named Fierlinger. Helmuth Weidmüller and the bookseller Herr Rothschild were in the audience too.

29 January 1954

Finished the *Vossische Zeitung* for September 1913. Frau Dr. Täuber gave me two more periodicals, both anticommunist. One was *Die Junge Welt*. On the outside it looks like the official organ of the FDJ, but inside are articles denouncing the communist regime of East Germany. The other was called *Tarantel*. It is a satirical publication filled with political jokes about the Stalinist system and presented in comic-strip fashion. Frau Dr. Täuber told me where it is made though this is supposedly a secret: in the *Telegraf* Building on Bismarckplatz in Berlin-Grunewald, third floor. Ask for either Herr Baer or Herr Wolf (these are their cover names). If you bring them a good idea for a joke, you're welcome.

The four-power conference does not seem to cause much excitement among Berliners. Only two days ago I overheard people in the U-Bahn wondering aloud whether there was much point in standing on the sidewalk in this cold weather to watch closed limousines drive by. Adenauer has asked the Berliners to show dignified reserve. What they are likely to put up may look more like a show of indifference. I think the Western powers and Soviet Russia approach the German and Austrian problems very differently. The Western powers want to put Germany and Austria back in order. Russia wants Germany and Austria to be ordered to suit the interests of the victors.[1]

30 January 1954

The weather is icy cold. I tried to read at home. Met Carol and Jay at Loden Frey at 3:30, where Carol bought a new overcoat. Then we saw the movie *Bis 5 Minuten nach 12*, the much-discussed but rather disappointing film about Hitler. The scenes shown were not very new and the editing poor. For example, there was much too much about the Japanese attack on Pearl Harbor, in which the Nazis had not been involved. With the exception of a few shots of Hitler and Eva Braun at the Berghof, nearly all the footage was from well-known newsreels. At the beginning, the film showed pictures of Germany

---

[1] The conference of foreign ministers met in Berlin from 25 January to 18 Feburary 1954. John Foster Dulles represented the U.S., Anthony Eden Great Britain, Georges Bidault France, and Vjacheslav M. Molotov the USSR. The Western proposal of German reunification following free elections was rejected by the Soviet Union. Konrad Adenauer (1876-1967) was West German chancellor from 1949 to 55.

Refugees in West Berlin

Refugee camp Berlin-Marienfelde, (15 Jan., 1954)

Fürsorger Exner and Ernst Gries

Taking a refugee to a police station (29 Jan., 1954)

AT THE BERLIN CONFERENCE OF FOREIGN MINISTERS

At the French press conference (10 Feb., 1954)

A debate with Vopos
in East Berlin
(5 Feb., 1954)

Adenauer speaking in Berlin
(23 Feb., 1954)

At the Soviet press conference
(5 Feb., 1954)

before 1914 and the narrator said that the whole story goes back to imperial times. But why? There was no explanation for the supposed continuity from Wilhelm II to Hitler. The historical thesis of the film was roughly like this: the Weimar Republic failed, unfortunately, due to the untimely deaths of Ebert, Stresemann, and Hindenburg. Germany's economy and her cultural life were soaring towards new heights when their élan was cut short by Hitler, who destroyed individual responsibility, human dignity, and God-fearingness. Having arrogated all power to themselves and wildly abused it, Hitler and his henchmen in 1945 evaded their responsibility by committing suicide. And so the entire blame for the Nazi regime is placed on the Nazi leaders with, at the most, this mild rebuke to the German nation: Don't ever again entrust your responsibility to others.

Technically, the film was dull. I also think more should have been shown of the regimented life of the Third Reich— secret police, education, concentration camps. The audience was sparse and quiet. Only a few people whispered. Yesterday the newspapers reported disturbances in some movie houses where the film was being shown.

Later we had coffee in a small cafe in Schlosstrasse. Carol said she was worried about Ernst Gries because he hadn't shown up last Wednesday evening. Jay will go to his camp to enquire about him.

Listened to a broadcast of the "Insulaner" cabaret over the radio in Frau Henninger's living room. As always, it was marvelous. The theme was the four-power conference, naturally. "Wir sind so bescheiden. Wir haben zwei Deutschland und wollen doch nur eins," (We don't ask much. We don't need two Germanies, one will do).

31 January 1954

The temperature is falling to minus 20 degrees! Absolutely freezing. I had lunch at the Schultheiss-Bräuerei opposite the Steglitz Rathaus. My neighbor at table was a young journalist who works for the International News Service. He lives in a small hotel opposite the Steglitz S-Bahnhof and his job, he told me, was to cover all Soviet press statements. Actually, I didn't like him much as a person, but he had some interesting things to say. For one thing, he told me where to go if I wanted to work as an interpreter for the English or the French. Then he told me about the news coverage for the conference. There are over 2,000 foreign correspondents in town, representing some 800 newspapers or news agencies. Some papers only have one or two representatives. The International News Service has 7 men. Their chief, Kingsbury Smith, will arrive in Berlin shortly. Sometimes several agencies cooperate with one another— for example, by taking turns to fetch the daily news releases from the various delegations. Interviews, of course, are treated as private property. He also told me that the Vopos are instructed to show special courtesy to all visitors from the West. When a reporter from United Press and his German cameraman were recently arrested by Vopos for photographing a poster in East Berlin— it showed a nasty caricature of Adenauer— the policemen were scolded by their officer, who then apologized to the two newspapermen.

I asked him why the West German government was against Molotov's proposal that both West Germany and East Germany be represented at the conference. My interlocutor was a CDU party man, and he admitted that Adenauer's refusal may have cost him some popularity among the people. On the other hand, you can't sit with the East Germans without recognizing them at least *de facto*, he said. Also, the Social Democratic opposition in Bonn would take advantage of such a contact with the East (one workers' party reaching out to another workers' party) to strengthen its position in West German politics. I wondered if this was all true, for it sounded quite extraordinary. Is this what the Berliners mean when they grumble about the narrow-minded politics in Bonn?

Afternoon tea with the Schmidts. I still don't know what job Papa Schmidt has, but it must be with the Ministry for Trade and Industry. He is a retired cavalry officer, that I now know. We didn't talk about the four-power conference (except for the crazy speed of Molotov's driver who drove at 100 km per hour down the Clayallee), but Papa Schmidt told about his attendance at the opening of the Grüne Woche (Berlin's yearly agricultural fair) and especially the riding tournament (both Carl and Sigrid love horseback riding). Sigrid mentioned a Spanish dancing troupe in town. Mama Schmidt complained about the abysmal ignorance of German history among the middle-aged Germans with whom she is taking a French conversation course at the Maison de France. "History has so often been rewritten," she sighed. "Under Hitler all books by Jewish authors had to be hidden. Now they can be displayed again and *Mein Kampf* must be put in the back of the shelf! The whole business of purging libraries with each change in regime is so stupid." But both Sigrid and her mother agreed that Heinrich Heine had no claim to be called a great writer. His poems are empty words. There is a history teacher at the Maison de France who is always urging his audience to read Heine's books on Germany. "This is unfair. Heine has nothing positive to say about Germany, nor about Paris, for that matter."[1]

Sigrid and Carl were more amusing to talk to. Sigrid told a joke that went: "Es war einmal ein Zwerg. Seine Eltern waren Schoten," (Once upon a time there was a dwarf. His parents were peapods). It took a long time before I laughed. And when she was small and played in the street, she once mimicked a man who was passing on a bicycle, singing. The man had bawled her out, Berlin fashion: "Du hast woll

---

[1] Heinrich Heine (1797-1856), German poet and publicist.

Lust mit 'nem verbundnen Kopp bei'd Charité zum Fenster raus zu kieken?" (Wanna look out the window of the Charité Hospital with a bandaged head?).

On my way home a tram conductor told me he had worked in France as a *chef de bâtiment* (*Baupolier*, or construction foreman) after his release from a POW camp. He had liked France. In Berlin he cannot have such a job. Not because of unemployment, but because to get a good job in the construction industry in Berlin you need connections.

I February 1954

A full day. First I went to the Senatsbibliothek. Because of the freezing weather, bought a black turtle-neck sweater which I saw on sale in a shop window for 25 marks. In the Senatsbibliothek, Direktor Zopf was exceedingly courteous. He himself went to fetch the trays of index cards and wouldn't hear of my helping to carry them. "You are our guest," he said. He has already selected some books which he thinks I should read and also wants me to look up old Rudolf Wissel.

I went to the press department in the Maison de France to offer my services as an interpreter. The lady there was very kind and took my name. She also called the Quartier Napoléon in Tegel (Berlin's French sector) to ask whether I might be useful to them, but it seemed not. Then I went to the Rankestrasse, where I looked for the association of foreign journalists. In the street I asked a girl wearing a white apron for number 19. A few minutes later she came runing after me to ask whether I was Chinese, Japanese, or Korean. When I said Chinese, she asked me to come with her to her father's restaurant, the Ritz, Rankestrasse 26. This is really a swanky place, and they have menus in Urdu, Korean, Japanese, and Chinese. The owner's name is Werner Fischer, he is from Stettin and learned cooking in England and in Egypt. His daughter is called Gisela, and she is in charge of Chinese cooking. The reason why I was hailed: they needed someone to rewrite the Chinese menu in proper Chinese characters. I was given a pen holder, nibs, black ink (*Tusche*), white paper, and a cup of tea, and so there I was, "am hellichten Tage," practicing Chinese calligraphy on the Kurfürstendamm. The result was not bad, but I must come back one of these days and correct one mistake I made. For my pains I was told to come and have dinner here and bring a friend. I asked whether I could bring two, and they said yes. So I'll bring Jay and Carol here.

At the Verband Ausländischer Journalisten I was received by a smiling elderly woman who told me to go to the Kathreinerhaus, room 9, and ask for Mr. Schulze-Werner. The Kathreinerhaus here in the West is more easy to get into just now, because this week the conference takes place on the other side, in Unter den Linden. I got past the door of the Kathreinerhaus by flashing my Chinese passport (it looks very foreign) and by talking to the German policeman in English. I didn't see too much of the inside though, except the big board in the hallway with a listing of all the offices of foreign and German newspapers in this building. As I left I noticed that at the gate the British and the American MPs were chatting with one another while the French policeman stood silently apart. Did they have a language barrier?

I got home by 3:30 and worked for the rest of the afternoon. At 7 o'clock in the evening I was off again, to Zehlendorf, to the American library where I was supposed to take part in Androwsky's advanced English language course. It turned out to be rather boring, but I do admire Androwsky's patience. His pupils range from age 20 to age 60 and more, mostly people with professional reasons for wanting to learn English. One woman was a doctor who wanted to emigrate to the United States. Her neighbor was a *Prokurist* (business executive), yet another man was an exporter. The topic of their conversation was the four-power conference, and I was surprised by their overall optimism that it will produce some good. They were, however, critical of the Hitler film which is currently shown in Berlin cinemas. This will strengthen Molotov's hand, they said, by reviving fears of German aggression. At the end of the class, everyone was asked to propose a topic of conversation for next time. I suggested a discussion of changes in German society since 1900, and it was accepted. It should be quite interesting.

Someone offered me a ride home in a marvelous brand-new Mercedes Benz. Klaus Androwsky came along too. He told me that at the last Kolloquium at the FU, which I had missed, there had been a discussion of Senator Joe McCarthy's investigations into loyalty in America. Fraenkel had defended McCarthy as not deserving all the abuse he got. Hofer had remained noncommittal, and Fischer-Baling had left early. I wonder whether the Meinecke Institut is very conservative and whether the students feel differently?

2 February 1954

In the morning called on Professor Direktor R. Scherhag of the Berlin Meteorological Institute. He was sitting at his desk doing nothing. A dial on the wall allowed him to see every change in the direction of the wind in Dahlem. An expensive radio was playing softly. Concerto for cello and orchestra. Perhaps he was only waiting for the weather forecast? He did not have much to say except that I might want to read something about the Berlin climate written by an American called Huntington.

Worked at the archives, combing issue after issue of the *Vossische Zeitung* for interesting news items. Telephoned Rudolf Wissel, but he has a cold and wants me to call again at the end of the week. Interesting that there should have been a picture of Wissel in today's *Illustrirte Berliner Zeitung,* showing him with President Theodor Heuss. The two are described as close friends. Heuss was once editor of *Die Hilfe* and is by training an historian and sociologist. Should I write to him?

At the archive met a Frau Dr. Barbara Pischel, who teaches at the FU and will give me some tips about workers' clubs and associations.

It's terribly cold. I think I've got some chilblains.

3 February 1954

In the morning I called Fräulein Dr. Weber at the Siemens works. She is going to call back and tell me when to meet Oberingenieur Hoefert. He lives in Wannsee. I also talked to Herr Biermann, head of the Siemens pension fund who will mail me the addresses of twelve retired workers. — Went to the Kolloquium. Very good discussion of the Trieste problem. Two interesting points were brought up: (1) Foreign Secretary Eden is supposed to have proposed in 1944 that Trieste should become a sea port for southern Germany in order to further the centrifugal forces separating north and south Germany; (2) the Italians propose a solution along ethnological lines in order to capitalize on the fruits of their Italianization campaign during the Fascist period. At one point Fraenkel raised his hands and asked dramatically: whom should the Western powers favor more, the Italians or the Yugoslavs? (As was to be expected, no one had an easy answer.)

In the evening, dinner at Restaurant Ritz. Jay came early since he had just been in town. Carol came around seven. I rewrote the Chinese menu in my best calligraphy, and then we were given dinner. Quite good, though the portions were small compared to what you'd get in a Chinese restaurant in the States. A good bottle of white wine came with it.

After dinner we went to the Maison de France, which has a French restaurant on the fourth floor. We had been attracted by the many cars with official French license plates parked outside, thinking an important function was being held inside, but nothing exceptional seemed to be going on. Lots of lively French faces, many British people in conservative tweeds. A four-man band played, but no one was dancing. We ordered coffee and some marvelous ice cream. Jay told of his latest exploits: he was at a youth camp for refugees yesterday (and will try to take me along next time he goes there), and he has met a Herr Laski, who is an editor for *Der Monat*, and Peter Herz from RIAS. Tomorrow we'll go to a meeting of Berlin's political youth organizations. Jay thinks RIAS is a real espionage agency. It knows who is going to escape from the Eastern zone long before the escape actually takes place.

I bought a copy of *Le Monde* in the vestibule for 35 pfennigs. Haven't read this paper in ages.

4 February 1954

Boring day at the archives. Sore throat. In the evening, went to Humboldtstrasse 26, here in Steglitz, where a meeting of the Ring politischer Jugend was being held. Present were a large delegation of British (and some American) youth organizers, who are spending a fortnight in Berlin visiting youth hostels and youth camps. It is a return visit, because some German youth organizers have just been to London. The British and Americans are paying their own way, but the Germans extend many invitations to them every day for lunches and dinners. The Ring Politischer Jugend, so I understand, is a kind of club where members of the youth organizations of various German parties meet and discuss political topics.[1] Today, representatives of the SPD and CDU were supposed to discuss the best electoral law for Germany. It never came to a real debate, however, since both sides were just discussing the pros and cons of either *scrutin de liste* or *scrutin d'arrondissement* (to use the French expressions) or a party vote versus a personality vote. No one was trying to explain his preference on philosophical or pragmatic grounds. They all might just as well have belonged to the same party, disagreeing only on a technical question. The English tried to explain to the Germans the British electoral system, but before they got very far they were disagreeing with one another, leaving their German hosts rather perplexed.

5 February 1954

Started early to go to Siemensstadt. Since I arrived early, I stopped for a coffee in a workers' pub. At 11 a.m. I entered the *Wernerwerk* of Siemens & Halske. The porter was already expecting me and a girl was ordered to take me upstairs to a Dr. Heim. I only saw Dr. Heim at lunchtime, however, since the man I was introduced to was Oberingenieur Reinhold Hoefert, who has spent 52 years at Siemens & Halske. He met me in a friendly, airy office where he readily and very openly talked to me for a solid hour about his experiences at Siemens before the war. (I took profuse notes in my little black book.) He told me to ask him anything I wanted though he became more guarded when the talk turned to politics. At noon, two gentlemen came in and insisted that I joined them and Hoefert for lunch. I said I had an urgent appointment (namely, with Jay and Carol) at Wittembergplatz at 1 p.m., but that didn't faze them; they

---

[1]Founded by the SPD, the CDU, and the LPD after the war, the Ring Politischer Jugend was meant to teach German youth resistance against dictatorship.

immediately offered me the use of a company car after lunch. ("Ja, einem Ausländer woll'n wir schon gerne einmal einen Wagen borgen! — Oh, we'd be glad to provide a car for a foreigner!") We had a marvelous lunch— I almost think it was more copious still than the one Eisele had offered me. (Soup, fish with mayonnaise and potatoes, dessert, cheese, coffee and cakes, cigars and cigarettes, sherry, white wine, and liqueurs.) The conversation was dull. My hosts were of the opinion the Americans have allowed the Russians to go too far ever since Yalta, and they did not expect the Berlin conference to produce any concrete results.

I got my car ride from Siemens. A very friendly chauffeur (30 years in the service of the firm) drove me in a small Mercedes to Wittenbergplatz. Jay and Carol were a little late. We went off to Thaelmannplatz, where we went directly to the Presse Zentrum Berlin, the Soviet sector's equivalent of the Kathreinerhaus. We also got into the International Press Restaurant without trouble. Jay ordered lobster tails with rice in a delicious sauce, and Carol Kamtchatka toast, which was very similar since it also had lobster tails on it. We bought cigarettes (yesterday I smoked my last American packet). I bought a pack of Bulgarian cigarettes, called "Derby," in an American-style package, which tasted too bitter after a while, and a pack of Russian "Drug" ("Friend") cigarettes made in Moscow, which I found quite delicious. Jay sauntered off to a neighboring table where English was spoken, and pumped the four men who were seated there for information. They were UP men, it turned out, and they told Jay something about the press conferences. Each delegation gives its press conference right after the meeting of the foreign ministers but in a different place (the Western powers presumably in the Western sectors), while the Russians give theirs right here in the Presse Zentrum. Then we saw a young-looking Asian sit down at another table and, thinking he was Chinese, I got up to talk to him. I was vaguely prepared to introduce myself as a Chinese student from Cambridge (to come from England seemed to me more innocuous than coming from America), but fortunately he didn't give me any time to say anything since he immediately took me for a Chinese Communist reporter. His name was Van Ky Tray, he was from Hanoi, and a reporter for the *Pho Thong* newspaper, and "had nothing to do with Bau Dai!" He was very pleased to meet me, wanted to know whether I also lived upstairs in the Presse Zentrum, then suggested we meet again later this afternoon or tomorrow because he was in a great hurry just then. When I told Jay he got worried for us and for my new friend and so we went to him again to explain that we were together, that we were students and not reporters, and that Jay at least was an American. At this point Van Ky Tray became much more reserved but he was too polite to withdraw his earlier invitation to meet again. In the meantime Carol also had wandered off to make contacts. She talked with an English journalist when we returned.

Well, we finally paid and left. Jay wanted to take pictures out in the street while the light was still good. Lots of Vopo trucks were driving around. Also very old, sturdy motorcycles thickly painted in olive green, driven by very young boys in brown leather suits and white helmets, but wearing no badges. Jay stopped a Vopo outside the Presse Zentrum and received permission from him to take photographs of some posters in the street. In a side street he came across another Vopo, this one an elderly officer with glasses, wearing the green uniform and lilac shoulder patches of the barracked People's Police" (kasernierte Volkspolizei). With a big smile, the officer told Jay he could photograph anything he wanted in the East sector since it had no secret installations. So off we went, taking snapshots of political slogans on walls and *Litfassäulen* (columns for advertisements):

Deutsche an einen Tisch

Berlin, voran mit dem neuen Kurs

Das Jahr der grossen Initiative

Weg mit dem EVG Vertrag, ein Friedensvertrag

Befestigt die unerschütterliche Freundschaft mit der Sowjetunion

Über Meinungsverschiedenheiten hinweg durch Verhandlungen

Wir fordern von der Viererkonferenz, Freiheit und Einheit für Deutschland[1]

One poster showed a photo of Molotov with a crowd behind him carrying signs demanding "peace" in four different languages.

We saw a number of American officers and men, one of them chewing gum, walking into the FDJ building. There is a clubroom there which was used by the drivers of the Western Allies while they waited. A British MP jeep was standing in the courtyard. The FDJ sentry was a dark-haired boy with a stern face who wouldn't let us in unless we first obtained permission from the main gate of the FDJ building.

A number of big limousines with blue flashing lights whizzed by as we crossed Unter den Linden. It was 3 p.m. and the conference was just getting under way. We asked a very young Vopo: "Do you know who just drove by?" He smiled in reply: "Ach, Regierungsfunktionäre!" He actually seemed amused at their self-importance. "And how long will today's meeting last?" we pressed him. "No one can say, but Molotov is in the chair, so it may take longer," he grinned.

---

[1]"All Germans at One (Conference) Table"— "Berlin at the head of the New Course!"— "The Year of Great Initiative"— "A Peace Treaty, not a European Defense Community!"— "Resolve Differences through Negotiations!"— "We demand of the four-power Ccnference freedom and unity for Germany."

This was the first time we walked the side streets of the Soviet sector. Unpainted, shabby-looking streets, no cars, almost no pedestrians, no signboards, no color, nothing. We went in the direction of S-Bahnhof Friedrichstrasse, and farther. Jay wanted to buy records and go into a big HO bookstore. We saw one big, very elegantly laid-out shop which sold books and cushions, tablecloths, room decorations, all very tastefully arranged. When we got to the record shop at last ("Schallplatten, Tonmöbel") we saw the iron grill lowered and the shop window empty. Some people were standing before the shop talking in hushed tones. Finally, a man in a shabby black cotton-padded vest (it looked Chinese) told us the shop owner had defected to the West ("hat sich abgesetzt nach den Westen") and suggested we tried some other place. Round the corner we saw a big store selling electric appliances, typewriters, etc. They also had a few records with songs such as "Herr Lehrer, wir wollen gerne wissen" (children asking their teacher about the *New Times*,) and "Das Lied des Teddybärs," but not what Jay was looking for, Russian songs like "Das Lied der Abendglocken" and the "International." The radios and typewriters in the shop looked a bit shabby. One typewriter for 300 East marks looked as if it were made of cheap metal. No television sets. We didn't buy anything.

I bought a pipe for 5.50 marks in a tobacco store because pipes can be had without showing your identity card ("nicht ausweispflichtig").

Then we went to a post office (Postamt 24), a big reddish building with minarets and crazy towers. Inside, big blue and red banners, Soviet and German flags, slogans, emblems. There were not many people about, so we looked at the stamps on display, many of them with patriotic motifs: personalities from German history like vom Stein, the brothers Humboldt, Cranach, workers at the barricades in 1848, and Marshal Blücher in the War of Liberation, 1813. We asked a woman behind a window— Frau Kollege Tepke— where we could get some of the communist emblems displayed on the walls. "Für Vereinszwecke (to use in our clubroom)," I said. She smiled and gave us an address, Rosenthaler Strasse 24, and told us to use her as a reference. She must have taken us for foreign communist youth workers collecting material to take home. We visited yet another post office (N4, at the Nordbahnhof) where Jay bought more stamps and a booklet *Karl Marx Jahr 1953*. He bought four of them and gave me one.

Back to the Presse Zentrum to meet our Vietnamese friend. On the way we passed the office of the Soviet High Commissioner Vladimir Semyonov. It was already dark. A small crowd had gathered in front and we all looked at the two big lighted conference rooms on the first floor where, from the distance, one could see big chandeliers and people moving about. The scene looked like Buckingham Palace when the king is ill and an anxious people waits outside for the latest news. The cars of the foreign ministers were parked in front of the entrance, with a number of Russian MP jeeps next to them. The pedestrians were restricted to the far side of the street, away from the conference building. The Vopos looked astonishingly young, real children.

Then we returned to the Presse Zentrum. This time we had trouble trying to get into the restaurant, for we were stopped and asked to show our press cards. Jay pretended to be angry and impatient, flashed his American passport and we were in. But then we had to leave again since there was no way from that entrance leading up to the first floor where we were to meet M. Van Ky. We entered the main building and I stopped to ask for the lounge. Jay thought we should have gone ahead as if we owned the place. However, since there was a second guard at the glass door at the top of the stairs, we may not have gotten through that easily anyhow. We had to go to the front office where I said I had a "very urgent" appointment with M. Van Ky. They fetched him and I think the poor man was not very pleased. We were really exploiting him since he obviously had little interest in us and was very busy, while our sole intention was to get inside. In his company we had no trouble getting past the second guard, but then Ky wanted us to wait on the first floor. This was a lobby. A whole mountain of bundled petitions could be seen here: the 9 million Germans who were demanding represen- tation at the conference. But being in the lobby was not enough; only when you got up to the second floor where the information bureau and the snack bar were did you have the freedom of the house. So, while M. Van Ky was running around to telephone, first Carol, then I, and then Jay slipped upstairs and stood by the snack bar. When M. Van Ky finally found us, we pretended to have come up to get something to eat for us all. (The official currency exchange here is 2.22 marks for one American dollar! I should have thought a dollar worth at least 25 marks!) Van Ky reluctantly led us into a lounge where we passed a painful quarter of an hour with him trying to put him at his ease. The poor man obviously wished nothing more than to be rid of us. From his conversation we learned that he lived in London and Paris and was reporting on conditions in Europe ("We know so little about Europe!"); that he sometimes goes to Madrid ("Spanish is very easy for us to learn because of our French") but does not like living there; that he has a 20-year-old son who is his assistant and that he himself is 40 years old (he doesn't look older than 25); that presently he lives near the Kurfürstendamm but disapproves of us for living in West Berlin (this inconsistency was not explained). Finally, we also learned that his paper was formerly a daily; that censorship under French rule is very strict; that his paper tries to be "unpolitical" (how??) and that he does not like to admit that he travels on a French passport. He didn't want to discuss Indochina.

He finally left and, of course, we stayed. Jay met a French student, Gérard, who writes for two French provincial papers. (Looks and acts much like Gérard Stephanescu, my old schoolmate in Bucharest before the war.) Gérard gave us a few tips. We had a snack and picked up two picture books on Berlin published by the East Berlin Magistrat which were given to all foreign correspondents. When the loudspeaker announced that the speech by Bidault was ready for foreign correspondents to pick up in room 2061, we joined the mob and picked up copies too. The speech was very sharp, and so was that by Dulles. Gérard thought this would spell the end of the conference.

We slowly drifted into the conference room. Carol and I waited while Jay and Gérard went to have a drink. At 8:15, the loudspeaker announced in four languages that the foreign ministers' conference was just over and that the press conference would begin in 15 minutes. Journalists began to pour into the room. Many of them Germans. Next to me were two men and a woman from the Agence France Presse. I also saw two Chinese and some Indians. The Russian spokesman, llyitchev, came in, smoked a lot, talked in short intervals while his words were translated into German (by a fat, determined-looking young man, Molotov's personal interpreter) and English (by a very incompetent young lady with a strong German accent who didn't know English well). A third interpreter remained completely silent. From time to time the projectors were turned on and the big camera in the back (television?) purred. A man took snapshots, two people (including myself) made sketches. Ilyitchev was very efficient. Gleaming, pale eyes like those of a lynx, bushy eyebrows. Occasionally a charming smile that still made you uncomfortable. Exuding intelligence. E.g., his answer to a question from an AFP man: "You said that the four ministers will meet in secret sessions to discuss the question of a five-power conference and disarmament. Will the German question also be debated at this secret session?" – Ilyitchev: "The aim of the four foreign ministers' conference is to find a solution to the German problem. The ways and means whereby this result shall be achieved is the affair of the four foreign ministers." In other words: "Maybe yes, maybe no."

The translation work was astonishingly poor. Molotov's bright young man made the *gaffe* of translating Molotov's statement, "Some people don't like the regime in East Germany, we don't like the regime in West Germany," as "I don't like the regime in East Germany... " (laughter in the audience). Twice he had to be corrected from the floor. The young lady *Dolmetsch* (interpreter) sometimes forgot what she was supposed to translate. "Les dettes de guerre de l'Allemagne" she translated as "Germany's postwar debts." *Vulgariser* was trans-lated as *vulgär machen* and she changed Ilyitchev's final statement, that his report had been his personal recollection of the conference, into "my view of the conference as I took it down in notes." The conference lasted about 1 $^1/_2$ hours.

We left to go to the Potsdamer Platz to take the S-Bahn home. On the way out an elderly man spoke to me. He said he had frequently seen me in Steglitz riding the tramway. Who could he have been? I didn't dare to speak to him for fear our unauthorized presence in the Presse Zentrum would become known.

Standing on the S-Bahn platform (the station is underground), Jay decided to photograph a sign which dangled from a lamp, reading: Letzter S-Bahnhof des demokratischen Sektors (Last stop in the democratic sector). Soon two Vopos, very young boys with nice smiles, came up from behind Jay and posted themselves in front of him. For a moment my heart beat faster and I think Jay also got a good fright. The Vopos said that normally it is not allowed to photograph on railway platforms, but when Jay pointed to the sign and assured them he had only taken a picture of that, they nodded generously. "Ausnahmen bestätigen die Regel" (Exceptions confirm the rules). Soon, we were chatting with them in a friendly way. Both Vopos held the rank of *Oberwachtmeister*, both were from Saxony. They said they did not see why police should be considered bad or something to be feared. All it did was perform a needed service to the community. "We want to encourage foreigners to see not only West Berlin but all of Berlin." They even thought we could visit Potsdam if we wanted to, but later they were not so sure about that. (They never speak of the Russian zone, but always of the DDR.) They called a third Vopo to ask him about trips to Potsdam. This third man was intellectually more aggressive, and also better trained politically. Soon it was he who acted as their spokesman. We have orders, he said, to treat all foreign journalists— or foreign nationals, for that matter— with the greatest respect and to help them wherever we can. Only during the conference? Jay asked. He seemed to resent this, but his answer, that it is very unusual to have that many foreign journalists visiting East Berlin, could be interpreted as an indirect admission that it was so. He also admitted that there were installations which we would not be allowed to photograph. Jay tried to ask him about his political opinions. He said that he believed there were good men in every country, only some countries are more peace-loving than others. "Why does the U.S. build military installations all over the world?" He had fought as a soldier in the last war, had served with the Wehrmacht in occupied Holland. "Another such war would be terrible," he said, "not to speak of an atomic war".

The conference? All three Vopos said that they were optimistic. Everything depends on the answer Dulles will give to the Molotov plan.

The main speaker said to us after a while that he had nudged his comrade when he heard us use the term *Vopo*. They prefer to be called "Volkspolizisten." *Vopo* has become an abusive term in the Western press. Jay apologized. The Vopo asked me what policemen are called in the United States. I told him they are called "cops" but that they also dislike that term. An American policeman would rather be addressed as "officer." "Even if he is not an officer?" the Vopo

VENTURING INTO EAST BERLIN

Woman in S-Bahn smuggling
a spare coat into East Berlin
(27 Jan., 1954)

Warning poster: No smuggling!
(2 June, 1954)

Distributing forbidden Western
newspapers (13 Sept., 1954)

Soviet war memorial in
Tiergarten (British sector)

A closed shop: The owner has fled
to the West (5 Feb., 1954)

At the Refugee camp in Kladow (25 Feb and 25 March, 1954)

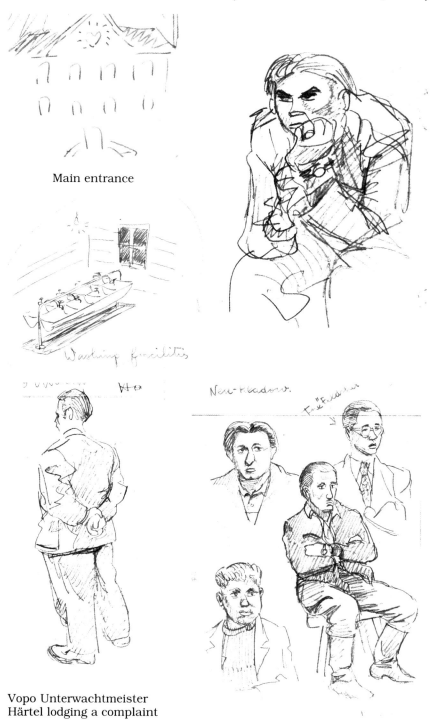

Main entrance

Washing facilities

New-Kladow.

Vopo Unterwachtmeister
Härtel lodging a complaint

asked me. "Of course," I said. "If he is not he will be the more pleased." The three Vopos were very amused by this and told me proudly that no one in the Volkspolizei had any vain pretensions of rank. Here they were all "Genossen," comrades.

The Vopo spokesman said something else that was interesting: he said he was not allowed to go to the West sector even when off duty because a Western secret service might arrest him. He said it was unfortunate that the conflict between East and West had reached the point where he no longer could move freely throughout the city. The Western press has painted so dark a picture of the Volkspolizei that any atrocity story about them is believed over there. "Das ist nicht schön, das sollte nicht sein" (That's not nice, that shouldn't be). His mother and wife, however, still can go to West Berlin.

I asked one of the other two Vopos why some of their comrades in the street looked so terribly young. He assured me 18 was the minimum age for entering the police. I suggested that during the conference even younger people might have been enlisted to help out temporarily. He seemed to take this as a criticism. "We don't take children, why should we?" "Well," I said, "to help regulate street traffic! Other countries do that in times of exceptionally heavy traffic." When I said other countries did likewise, he seemed to relax again. But, he repeated, there are no children in the Vopo.

A lot of people stood at a distance from us, watching. Perhaps they were astonished to see us talking in such a friendly manner with policemen. We left with lots of hand shaking. Carol even ran back to shake hands with one whom she had forgotten to say good-bye to.

I had two sausages at the railway snack bar in Steglitz. Met a disgusting elderly man who at first seemed quite nice, but turned out to be drunk and morally not too sound. A Roman Catholic. Said he loves China. Has read a lot of gangster stories set in China. He told me he had been married once, that his present (second) wife was about to die, that now he wanted to marry a third woman, and that he had an illegitimate daughter. He wanted very much that I visited him but I had absolutely no desire to. Got home very late and very tired.

8 February 1954

There has been a short pause in my diary writing since I ran out of paper over the weekend. Saturday I couldn't do much work since I had to spend the afternoon and evening with the Henningers. It was the birthday of the elder Henninger daughter, Ingrid. There was supposed to be a costume ball and some costumes were quite good, especially little Esther's, who came as a little negro. But I soon became bored with playing parlor games and listening to silly jokes. One piece of information I found interesting: the father of Helga, one of the invited girls, has been a political prisoner of the Russians since 1945 simply because he held the rank of *Regierungsrat* under Hitler.

Sunday was more fun. The weather was bright, and relatively mild. I had tea with the Cerfs, and Herr Ossowsky from the RIAS school program was also there, together with a friend of his, Fräulein Huss. Ossowsky was jovial and relaxed, the talk was interesting, and it grew so late (9 p.m.) that Jay had to make some soup and toast as a light supper. We played some of Jay's communist records, which amused Ossowsky and Miss Huss very much, especially Ossowsky, since he has not been to the East sector for the last 7 years and had not heard them. Apparently there has been new unrest in the Russian zone and in East Berlin with many arrests. SED agents have tried to initiate the plebiscite which Molotov wants in place of free German elections, and the workers in the factories have shown their discontent by asking "improper" questions and by walking out of political meetings. Jay and Ossowsky both believe that if the conference fails, as seems likely now, visiting the East sector will become more hazardous again. Ossowsky thinks that RIAS will have a difficult psychological task on hand following an unsuccessful conference, because its listeners in the East will have lost all hope of liberation from Soviet rule in the near future.

Today I worked in the archives. Dr. Lachmann is back. Friedrich Meinecke, the great historian and old teacher of my own Doktorvater at Yale, Hajo Holborn, has died two days ago.[1] Lachmann thought I should go to his funeral on Friday. I will certainly try. I called Dr. Rudolf Wissell and he asked me to come and see him right away.[2] He turned out to be a nice old gentleman, living in a suburban apartment house (Tempelhof, Wiesenerstrasse 22) which has been his home for 30 years. A housekeeper opened the door. In the hall, stone slabs and an old trunk or two. At the top of the stairs, a cozy study next to a small dining room. The study was quite modern and comfortable. With the typewriting table and chair in one corner, the brass pewters on the shelves, the red carpet and yellow paper lamp shades, you could think yourself in the study of a Yale professor. Wissel was kind to me but not well prepared for our discussion. He showed me his library upstairs and recommended that I read the *Sozialistische Monatshefte*, the *Correspondenzblatt der deutschen Gewerkschaften*, and *Die Glocke*. When he tried to tell me his ideas about the workers before the First World War he seemed not to be able to concentrate very well. In the end he changed the subject and asked me how I liked Berlin and to my astonishment inquired whether I came from South America. But I am invited to call again and I may use his library if I cannot find enough books in Berlin.

---

[1] Friedrich Meinecke (1862-1954), eminent historian and in 1948 cofounder of the Free University in Berlin.

[2] Rudolf Wissell (1869-1962), SPD politician, Reich minister of economics (1919), Reich labor minister (1928-30). Active in postwar trade union movement.

While changing from the S-Bahn to the U-Bahn in Schmargendorf, I had a quick cup of coffee, then hurried on to the Breitenbachplatz. The Leuschnerhaus is at Lentzeallee 7-9 and was formerly the mansion of the Nazi foreign minister, von Ribbentrop. Today it is owned by the German Trade Union Association (Deutscher Gewerkschaftsbund, or DGB). The Free University's Students' Trade Union Society (I didn't get the exact name) were showing two films in the hope of making their club better known. Jay and Carol were there, and we had a lively talk with a group of students after the show. The head of the group is a Frau Christine Häker. She told me I must get to know a Herr Pietsch, who directs the Workers' Educational Institute (Institut für Arbeiterbildung) here in the Leuschnerhaus. The library of the DGB is also in this building. I must come back on a Thursday between 2 and 4 p.m., when the student club has its office hours.

9 February 1954

Spent the day in the archives. Herr Siewert admits that Russian war prisoners were badly treated by their German captors. He is not uncritical of what Germany had done to the world. Called Ossowsky. He is going to arrange for me to listen to four recorded radio programs at RIAS next week, which he thinks should interest me.— After the archives I had two cups of coffee and a doughnut at my Stammcafé in Steglitz, then I went to the Cerfs' for dinner. Peter Herz of RIAS had not come, but a Herr Wolf Libal, correspondent for the Deutsche Nachrichtenagentur (German News Agency) who is covering the French angle of the conference. The French, according to Libal, are not very talkative. I'll try to attend the French press conference in the Maison de France on Thursday. Today little Randolph stood up for the first time.

IO February 1954

Worked at home, then went to the colloquium at the Free University. Professor Walther Hofer introduced a French journalist, Jo Latour, who gave a very good talk on French Indochina. He described to us the difficulty of drawing up an armistice line in a territory where many parts are controlled by the French only during the day and by the Communists at night. He described to us the "pourrisemement du delta de la rivière rouge," which is political as well as ecological. Latour said the French know that they must quit Indochina sooner or later. "The Navarre plan is a mere propaganda stunt to get more Western support." At lunch I met a boy whom I had seen at the Leuschnerhaus two nights ago. His name is Jürgen Molkenthil-Böhme. He wants me to meet a Russian doctor, Vladimir Liebberg, who invites all sorts of weird characters to his house and believes in mysticism.

After lunch, tried to work at home, then proceeded to the Kudamm. First I had a coffee in a strange cafe near the Rankestrasse, whose guests appeared unusually gregarious, then I went to keep my appointment with Dr. Barbara Pischel at Schaperstrasse 21. She is a real "Blaustrumpf," a bit pedantic, lectures too much, but seems to be very competent. She lives in a large room stuffed with books and papers. She gave me some good tips regarding registrar's offices (Standesämter) and singing clubs in working-class districts. However, I fear that in her enthusiasm she underestimates the difficulty of finding 40-year old documents in workers' clubs and churches.

Following a quick dinner at a snack bar (*Schnell-Imbiss*) on the Kudamm, I wound up in the press conference room of the Maison de France. I was there at 7:15 and had to wait an hour since the foreign ministers' conference was still in session. After that journalists began to pour into the room, among them Jo Latour, who had talked to us at the Meinecke Institut this morning. We chatted together for a while. A native of Alsace Lorraine, he is rather shy by appearance. One wonders how he can have crossed from Indochina into China on horse back to visit anticommunist guerillas in Yünnan province, but that's what he says he has done. Liebal was there too. He gave me Dulles's speech to read. The great topic of conversation was Molotov's new proposal of a "European Defense Pact" that would include the USSR, France, England, and Germany, while the U.S.A. and China would serve merely as observers. According to Latour this proposal has found widespread interest among French journalists because France is the one Western country that is interested in this idea.

I am astonished how fast things get done here. The reply by Dulles to the speech by Molotov early this afternoon was mimeographed and distributed in time for this press conference. And when I left at 9:30 p.m, the evening newspapers in the street already carried the news of the new Molotov plan.

The press conference at the Maison de France was very cozy and informal. Only one man was in charge, Monsieur Bayens of the Quai d'Orsay, a man of about 55 years with kindly features and amiable manners, wearing a bright yellow overcoat. He sat at the center table, dropped his head very low, fumbled through his notes, and reported on the conference in a moody monologue. He was constantly interrupted by reporters who wanted to know the exact time when somebody had said something. It was like being in school with a very indulgent teacher. When one journalist got impatient, Bayens calmed him down with: "Allez, attendez, c'est moi qui vous raconte des histoires!" Journalists who tried to pull his leg, he rebuked with "Allons, allons, pas d'histoires, hein!" "Continuez, continuez!" he was urged. His reply was "Ba...b...b...b!" When Bayens told us that Dulles had declared that the U.S. had no interest in Europe, a roar of laughter went through the room. It was all finished in one hour. No questions at the end. No interpreters. Everyone spoke French.

And finally Bayens announced: "Demain, Bidault va rendre visite au Quartier Napoléon." Then he imitated a bugle, "ta-ta-ta, ta-ta-ta-ra!" and presented arms.

II February 1954

I have a sniveling cold and my head feels heavy. It must be the break in the weather. Spent most of the day at home. Only went out at 11:30 to return some books to the Senatsbibliothek and talk once more to Direktor Zopf, who gave me kind counsel. He mentioned a Dr. Bruno Kaiser, 100% communist, who heads the Marx-Engels Institut in the East sector. He said it was a pity I couldn't go there for the Communists have spent fabulous sums to replenish the library there. I then tried a goulash soup at a stand near the Gedächtnis-kirche that specializes in Hungarian snacks. Since it left me still hungry, I went into an Imbiss-Stube in a dirty rear courtyard in Joachimsthaler Strasse. Very interesting *intérieur*. There was a fat and grimy proprietor in a big pullover with a reddish, bloated face and curly hair who smiled at me sweetly. Coca-Cola advertisements on the wall and AFN music from the radio. Strange, swarthy men were conversing rapidly in a tongue that I couldn't identify. In one corner, some men were playing cards. One of the gamblers talked to me.— Now I've got a headache too.

12 February 1954

A wasted day. Went to the Freie Universität to hear Sir Anthony Eden give a talk, but he canceled his visit because of an unexpected secret conference he had to attend this morning. Jay had come too, and since I wanted to go to Friedrich Meinecke's funeral here in Dahlem later, I agreed to accompany him on various errands. We had a super-duper hamburger with coffee at the Harnack House (which is reserved for American officers and U.S. civilians), where we also picked up a copy of the Army paper *Berlin Observer*. Went to get Jay's photos at the photo store and found that the entire film which he had shot in East Berlin had been spoiled. (Jay doesn't believe it and is suspicious.) We finally wound up at the PX store, where we met Mr. and Mrs. Walter Sullivan in the cafeteria. The sky was grey, everything seemed rather gloomy. Jay asked what makes people in Berlin so interested in politics. My guess is that they are forced to by their circumstances. In the U.S. you can buy groceries without thinking about the world situation. In East Berlin you buy eggs at the HO store and think about the reconstruction program, the Communist party's "Neuer Kurs," and about the Soviet Union's relations to her satellite countries.

Meinecke's funeral was simple. There was a quartet playing chamber music from a balcony in the communal hall (*Gemein-*

dehaus) of Dahlem, which is an elegant residential suburb but calls itself a village. They played loudly and harshly, and the music seemed to me somehow inappropriate for a funeral unless it was thought something "highbrow" and "detached" was suitable for an historian. A pastor delivered a funeral oration that was a bit stilted compared to the elocution by Rektor Ernst Hirsch, which was brief but good. He and a number of his colleagues had come in full academic dress: velvet bonnets and long gowns with stripes. Someone I didn't know spoke after Hirsch, and after that Professor Hofer in the name of the younger academicians, and he was quite good.

One hour later we all followed the coffin across the street to the Sankt Annen Friedhof, where it was immediately lowered into the grave. Children stood on the stone wall and gaped, and there were press photographers. I wanted to but didn't dare to go and throw earth on the coffin, and much regretted my shyness when I got home.

13 February 1954

Returned books to the Wohlfahrtsarchiv. Sent a postcard to the Milkana-Preisauschreiben (a lottery) in the vain hope of winning an automobile. Heard the French foreign minister Georges Bidault talk in a former riding hall (*Reithalle*) in Ihnenstrasse, Berlin-Dahlem. It was terribly crowded. I was lucky to stand in the gangway where Bidault had to pass on his way to the podium. Coming and going he passed me only 3 inches away. He spoke briefly and seriously about the fight for freedom of students in West Berlin. "There can be no *égalité* and no *fraternité* where there is not *liberté* as well!" he exclaimed. He also said a few grave words about the foreign ministers' conference and his hope that something will still come of it, for the good of "votre pays et le mien." Great applause.

15 Februarv 1954

The weekend was "shot." But today things looked up again and I think the next few days will be busy and interesting. Met Carol and Jay early in the morning at Steglitz Bahnhof and while Carol and I proceeded by S-Bahn through the Soviet sector up to Reinickendorf in the French sector; Jay left us in Schöneberg to go to RIAS, where he met Ossowsky. Together with some Americans they were to be driven in a U.S. State Department car to the same place where we were going: the Bertha von Suttner Oberschule (Wissenschaftlicher Zweig) in Emmentaler Strasse 67.

The school itself was a big, grey building, not very cheerful, but rather like so many other ill-kept, impersonal, and ill-heated German office buildings in Berlin. On the walls hung prominent signs reading "Rauchen polizeilich verboten" (No smoking by order of the police). Cheerless corridors with peeling walls made me expect to see spitoons in the corners. We waited in the office of director Dr. Hübner for the recreation period to be over and for the microphones to be set up in the classroom. Hübner (who looks like a small employee with a collar that was much too large) explained to us that in the special class for East German boys and girls that we were about to visit, about half the children still lived in the Soviet sector of Berlin or in the Soviet occupation zone (DDR). Those who live in the zone have to leave home as early as 5:30 a.m. to arrive in time for their classes here at 8 a.m. They all have made their Abitur in the East, but to be recognized as graduates from secondary school in the West they must attend more classes. This is not easy since most of them still live under the pressure of the totalitarian regime in the East. One boy not too long ago got into trouble with his former school headmaster in East Berlin. This headmaster had learned that he now attended school in the West and denounced the boy to the police. The boy however was lucky and managed to escape from the police station. While waiting in the courtyard of the police station he had noticed many Vopos going in and out a gate leading to the street, and in an unguarded moment had slipped out. He made it to the West, where he asked for political asylum. When we finally went into the classroom, Ossowsky first made it clear that though the interview was to be recorded (there was a RIAS recording van outside the window), the tapes would not be broadcast over the air.

The discussion was slow in getting under way. There were about 20 girls and 60 boys ranging from about 17 to 21 years of age. (This is according to Hübner. Some of them looked much younger to me.) They had no satchels, no books or papers or pens on their benches. The first questions they asked were practical in nature and concerned job opportunities in America, whether American universities recognize German state examinations, and whether in the U.S. washing machines are for everyone or merely for the affluent woman ("die besser gestellte Frau") as in Germany. One boy asked what gadgets Americans were so proud of? But slowly the questions became more political. Could the "German question" be resolved by next Thursday? What had we to say about McCarthyism in America? Are Americans really less interested in politics than Germans? Why is America so "cowardly" and always gives in to the Russians?

One boy, his voice ringing with emotion, asked why the U.S. fought on the French side in Indochina, where a colonial people were only struggling for national freedom? This question provoked a roar of laughter from the other students, and I didn't like it. The merits of the question apart, I fear that such laughter discourages more questions along this line, questions that probably really trouble many youngsters and which ought to be asked and answered. Moreover, it may indicate that there is a psychological pressure to ridicule anyone whose ideas seem to reflect the schooling he (or she) has received in the East. Are these students vying against each other in demonstrating how "emancipated" they were from communist propaganda? Are they then not in danger of trading in one set of political slogans for another, at the expense of learning what a liberal education really should give them: the ability to think and discern by themselves?

I don't think John Albert, one of the Americans Jay had come with, was very good as the spokesman for the Voice of America. His answers were not simple and straightforward enough. He spoke too fast, he got lost in side issues which he illustrated with too many examples, and he often missed the point of the question. Example: one boy criticized the low quality of American magazines like *Life* and *Holiday*. He didn't like the advertisements and the poor quality of the articles. Albert explained to him the advantages of advertisements (it makes the magazines cheaper), talked extensively about radio commercials, and never answered the question about the poor articles. Another boy asked whether America has not a vested interest in the armaments race in order to prevent an economic crisis at home. Albert brushed him off by telling him that he was confusing "economic crisis" with "inflation" and left it at that. I don't think he won the hearts of his audience, though he managed to make them listen to him with keen interest.

While Carol went home (Ossowsky gave her a ride part of the way to Wannsee), I spent the rest of the day with Jay. First we had a good lunch at a nearby restaurant, then we went into town. Jay wanted to go to the "Goldener Pfeil" (a shop selling leather goods) in Tauentzienstrasse to buy Carol a birthday present, and I went to Charlottenburg, first to look up Konstantin Kurtz, a Siemens pensioner, to tell him I won't be able to see him on Wednesday. For on Wednesday the Cerfs are planning one more trip to the East sector and I want to go with them. This will be the last time the foreign ministers meet in the Soviet sector and we want to take advantage of the Vopos' special order to be courteous to foreigners while it lasts. Kurtz was not in, so I left a note. Then I went to see an exhibition called "Berlin um 1900" in the town hall of Charlottenburg. It mainly showed photographs of street scenes from that period. Thus you saw the Steglitz Rathaus with the trees outside in full bloom, the square without the neon lights of today, and instead of large stores, old-fashioned bourgeois mansions and horse carriages where today there are electric streetcars. The visitors to the exhibition were mainly elderly people who obviously enjoyed seeing the Berlin of their childhood days again.

I rushed over to the Reichskanzlerplatz where the British have their clubs, cinema, and other facilities for their armed forces. The Jerboa Cinema is very well appointed: big, well furnished, with excellent projectors. Jay met me there. He had gotten hold of some "Bafs" (British Armed Forces currency) and so we went in to see *The Conquest of Everest*, a magnificent documentary film. The British newsreel, however, was interesting mainly because of the selection of its topics: about 85% was sporting events (rugger, football, and the British armed forces skiing competion in Austria) and only a few shots of the Berlin conference.

Then we went to the restaurant of the Army Club. Much better than the American PX in Clayallee. Maybe this is the reason why so many American officers were eating there. On the first floor, a very comfortable club room with a counter selling English papers. On the second floor, the restaurant, tastefully arranged though not extravagantly so. Good sturdy British women having their meals. The waitresses were German and we made friends with one called Uschi (Ursula), 29 years old, who told us she is engaged to a Jewish waiter. We gave her a big tip in the end so that she can play Toto, the favorite Berlin lottery, and perhaps buy herself the furniture she wants for her future home. We spent a long time in the club, first at the restaurant (I ordered kidneys with potato chips and lots of Worcestershire sauce, followed by a good cup of "char" with milk and sugar and an English doughnut), then at the bar in the sergeants' mess a floor higher (where I had a gin with orange juice). Uschi was also serving there and she offered us cigarettes.

Jay and I talked about Yale and his plans for the future. Jay is getting tired of living like a graduate student and has resolved to wear only suits when he gets home to the U.S.A. (Though Carol doesn't mind living in the style of poor scholars, Jay admits.) He also intends to become rich, even if this means having to go into the business world. He has an idea about selling educational films for the *Encyclopedia Brittanica*. I personally think Jay would be better as a teacher or a journalist, perhaps a foreign correspondent.

We left close to eleven. I accompanied Jay by S-Bahn as far as Wannsee, then changed into what I thought was the train to Steglitz. It *was* a train to Steglitz, but I didn't know that it would first go into the Russian zone (the DDR!) for cleaning. My heart sank as I saw the carriage leaving the station in the wrong direction. I was the only passenger. As we left the well-lighted station and rolled into the dark night towards the "forbidden" land (I was afraid we would go to Potsdam) I began to think very fast, faster than I've ever done before. My first thought was: "What will Jay and Carol say when I don't show up for dinner tomorrow?" because I was sure that in Potsdam I would be arrested. My next move was to pocket a communist matchbox with a propaganda cover which I saw lying on a bench. It might come useful, I thought. Then I decided that the copy of *Foreign Affairs* and all my notes taken at the Suttner school this morning would have to disappear under the radiator under the bench the minute police came to get me.

But no police came. The train slowed down and entered a hangar. I was spotted by some railway officials who shouted and gesticulated.

I opened the door and explained that I wanted to go in the direction of Schöneberg and had gotten on the wrong train. (Had I not been spotted, I would have tried to spend the night in this carriage.) Then they quietened down and told me to sit tight, the train would leave for Schöneberg in 20 minutes. I was greatly relieved. The carriage was dark and I sat smoking cigarettes, now able to enjoy this little adventure. A sloppily dressed woman climbed into the carriage to sweep it and she confirmed that I was now in the DDR. Soon the train left again, this time in the right direction, and I returned to the safety of West Berlin.

Tuesday, 16 February 1954

Spent the morning in the Landesarchiv. Then hurried by U-Bahn through the East sector up to Wedding. I had wanted to see the OSRAM works, but found to my dismay that the tour which I had seen advertised had taken place yesterday. Then I decided to visit two Siemens workers who lived in Wedding. First I had a meal at a big proletarian restaurant (though that didn't make it cheap), erred around in the intense cold— it snowed— and at 2:30 finally went to Malplaquetstrasse no. 9 to ask for Herr Görk. Görk lived in the rear wing of a tenement house up a dark stairway, the door opening into a smelly kitchen. He wasn't in, so I left a note and went to Genterstrasse. Luckily Herr Bohn was at home. His wife immediately guessed who I was. Bohn was very lively. We sat around his table for an hour and I took lots of notes.

The Wedding has very wide streets, I discovered. This gives the whole district the appearance of spaciousness. The high houses, however, are drab and grey, the court yards (*Hinterhöfe*) are depressing. Lots of children could be seen playing in the streets.

I went to Wannsee for dinner. Peter Herz had come. Like Ossowsky, he's from the RIAS Schulfunk. About 26 years old, chubby and a bit pompous, but very well informed on current affairs in Germany. A Socialist party man. His job is not only to broadcast programs for young people but also to collect information and to undertake propaganda in the fight against communism. He visits jails where he talks to communist youths who have run into trouble with the police, trying to win them for the West. He says there are FDJ boys who believe in communism yet who still will come to see him at RIAS, as for example during a recent rally of the World Federation of Democratic Youth. He doesn't think the youth in the communist countries is "lost" to the West. According to him, 50% of the boys and girls who graduate from the children's organizations in East Germany do not enter the FDJ. (He says he knows this from secret communist documents that he managed to obtain.) Some two years ago, he and some colleagues decided to reach Eastern youths by way of their hobbies. They started a philatelic society and Peter contacted philatelic clubs in the East sector and the Russian zone under the assumed name "Peter Albert." No one knew, of course, that this was just another RIAS undertaking. He now has some 4,000 boys in the Russian zone with whom he trades stamps. Trading postage stamps can be a form of propaganda since foreign stamps can make the boys over there think about the rest of the world. Why don't Western stamps carry political slogans? Why is everything in the East so political? Recently Peter Albert furnished a batch of stamps for an FDJ stamp exhibition and it won a prize! I asked him where he got the money for doing all these things but he wouldn't say. "There are sources…"

We also talked about the revival of the German student fraternities (*Burschenschaften*), a subject Jay is very sore about just now. The Burschenschaften were outlawed in Berlin after the war, but the FU authorities, apparently, are turning a blind eye on their continuing activities. Recently there had been a meeting of Burschenschaften in Berlin, and Adenauer and several Bonn ministers are said to have sent telegrams with good wishes. (When the FU celebrated its 5th anniversary a few days later, however, only one federal minister had cared enough to send a cable.) Since the Burschenschaften claim that they are no different from American fraternities, Jay has written them a letter as an American fraternity student, asking permission to attend a meeting. If he can get evidence of inadmissible doings on their part, he will inform Rektor Ernst Hirsch about it, and if that doesn't help, write to his senator in America and to the Ford Foundation, which finances the FU. The Burschenschaften are said to cultivate the old nationalist and military spirit. Peter Herz had once been invited to join one, but the invitation was withdrawn when it was found that he was half Jewish.

Peter took me home in his car. He told me that I should make sure to meet Rudolf Wissel. We made a stop at RIAS where he had to pick up some work to take home. Got home very late again.

Wednesday, 17 February 1954

A great but exhausting day. I got up earlier than usual to go to RIAS, which I reached by 9 a.m. I was immediately taken to a studio ("Tonträgerraum 2"). Ossowsky had arranged for me to listen to the tapes of 4 programs that describe welfare provisions for workers in present-day Berlin. They were, unfortunately, not historically interesting. Ossowsky himself arrived at 10. He agreed that the tapes were chiefly intended as propaganda: they were meant to inform people in East Berlin what social security the workers in the Western sectors receive. When he heard that I was about to go to the East sector, he asked me to buy him some music records and pictures of pieces of French sculpture.

At 11:30 I met Carol and Jay, as arranged, on the platform of S-Bahnhof Schöneberg. The weather was intensely cold and I was wearing only a mackintosh. We rode as far as the Thälmannplatz and then proceeded on foot towards the Lustgarten and the site of the former Berlin Castle. When you walk here you are surrounded by gigantic ruins of royal mansions, opera houses, theaters, and churches, all at one time conceived on a monumental scale but today little more than burned out, hollow shells with twisted rusty steel girders. Near the bridge we found a Russian sentinel, the first Russian soldier on duty we had seen except for those at the Tiergarten memorial. When Jay asked him for direction the Ivan muttered a gruff "Njet versteh." Jay said he had heard Russian soldiers were back on the streets of East Berlin in large numbers to prevent another popular uprising like on 17 June last year.

Where formerly the royal palace had stood a large tribune has been build, with a huge poster announcing 1954 as "The Year of the Great Initiative." All around the square were more posters with gaily colored political cartoons, and stands for selling sausages and lemonade (though these were closed). I was anxious to return to where, last time, the postmistress had told us we could obtain propaganda materials. We couldn't find Rosenthaler Strasse no. 24, but finally came to the Society for German-Soviet Friendship in another house. (Before venturing inside we first had lunch at a HO restaurant and bought some Russian cigarettes. The meal was quite good and cheap if you pay with West marks.) Thus reinforced, we walked into the German-Soviet Friendship Society. It is on the first floor of a former patrician house, having once belonged to a rich textile merchant— "the richest man in Berlin," we were later told. A very pleasant young man received us. He was very thin, shabbily dressed, pale, but he had a friendly smile. I introduced ourselves as foreign students who are in Berlin for only a short time and anxious to see what our German comrades were doing. Might we have some of their political posters to decorate our own club rooms with? I also vaguely talked about amity between all democratic and peace-loving nations. Jay thought I laid it on too thick, especially when I exclaimed "my hero" at the sight of a Mao Tse-tung picture, but the main thing is that it all went down smoothly. The man never asked us any questions (what would we have answered had he asked us for an address in Berlin?). He showed us cardboard emblems of the Soviet Union, the DDR, and of the Society for German-Soviet Friendship (I bought one of them), emblems of the East German Five Year Plan, pictures of Marx, Engels, Lenin, and Stalin in one row, and lampions with hammers and sickles. We bought little insignias of their society, which we pinned to our lapels for the duration of our tour in the East sector. On the way out, to my horror, Jay stole a pocket diary of the society and an empty membership book from a desk.

Next, we went to the Theaterkasse. I wanted to invite the Cerfs to

WORKING-CLASS STREETS IN BERLIN—WEDDING

Afrikanisches Viertel

Reinickendorfer Strasse

BERLIN SOCIAL DEMOCRATS

In former days Liebknecht used to sit in a Café and, over a cup of coffee, talk to the simple workers to ask them about their opinions and to give information."

In der "Tonne"

**Speaker at a Conference of Party veterans
(14 July, 1954)**

**Wilhelm Miethke,
founder of Workers'
Abstinence League
(2 and 11 Aug., 1954)**

Paul Löbe (7 July, 1954)

**Rudolf Wissell
(12 Feb., 1954)**

Willy Brandt (4 July, 1954)

a good communist play as a birthday present for Carol but it turned out there was no performance today. We went on to the Alexanderplatz, which surprisingly looked like a small, unimposing square. There are some better looking modern shops at the corners, but very little traffic. All around you see mainly ruins and streets that look as if the Battle for Berlin had ended yesterday. We went into the Marx-Engels bookstore, where I bought a record with "Ami Go Home" and "Kalinka," then to the Soviet bookstore where I got a record with a Caucasian cradle song for Ossowsky.

In Stalinallee Jay stopped to take a picture of a construction site. An old man with a red armband asked him whether he had a permit. "Njet versteh," Jay answered, then the three of us departed very quickly. Loudspeakers along the Allee were blaring away the "Song of Democratic Youth," children were playing on the broad pavement, a box-shaped Russian plane flew over low, and a Russian jeep hurried past, looking much clumsier than the American original.

We entered the Café Budapest, which we found luxurious and elegant. It is not allowed to put your overcoats on chairs. Glass vitrines diplayed samples of popular craftsmanship from various "democratic" countries. The guests were all elderly. A few Russian officers, a Chinese in a raincoat (he looked exactly like me!), a few distinguished looking gentlemen with white hair (comrade academicians?), and two women who seemed to belong to the proletarian class. Next to me sat a very elegant young lady whose escort, however, was in a drab grey suit. He had no tie and his shirt was positively dirty. The two were drinking Hungarian wine. In this restaurant, waiters who go on duty take cards out of their wallets and place them on the tables before they wait on you. Our waiter was "Kollege Kunkel." We were also given the names of the manager and the cook.

After we left we peeked quickly in the Café Warschau next door: even more posh than the Budapest! Beautiful wall decorations in the Polish style, cozy little *chambres séparées* with pictures of Chopin and other famous Poles. Delicious-looking cakes.

It was getting dark. We looked for a cinema in the hope of seeing a Russian film. Ended in a miserable little movie house on a side street near Alexanderplatz. It showed a Czech film, *Revolt in the Village*, the story of how the women in one village won a fight with their menfolk in a dispute over whether the village commune should buy a tractor or a washing machine. Technically the film was very poor. But there was an interesting short film beforehand: a satire about an HO store where a customer was not allowed to buy a winter coat made in the winter (why?). The tailor who refused to sell is in the end sent off to a lunatic asylum. The newsreel showed the same explosion of a British A-bomb in Australia that could be seen in the West sectors, only here the commentator talked about murder weapons designed by the imperialist warmongers. They also showed the catastrophic snow avalanche which was shown in the Western cinemas some weeks ago, but without the shots showing U.S. helicopters evacuating the wounded.

Got back to Wannsee, had a Chinese chop-suey dinner which was really toi-toi-toi, returned home late, as usual.

Thursday, 18 February 1954

Worked in the archives. Had planned to go straight from there to interview two more Siemens pensioners, but was forced to go home first since I had forgotten their addresses. My first interviewee was Konstantin Kurtz, a verbose, expansive man of over 70, who is Catholic and loves Charlottenburg. By contrast Richard Wels was a careful, reserved man, a stolid Socialist who still has the accounts of his wages from the year 1914. I was surprised by the comfortable— indeed, the bourgeois— appearance of their rooms. Both men lived in well-heated flats furnished with carpets, lace curtains at the windows, sideboards with glass vitrines containing pieces of china, and nice radio sets. Mr. Kurtz had a beautiful blue tile stove.

I left Wels in somewhat of a hurry because I didn't want to miss the "Schweigemarsch," the silent protest march called by the trade unions to protest the failure of the Berlin conference. (Another procession is supposed to be staged for the same time in East Berlin). Arrived at Wittenbergplatz by 6:30, just in time to catch the tail end of the procession. All the tramways and automobiles had stopped as thousands of people shuffled towards the Schöneberger Rathaus. I saw one man distributing leaflets. Flanking the procession were people carrying burning torches. The procession was made up of people of all classes and all ages, including whole families, workers and intellectuals. They were not really silent but they talked to one another quietly and a bit listlessly, like people at a funeral of someone they hadn't known too well. A blue police van brought up the rear. I joined the marchers and tried to talk to some of them. One girl said she belonged to a trade union, a worker told me that he belonged to no union but wouldn't say why he had a torch and why he had joined the procession. A boy said he was a music student and felt he must march because he was a refugee from the East. He also said he was disappointed by the lack of interest shown by the participants. I only saw about 5 or 6 posters: Youth Does not Want War but a Free Europe! The Landowners of West Berlin Want to Use Their Land in the Russian Zone and the East Sector. The Construction Workers Want Unification. Don't Forget Our Sisters and Brothers in the East!

I rushed to the head of the procession where students marched with the green-white banner of "United Europe." I talked to a girl student who was obviously having a good time. No one seemed bitter about the conference, they didn't even talk about it. I stood very close to the podium of the speaker, in the front rank of the marchers.

Journalists were taking pictures and there were newsreel cameras. Then the mayor of Schöneberg, Kressmann, introduced Berlin's Lord Mayor Schreiber, Otto Suhr, and Scharnowski, who all spoke of the West Berliners' determination not to give up their hope for a peaceful reunification of Germany. But Scharnowski was the only one who tried to stir up some enthusiasm. "In the battle between East and West, Germany has no intention to play the part of the buffoon [*Hanswurst*]!" He wanted to introduce a new symbol, the raised hand with three pointed fingers, to represent Berliners fighting for their good cause, but very few people took him up and saluted in this fashion. Some students started to sing the old socialist song, "Brüder zur Sonne, zur Freiheit!" just when Kressmann dissolved the meeting, and only a handful of people stayed behind to sing.[1]

19 February 1954

Spent the morning going to the Wedding interviewing another old Siemens worker, Richard Görk, in the Malplaquet Strasse no. 9. (According to the newspapers, a little girl had been found murdered a few houses away, at No. 24.) It was a very good interview that lasted two hours. I was given tea, biscuits, and cigarettes. Very cosy living room, though the house itself was by no means inviting: Görk lives in the rear wing of a tenement with a dark staircase. He owned a big fishbowl, a black dog, and quite nice furniture. The flat itself is sunny and clean. The rent for this one room, kitchen, and toilet is only 28 marks a month.

Had a turnip cabbage soup with pigs' knuckles for lunch, then went back to the center of town. Since I had time to kill, I visited the Amerikahaus on the Nollendorfplatz but was greatly disappointed. I didn't like it at all. I found its design tasteless, cheap, and almost shabby. I only stayed to see two very boring films (one on New York harbor, the other on Rockefeller Center) because it was so cold outside.

Then I went to Ziethenstrasse, the main office of the Social Democratic Party in Berlin. Met a very interesting Herr Eberhard Hesse in room no. 11. (Kind man with a brutal face, a flat broken nose.) Hesse is a journalist. The office looks shabby (the Ziethenstrasse is in a proletarian quarter) but he was talkative. He didn't expect me to know very much for he told me some elementary facts on German history and was stupefied to find that I had heard of the old three-class voting system in Prussia. As to archival materials: he said they had all been lost in the war. A complete set of the SPD newspaper, *Vorwärts*, exists only in Tübingen. (Here Hesse was wrong: the Berlin Landesarchiv also has a set, though it is not complete.) Then he told me that older SPD men like him feel

---

[1] Ernst Scharnowski (b. 1896) was chairman of the DGB in Berlin.

melancholy when they compare the political climate today with the lively atmosphere within the socialist movement before the First World War. In the old days workers spent their whole free time with party organizations: attending club meetings or talking with each other in SPD pubs (*Kneipen*). This tradition no longer exists. The reason may be the German working-class movement's failure to fight fascism arms-in-hand, the way the Austrian comrades had fought in 1934. Hesse thinks it will take decades before the German Socialists can overcome the memory of their weakness in the face of Nazism. Today, Austria with some 6 million inhabitants has 650,000 SPÖ members, which represents 10% of the population. The Federal Republic of Germany has more than 40 million inhabitants, but the SPD members number only 650,000. Hesse also told me that the *Mietskasernen* (the worker's tenements, designed in the 1860s) were built five storys high in order to render barricades less effective. He will introduce me to someone who can conduct me through the working-class districts and show me their problems.

Met Jay at 6 o'clock at the Reichskanzlerplatz to see the British film *Desperate Moment*, because it is set in postwar Berlin. Very disappointed since it was no more than a thriller.

20 February 1954

Nothing important happened. Read an article from *Harper's* magazine which Jay lent me: Milton Mayer, "The Germans, Their Cause and Cure." Found it titillating. It is a study of the mentality among "little people" in a small West German town. Meyer limited his survey to just 10 individuals (is that sufficient?), but his remarks are all very shrewd. He obviously dreads Nazism more than communism and he denounces the U.S. for not "reeducating" the Germans thoroughly enough. In place of free lectures on democracy, the Amerikahauses in Germany should offer political debates. There is a resurgence of fascism, he claims: is this because of American ignorance or cupidity?

Sunday, 21 February 1954

Afternoon tea with Klaus Androwsky in Mariendorferstrasse 33d, Steglitz. Present were his mother, his grandmother, Simon Warrington-Ward (an English boy from Cambridge University), and Harold Craig, an American working as a clerk for the U.S. Military Police. The conversation was interesting. Klaus's mother taught in a secondary school (*Oberschule*) in the Russian zone until 1951, when she came to the West as a refugee. She claims that before she left, the older children she had in her class still resisted communist indoctrination. They would come to class and put anticommunist pamphlets on her desk to test her: would she go and denounce them to the headmaster as was her duty? (She threw them in the waste bin.) As a result her class cooperated well with her and would not let her down during political inspection tours by Party functionaries. Among the teachers there had also been many who were not communist. And yet, because of fear, some of them turned in students to the police who would not toe the party line. One teacher called the police because a child had pinned a caricature of President Grotewohl on the blackboard. However, Frau Androwsky believes that the elementary schools are now producing a younger generation of children who will be thoroughly indoctrinated. At that point, reunification of West and East Germany may become impossible. There is also a growing disenchantment with West Germany among the East Germans: Adenauer and the CDU are believed not to care about Germany's division any more (the people in Bonn had held only a very modest "Schweigemarsch"), and the SPD is seen as too unimaginative.

Saw the movie *Geliebtes Leben*, and found it rather thought-provoking. It tells the story of a German family from the 1890s to the present. What do you do when your children become Nazis, and when you are ruined by wars and financial crises? The closing scene was touching: Luise, now an old woman, goes to the refugee camp Friedland to meet her husband who is a returning POW, now also old and worn out. And both of them say: "We must make a new start." I left in a pensive mood. It seems to me that I have enjoyed Berlin so far without quite thinking that all my exciting adventures are related to the very things that cause sorrow to thousands of Berliners. There must be many old people like Luise and her husband among the older people I have met in the past weeks.

On my way home, around 9 p.m., I observed a young man fleeing through the park. A few minutes later a girl, her mother, and a porter ran towards me, gesticulating wildly. The girl had been attacked but she had managed to scream and her attacker had fled. I waited until the police came (a Volkswagen and a Mercedes Benz patrol car coming slowly down the footpath), and I told them the direction in which I had seen the man flee.

Monday, 22 February 1954

An arduous but very satisfying day. Went to Siemensstadt and to the neighboring district of Haselhorst to interview four old Siemens workers. I was well received. All of them live comfortably, though not luxuriously. Their rooms were all remarkably tidy though over-stuffed and a bit smelly, but at least they did not live in attics or humid cellars. Everyone seems to have a big clock, a sideboard, some dainty china for display, table cloths. The poorest of the four was probably Hugo Hoppe, an old monarchist with a broad, reddish face whose father, however, had been quite well-off (he had owned four houses). Hoppe told me he is still a Nazi. "We need another Hitler now," he said. The only reason why he hadn't joined the NSDAP in the thirties was because his boss at Siemens had been anti-Nazi and joining the Party could have cost him his job. "But otherwise," he said, "Ph...! Hitler should be here now, he wouldn't stand for such a nonsensical conference! He would bang his fist on the table!" Hoppe also told me he admires Chiang Kai-shek. Oh dear.

Two of the Siemens workers offered me some refreshment. The one in the Wattstrasse did decorative woodwork (*Laubholzarbeiten*) as a hobby. He was also the cheekiest of the three and wouldn't let me ask him about his SPD membership. Actually, all of them except Hoppe were taciturn when I asked them about their political or their trade union affiliations.

I had no time for dinner and had to rush straight to Zehlendorf in order to make Klaus Androwsky's evening class in time. We had a very stimulating discussion on German society but of course reached no conclusions— except that all social classifications that had once existed no longer apply today.

23 February 1954

Went to the archives, then borrowed some books from the Stein Bibliothek. After a lunch in the FU Mensa, went to interview my last Siemens worker, Kurt Kaczmarek. (He turned out to be a kindly old fellow.) Then I rushed to the Funkturm to hear Chancellor Konrad Adenauer speak. The event took place in a huge exhibition hall, but it was not overly crowded. At one end, on a balcony, a band played marches, waltzes, and Wagnerian music until Adenauer arrived shortly after 6 o'clock. There was a rousing reception. Adenauer reminds me of Vicar Hewitt in Felbridge, Suffolk (where I spent two holidays as a schoolboy in England): a strong, vigorous old man with huge hands. He spoke firmly about his government's resolution to reunite Germany in freedom, be it by means "straight" or by "roundabout ways" (*auf Umwegen*). He brought a "Hoch!" to the three Western foreign ministers who had stood up for German freedom and promised the East Germans that they would share in the prosperity of West Germany after unification. West Berlin was told to expect more economic help in the form of orders placed with local firms and a continued policy of special tax reductions. The audience responded vividly: when Adenauer spoke of Molotov's aims at the Conference people shouted "Pfui!" He mentioned the several cabinet ministers who had come with him to Berlin and one joker in the audience shouted "Introduce them!" (Vorstellen!). For Adenauer, this appearance was politically important because there are people who think he does not care about reunification.

24 February 1954

A wasted day. Went to the FU Kolloquium at 11 a.m. but it was canceled. On the way home with Androwsky I got lured into an old car park. A small 1938 Fiat four-seater limousine, light grey and sturdy, attracted my attention. It cost only 1,250 marks, or a little over U.S. $300! The sudden spring-like feeling in the air must have made me dream of traveling out of Berlin to distant places like Avignon in Provence, or to Italy. After all, I don't know when I can come to Europe again. By contrast, a second-hand Volkswagen at the VW dealer near Rathaus Steglitz costs 3,000 marks.

Went to Loden Frey and decided to buy a new coat. Mine is getting too shabby and worn out. To make up for this extravaganza I had only a cup of coffee at Konditorei Rabien as my dinner.

Jay called. He and Carol have been asked to make the rounds of all the political cabarets in West Berlin for the *New York Times*. How marvelous!

25 February 1954

Worked in the archives. There is tension in the reading room because Dr. Lachmann is angry at Frau Dr. Täuber, who has made many mistakes in her files.

After lunch I went to the Leuschnerhaus. Met a Jürgen Eppe who invited me to a trade union meeting in the Kliems Festsäle, a popular workers' meeting hall, on Thursday. Returned books to the Senatsbibliothek and noticed that the Tiergarten smelled so fresh and clean. Spring has come at last and the air is quite mild. Dropped into the Ritz Restaurant to write down some more Chinese words for their menu. I was taken up to the private apartment of the Fischers in the house next door. Herr Fischer in shirt sleeves gave me a pen and black ink, while his daughter Gisela was making lampshades for her room. We chatted and Fischer said I could ride with them to Italy in the summer if I wanted to.

After a quick supper of pea soup and pigs' knuckles (which cost 80 pfennigs at Aschinger's), went to RIAS where I met Herr Herz senior (a well-known news commentator for RIAS and for radio NWDR), Frau Herz, and Peter. Jay almost came too late. Carol didn't come since she had to attend the Ring Politischer Jugend for Jay. We proceeded in two cars to a boys' refugee camp at Kladow, a country seat that once belonged to Prince Bismarck. It is quite far outside the city, close to the British military airport. It was already dark by the time we got there and we couldn't see much of the open country around us. At the camp was a gate with a gatekeeper. (The boys are not allowed out at night. When they go into town they must give notice beforehand.) Inside the camp stood a few houses among big trees. The main building has a red neon-light heart over the front door. We were met by Frau Bachhofer, a sweet old lady who is the *Lagerleiterin* (director), an American preacher from Ohio and his wife, and by a very young Herr Heim, a rather pompous clergyman who called himself "Lagerpastor." (It turned out he had no sense of humor!)

We went inside a wooden barracks. By then it was around 8 o'clock. In the front room a boy sat at a table writing a letter to the dim light of two electric bulbs dangling from the ceiling. Then came a room with wash basins of metal looking like troughs in a cowbarn. This depressing scene reminded me of a borstal institution for juvenile delinquents in Suffolk that I had visited some years ago. Later the boys told me they lived 80 to a room, in bunks one atop the other.

In the main assembly room sat about 200 boys. They had waited for us for close to an hour. Peter presented himself as the spokesman of RIAS, the bridge between their old homes in the East and their new ones in West Germany. He told them to be politically conscious, to think of themselves as missionaries or ambassadors of East Germany to the "so often near-sighted and self-complacent West." He also admonished them to give up drink. Alcohol, he later told us, is the symptom of the general malaise of young people under communism. Drunkenness gets them into fights with the police and forces them to flee to the West. Which means that many of them are not really "political" refugees. He was later borne out by the things the boys told us about themselves. Most of them had learnt simple manual trades and wanted no more than an easier life in the West. Only two or three had received an advanced education.

One case was particularly interesting. This concerned a boy who had served in the Volkspolizei and then escaped. At the Marienfelde refugee camp the American CIA asked him to return to the East zone to spy for them. But to save paying him travel expenses, he said, the Americans asked him whether he had a bicycle or a motorbike that he could use. So he had refused their offer. (I am not sure this story is accurate. Can the CIA be that dumb? Maybe the boy had simply misunderstood them?)

The boys did not appear to be very interested in Peter Herz's political preaching. Their chief concern was their personal future (Where in the Bundesrepublik will we be going? What chances will we have there?) and many complained about the rudeness of camp officials here and in Marienfelde. When one of the boys got up and spoke bitterly about being treated like a fourth-class person and said he now wondered why he had bothered to escape to the West, all the other boys listened intently. Frau Bachhofer quietened the boys by reminding them in a tactful tone that there had been some unruly elements among them (equipment that had been broken, blankets that were torn up, bedsteads that were taken to pieces) and how important it was that the camp officials retained overall control.

Peter promised to report the complaints to higher authority and urged them to insist on their right to treatment as equals. "Wir sind doch alle Landsleute" (Aren't we all fellow citizens?). But he seemed to be on the defensive. A thick-set, muscular young ex-Vopo Unterwachtmeister accused Peter of not answering their questions (he was referring to an earlier session) and of intimidating his audience by mocking their questions as "Party jargon" (Parteichinesisch). I must admit I don't understand why Peter at the beginning of the meeting insisted that all boys had to take off their caps. Any familiarity between him and the audience— a joke, for example— had to be on his terms. Far more successful than Peter in producing a good contact with the boys was the American padre. He talked in quite good German about his belief in God and in human freedom and sincerely wished them well. Unlike Peter, the padre spoke with humility and his sympathy sounded true.

The session ended around 10 p.m. Some of the boys wanted to talk to us as we got up. I spoke with one boy who said he was 19 but looked like a 12-year-old kid. He had dark, frightened eyes, and a yellowish skin. He said that he had learned the trade of cobbling and escaped from over there less than one week ago. When I asked why, he just looked at me with an open mouth and said nothing. Some comrades patted him on the shoulder and laughed: "Hab' doch keene Angst, sag's doch!!" (Don't be scared, tell him!). But he just continued to stare at me like a frightened rabbit. Would he have stared liked that had I been a communist policeman? Had I been a communist policeman, would I have considered him an enemy of the state and imperialist agent?

We had a late supper at the Paris Café in Rankestrasse. We were served excellent filets with French fries, and glasses of red "pinard." But I had to think of the refugee boys who will wait a long time before they get a supper like this.

26 February 1954

Left home early to go to the General Electric Company (AEG) at Hohenzollerndamm in the Grunewald. Since I was a bit too early to see Herr Domschke, I walked around the suburban streets looking at the big crematorium and the Russian Orthodox Church at Fehrbelliner Platz. The AEG office building was smaller and less impressive than that of Siemens, but easier to get in past the doorman. I found Domschke in the office of a young Dr. Matz, who is in charge of economic matters. Matz said he would get me in touch with a Herr Schwandt and Herr Möbius who had written a small brochure about the history of AEG. Schwandt could also get me in touch with old employees. A Herr Dr. Deter promised me reading materials, among them a hand-written essay by an "educated workman" (*intelligenter Arbeiter*) named Wilhelm Wahrmund, who has written a political history of Germany from Weimar to Hitler. A visit to a factory may also be arranged.

Met Jay at RIAS where the two of us invited Peter Herz for lunch in the RIAS casino on the top floor. (This turned out to be quite expensive.) Peter told us how Marshall aid money is being squandered here. Once he was asked to write the script for a political cabaret. Before long he was approached by a man who seemed to be walking around RIAS with his pockets stuffed with money to hand out. He asked Herz what he needed, Peter said 100 marks, and the man gave him 200. He treated everyone who worked for the cabaret like that, paying them large sums for the smallest contribution, even if they had only carried a few chairs.

After lunch, walked Jay to the Bundesallee where the Bonn government has its main Berlin office. Jay is looking for an archive that collects information on the Soviet zone. I continued by myself to the SPD library in Zietenstrasse. Found some interesting material there, namely a wad of police reports dating from the 1890s in manuscript form (mainly accounts of May Day celebrations) which some Socialist must have stolen from the police headquarters in Berlin-Weissensee during the 1918 revolution.

27 February 1954

Got up especially early so I could meet Gustav Pietsch at the offices of the German Trade Union Association (Deutscher Gewerkschafts- bund, or DGB) in Schlüterstrasse. Gustav Pietsch is the second-in- command of the DGB, directly under Scharnowski. The building is modern and big. It houses the head offices of some of the largest German trade unions like the ÖTV (the union of civil servants and transport workers). Pietsch is a kindly elderly man, rather jolly, who reminded me of Papa's old friend, Nationalrat Hans Müller in Berne. He was especially cooperative, I believe, because he has fond memories of Tsingtau which he had visited as a merchant seaman in 1912-14 and loves China. He wants to take me to the Leuschnerhaus next Tuesday to look through the Institute for Workers' Education and ask all trade union offices there what materials they could give me for my thesis. It is strange that Pietsch has never heard of the Stein Bibliothek. The DGB library has pitifully few books. Most of its collection are today in the East sector, in the library of the *Free* Trade Union Association (FDGB).

Had a cup of coffee at an snack bar after leaving Pietsch. A man sat next to me and we started to talk. He had been a POW in Russia, and in order to please me, he told me how much he had respected the Russian guards of Mongolian origin. They were much cleaner than the Great Russians, he said, and they could not be bribed. They have an extreme sense of duty (*äusserste Pflichttreue!*), he emphasized. There is a Russian army rule, he continued, that says prisoners of

TOURING BERLIN'S ELECTRICAL COMPANIES

The Siemens-Schuckert Works (19 Jan., 1954)

Director Eugen Eisele

In the Siemens library

262

Lombacher said there are still thousands of Swiss living in the DDR. They are not allowed home to Switzerland. the grown ups are immune to to Communism, but not their children.

Ordered his maid to get him young eels to eat within the next few days.

Jay wants to marry him off to one of the secretaries of the Aussenkommission of the F.U. Poor Hartel!

Interviewing the works' council at AEG (7 Apr., 1954)

Investigators at scene of a factory fire
(2 July, 1954)

84

Factory inspector Bindel

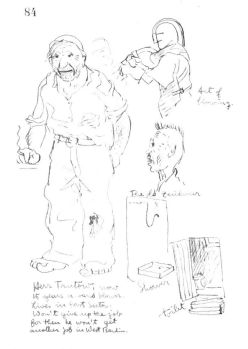

In a sand-blasting shop (24 June,1954)

At a labor court session (24 Sept., 1954)

war on the march may not be overtaken by any vehicles. One day, a truck delivering bread to a neighboring town overtook the prisoners marching back to camp. The Mongolian guard simply shot the rear tires of the truck to pieces. When the driver got out and screamed abuses, the guard promptly threatened to shoot him dead. "Äusserste Pflichttreue!" my companion repeated, full of admiration.

Spent the afternoon at home, then went to the Cerfs' to prepare them my version of a Chinese dinner (not very successfully.) Jay was at an artists' ball at the Hochschule für Bildende Künste yesterday. He had gone with Bruce Wilson, an accountant for the U.S. Army. Coming home in the early morning he didn't want to wake Carol, so he and his cab driver had stopped for a drink. The man, Jay said, had suffered 60% disablement in the war, yet he only receives 47 marks in pension money per month! Had he been a high-ranking Nazi officer, he surely would receive much more.

Jay also said he didn't dare to go back into the East sector any more. Because a Russian consular officer defected in Tokyo a few months ago, the Russians are now said to be looking for a hostage to trade for him. Besides, the Communists must by now have learned about Jay's research on the FDJ and are likely to think him a spy.

Sunday, 28 February 1954

I tried to work a little in the morning. In the afternoon I wanted to see something of the German carnival, the "Fasching," so I went to Ernst Reuter Platz at 2 o'clock. Alas, it was most disappointing. The procession consisted of a few riders on horseback in medieval costumes, a camel from the Berlin Zoo, two horse-drawn peasant carts with revelers, and a few lorries with funny figures. The public smiled, but there was no real rejoicing as in a Catholic town like Fribourg which I remember from 1946. There was a speech over the loudspeaker which ended with three cheers for the "young Berlin carnival" (introduced from the Catholic Rhineland only a few years ago, no wonder!), but no one listened.

Went to see the movie *Die letzte Brücke* in Steglitz. Very sentimental, and yet impressive. It shows Germans and Yugoslavs during the fighting in 1943 without any embellishments. To the German army doctor and the young soldiers the Yugoslavs are no more than bandits because the regular Yugoslav Army had officially surrendered in 1941. The doctor concedes that the Germans had not come here as tourists and that the partisans might be seen as patriots but, pointing to the red star on the cap of a captured partisan: "These people are not nationalists, they are *inter*nationalists!" Even the nurse, Helga (played by Maria Schell), says something like "Look, how strange they appear with their high cheekbones," which was presumably a negative remark. In the end she delivers medicine to the Yugoslavs and is shot in no-man's-land. Helga is the unpolitical

German who truly and simply has no answer when her Yugoslav captors ask: "Surely, you too must be against fascism?"

I think this is as far as the Germans will ever go in apologizing for the last war. They will never make a film in which the hero joins the Allies to fight fascism. Helga can be a hero precisely because she did not betray Germany; indeed she tried to escape from her Yugoslav captors. In the end she did help the partisans, but not because she had turned against her country, only for humanitarian reasons. At the most the Germans will acknowledge that the invasion of Yugoslavia had been ruthless.

Had dinner with the Lachmanns. They live in a small but comfortable place. The other guests were the bookseller Herr Rothschild and his wife, a Frau Kunkel, and a Dr. Schulz from the Hauptarchiv. The conversatioin turned around conditions in Berlin. Dr. Schulz said the average employee in Berlin cannot afford to spend 1 mark (25 American cents!) for lunch.

1 March 1954

Went to the U.S. consulate in Dahlem to ask about my visa to America. Outside the consulate I met a refugee boy from the Gatow camp. He was gaping at the shiny, big American cars at the curb: "Hot cars!" (*scharfe Wagen*).

In the evening I decided to see something of working-class Fasching, so I went to the well-known proletarian dance hall "Die Neue Welt," in the Hasenheide, district of Kreuzberg, but it was closed. I continued to Neukölln, where I went into a small, dingy pub in a dark side street off Karl-Marx-Strasse. This was a bar owned by a Tante Emmi. Regular customers come here to meet one another after work. The clientèle seemed not to be strictly working-class since some looked like lower middle-class, possibly businessmen. I got into a conversation with a man named Bodo Voigt, 52 years old, an official of a coal mine (Hedwighütte Kohle und Kokswerke) and seemed to be the kind of rough customer so well described in Erich Wildberger's novel about post-war Berlin, *Ring über Ostkreuz*. He offered to show me around Neukölln's *Kaschemmen* (dives) because he was proud to take part in my "scientific investigation for Yale University." First we had a bite at his home, which was in a dark street up a dark stairway (he locked the door behind us, which made me worried), but the flat itself was nice. There were books, paintings, a chandelier. The paintings were his own work, the furniture he said was rented. While he did not seem very well-off, he seemed to live comfortably. His wife was much younger than he. What I found refreshing was Bodo's attitude towards the recent war. He thinks the German cause was quite indefensible. He hopes that Germany will make up for what she owes the world through hard work.

First we went into a dubious looking pub called the "Rollkrug."
Rather spacious, it even had something of a soda-fountain atmosphere. A drunkard sang Léhar to the accompaniment of a violin and
an accordion. A fat and heavily painted old lady teased him, and a
waiter whispered to me that if a police inspector came I should say
that I was over 18. We moved on to the "Zum Goldenen Stern," which
is a *Nuttenlokal* (a hangout for prostitutes), my companion told me,
but was practically deserted when we looked in. (It was a sinister
place, but there was a police station right next door.) We entered a
number of other pubs too, each time asking for an acquaintance of
Bodo (Fritz, Horst) to allay suspicion and also to show that we
"belonged" to the milieu. In one of the dirtiest and smallest pubs, a
little boy of about 5 was still up, playing with the gambling machine
(it was 11:30 p.m). I asked the innkeeper's wife why the boy was not
in bed. "Not my son, it's hers," she grunted, pointing to a thin woman
sitting in a corner drinking.

The most rewarding visit was the one to the Familien Restaurant
"Zum Sängerverein," where the "Musikverein Echo," a workingmen's
music club, celebrated the birthday of one of its members. A
trumpeter and a clarinet player, both with very serious faces, made
awful village green music (old polkas) and couples of very ancient
vintage gaily performed the old dance steps. When I was spotted
drawing pictures of them in my notebook I was kissed and stroked
by one of the grandmothers. Then she peeked at my drawing and
said, "Next time I bring my glasses." I had to promise to come back
Friday to hear the orchestra perform. Got home very late.

2 March 1954

Morning in the archives. Frau Dr. Täuber's latest theory is that
people from the West who were in the East sector to observe the
foreign ministers' conference are now being watched by communist
spies, and that I most likely am being watched too. I don't believe it.
Went to see Pietsch at 2 o'clock. Fortunately I was on time, for he was
already waiting for me and fussed over me like a father. He took me
by car to the Leuschnerhaus, introduced me to the staff, had books
brought to me (though they were, alas, not very useful for my thesis)
and finally had me sit in on a training course for unemployed
workers, men and women. This course lasts for eight days and is
given here in the Leuschnerhaus with the "students" living in. They
all looked happy and content (the women all wore makeup), like
tourists on holiday rather than workmen out of a job. That's partly
because the Leuschnerhaus looks like a country home. Pietsch told
me that Bonn is thinking of ending food subsidies to West Berlin, in
which case the West Berlin trade unions would have to renegotiate
all the wage contracts and there could be labor unrest.

As I walked into the training course, a Kollege Modell was acting
as *referent*. He was lecturing on political strikes. Political strikes are

not admissible, he explained, if their purpose was to replace existing political institutions, however "democratic" the intent— such things must be left to parliament. Political strikes are admissible only *in defense* of democratic institutions should they come under attack. He gave as an example the militarist Kapp Putsch of 1920, which was brought down by a general strike. I talked to some of the participants, who all assured me they were here only to find spiritual and personal stimulation and to enhance their general knowledge. They all denied that these courses amounted to political training.

I was interested to learn that West Berlin tries to keep the door open for contacts to East Berlin workers and East German trade unions. Thus East Berlin workers can belong to Western trade unions, only if they join they prefer to hold their meetings clandestinely. (Pietsch said he would try to get me into one such meeting.) And while the Western DGB is banned in the communist sector, the East German trade union, the FDGB, is not outlawed in West Berlin except in the American sector.

Kollege Modell promised to arrange a tour of Berlin factories for me. A Fräulein Winning, who is the director of the Arbeiter Bildungs Institut, said she would let me see a study on "workers' aims in life," which a Dr. Stammer is currently preparing.

Pietsch drove me to Siemensstadt where I had an interview arranged with Max Müller, another Siemens pensioner. But I found Müller disagreeable. He was suspicious and a bit arrogant, and quite unwilling to talk about himself or about anything that was political. So I gave him up. On the way home I stopped in Steglitz to get my new Loden coat.

(P.S. I finally found out who Wilhelm Leuschner was: a well known TU leader who in the 1930s had spoken up against the Nazis at the World Health Organization, was arrested on his return to Germany, and executed by the Nazis during the war.)[1]

3 March 1954

Met a Herr Heinrich Kuhn at Wundtstrasse 46c. He is SPD Abgeordneter for Charlottenburg at the Berlin city parliament. But Kuhn was as difficult to interview as Müller was yesterday. He only wanted to talk about his recent trip to Africa.

So I went back to the Landesarchiv, worked, and then went home. In Steglitz I stopped at a photo store to order pictures for my American visa application. Met an American there who also needed photos. Sad to say, this American made a very poor impression on me. I learned that he lives in Wielandstrasse 17, not far from the Kudamm. "Just ask for Charles the Greek," he told me. He was formerly a bartender in Chicago, now a cook with the U.S. Army. He has every other day off, he said, buys himself a new suit every month,

---

[1] Wilhelm Leuschner (1888-1944).

and spends every evening in the bars and nightclubs of the Kudamm. He also hates Germans. Though he has been here for eleven months, he knows not one single word of German. To him all Germans are arrogant and cold, the men are Nazis, the women are immoral. He himself is thriving as a blackmarketeer. He offered to sell me a small car that he and a friend use for black market deals, and also to give me the address of a U.S. sergeant who runs a military gas station and sells American petrol and cigarettes illegally. I think this GI is a disgrace for the American forces in Berlin.

4 March 1954

The day was again mostly spent in the Landesarchiv; then I met a student from the Freie Universität named Ernst. He recommended that I should go to the newly reopened art library behind the S-Bahnhof Zoo. He himself often works at the city archive in the East sector. The communist archivists are burning documents from the 17th and 18th centuries if their content is incompatible with the Party line, he said.

Went to the Hasenheide in Kreuzberg, later in the afternoon, to listen to the speeches in the Kliems Festsäle, a traditional trade union meeting place. This was a meeting of the Metal Workers Union of West Germany (Industrie Gewerkschaft Metall für die Bundesrepublik) to discuss the prospect of higher bread prices and rents in Berlin. The meeting hall was huge and at first glance quite elegant, provided you don't look too close, for then you see a thick layer of ashes and hundreds of cigarette stubs all over the carpet. As one enters, the entire hall looks very much like pictures I have seen of political rallies in Soviet Russia: red carpets, elaborate chandeliers, a huge red banner with "Industrie Gewerkschaft Metall für die Bundesrepublik" inscribed in yellow letters. All the speeches were delivered in loud, ferocious tones. The audience looked mixed. There were workers in short overcoats and peaked caps without ties, factory girls in fashionable but cheap dresses and dirty fingernails, and elderly, white-haired trade union theoreticians with strong faces. The meeting lasted from 5:45 to 9:15 p.m. Three or four policemen were standing at the rear of the hall. The audience was very attentive and by no means docile. There was heckling, clapping and booing. Scharnowski was attacked and also Adenauer, and one sensed that the workers had a mind of their own, each thinking for himself. (One of them said: "Adenauer should not surround himself with police the way Hitler did. Let him come to the Kliems Festsäle and listen to the Berlin workers! We won't hurt him!") Many workers knew one another, friends sat together at one table, ordered beer and smoked and smoked and smoked. (The air was so foul that I twice had to go out for fresh air.)

I invited one boy to a cup of coffee. He told me that he regarded all employees (*Angestellte*), policemen, and officials as belonging to the employers' camp and so outside the working class. His brother is a professional cyclist, but considers himself working class.

The meeting began with four speeches about the threatened rise in prices. More than 20 workers asked for the podium. They all said about the same thing: they were discontented because West German workers got higher wages than workers in West Berlin while the cost of living was about the same both here and in the West. They were sick of being told that Berlin must fight as the outpost of liberty; instead they wanted to share in the prosperity of the West Germans. The recent "march of silence" was disappointing. Why hadn't it been organized by the political parties? Should the Berliners march in protest against higher bread prices? (This proposal was loudly applauded, but it was never voted on.) I was especially impressed by the high standard of oratory among the Kollegen from the *Betriebsräte* (works councils). They spoke with passion, very clearly, and without notes.

I sat with a young worker named Erwin. Since I told him I was "from the Gewerkschaftliche Studenten Gemeinschaft," he immediately called me "du," because trade unionists never say "sie" to each other.

5 March 1954

The whole day was spent just to arrange and hold an interview with Max Urich. True, the interview was very useful and Urich most cooperative. Urich lives in a settlement built by the Metal Workers' Union before the war. Many such public projects were later claimed by the Nazis to give credit to their Kraft-durch-Freude program (for example the public beach in Wannsee and the Jungfernheide park). Urich served a sentence in a concentration camp under Hitler; after the war he was made police president in a town of the Russian zone. When he refused to cooperate with the Russians in founding the SED party, he was thrown in jail for 29 months.

8 March 1954

Went to the Police Presidium in Tempelhof to get my formal residence permit. Dashed over to the American consulate. They want a Swiss police statement of good conduct for the years I spent in Switzerland after the war (!) and also from the New Haven police for the time I was at Yale (!). Got angry when the receptionist wouldn't let me speak to the vice consul, Mr. Bradford. Wrote to Onkel Müller in Berne to ask for his help.

Went to Professor Grottian's party at 4 p.m. A fairly young bachelor, he lives with a family in a rented room at Irmgardstrasse 57, Zehlendorf, near U-Bahnhof Oskar-Helene Heim. Nine students were there. I found out it was not a regular seminar but an end-of-semester party. There were generous mounds of cakes and lots of coffee. The conversation however was dull. Lots of shoptalk about the Hochschule für Politik. No serious discussion of Asia (which I had thought was why I had been invited). One rather aggressive young student was more talkative than clever. Mr. Grottian was extremely friendly to me, but I doubt whether all the secondary books on China he has read can make up for the fact that he knows no Chinese and has never traveled to China. I was, however, impressed when he told me that he daily reads *Pravda*, the *New York Times*, and the *Manchester Guardian*.

Maybe the party got more interesting later, but I had to excuse myself early because I was expected in Wannsee for dinner. The evening with Jay and Carol turned out differently than expected because our planned meeting somewhere in town with Ernst Gries and a communist secret agent didn't come off. Ernst had told Jay that this man, while still a believing Communist, was nevertheless a possible defector. Jay wanted to interview this man somewhere in town but not here, because Jay did not want him to know where he lived. Well, just before I arrived, Gries had met Jay outside the Wannsee S-Bahnhof. The man in question, Gries told Jay, is registered as a political refugee in West Berlin (which contradicts something that Gries had said earlier), but recently he had been spotted by one of Gries's men in Dresden, in the Soviet zone! Could he be a communist agent posing as a refugee? On reporting this to the American counter intelligence (CIC), the man had been arrested and Gries himself was driven home in a big CIC car.

Jay doubts this story. I think it might be true, but greatly embellished. At any rate, I am glad the CIC did not seize him just while we were chatting with him in some obscure dive downtown, looking like fellow conspirators.

9 and IO March 1954

Spring has really come now. This may explain why I am so tired these days. Got little accomplished. Went to Leuschnerhaus yesterday and today to meet workers. This was quite useful. Alas, Kollege Modell no longer thinks that he can arrange visits to factories for me.

Had tea at the Schmidts' yesterday. They had also invited a friend, a young nobleman named Klaus von Wahl, who says he is the direct descendant of the Princess von Lieven. He has spent a year at Yale (Berkeley College) studying at the Drama School and now works at the Renaissance Theater in Berlin. I am to call him up sometime so he can tell me more about the Volksbühne, a theater for the common people. The conversation centered around the theater and ballet, especially around modern dancing (the schools of Mary Wigman and Tatiana Gsovsky). Incidentally, the Volksbühne is SPD and so the famous Tatiana cannot dance there because she is not a Socialist and has no connections to the party. The theatrical world in Berlin, I was told, is very narrow-minded.

Sigrid Schmidt used to play with the Ribbentrop children. She still calls their old villa, now the Leuschnerhaus, the "Ribbentropsche Haus." I for one think it marvelous that simple workers are today sunning themselves in the garden of the "Ribbentropsche Haus."

With the coming of spring work has resumed on clearing the rubble from the site of bombed-out houses in Steglitz. The other day I saw part of an automobile engine being dragged to the curb. Do autos decompose like human bodies so that only their skeletons are left over?

11-13 March 1954

Not too much is happening. I went to Neukölln to get some more addresses of trade union people to interview from Herr Urich, who was just in a session with fellow TU people in Niemann's restaurant, Hobrechtstrasse 70a. Though both districts are considered proletarian, Neukölln is so different from the Wedding. The Wedding looks open and suburban with its wide cobbled streets and plain, though ugly, grey house fronts. The streets in Neukölln are more lively. They are narrower and twist more and there are many more shops and beer houses. The facades are ornamented with cheap stucco. The people also seem more talkative.

The Russians deny all responsibility for the shooting a few weeks ago of a 16-year-old boy from West Berlin. Most papers here are indignant.

Tante Müller wrote. She will ask Onkel Müller to get me the necessary certificate of good conduct from the Bernese police. Jay also said he would write to the mayor of New Haven for me, Richard Lee, whom he knows.

Went twice to the SPD offices in Zietenstrasse. I am combing through their archival materials. I also dropped in at the Wasmuth bookstore. Miss Hagemann at the Wasmuth Antiquariat was horrified when I told her that the Socialists I meet call me "du" and "Kollege." This, she said, destroys individualism and reminds her of the Nazi "Volksgenosse" idea. I also visited the art library in Jebensstrasse behind Bahnhof Zoo, but they had nothing that interested me.

Went to see the French-Italian film *Lukrezia Borgia* on the Kudamm on Saturday night, and afterwards chatted with people at Aschinger's.

14 March 1954

I was up early to go to Gesundbrunnen to attend the members' meeting of the metal workers' union (IG Metall) for the district of Wedding. The meeting took place in a pub in Swinemünder Strasse 42, an old-fashioned hall with green pillars and walls painted brown.

Much more "atmosphere" than in the Kliems Festsäle. While people did not drink as much, they were less attentive than at the meeting of trade union functionaries ten days ago. This time the assembly debated the resolution proposed in the Kliems Festsäle. There were speeches by Hans Warnke (the chief of IG Metall) and Urich. (Urich recalled how during the Hitler period he had refused to celebrate the Nazi version of May Day and told his colleagues that they might as well go to the zoo and watch the brown apes over there.) Someone proposed to ban reporters of the *Berliner Stimme* because their reporting has been "unfair." Several people called for Scharnowski's resignation because he allegedly tried to tone down the workers' demands. I was intrigued when one worker got up and said that trade union pamphlets for workers should not be couched in Berlin dialect and "baby language" any longer. This insults the workers, who are much better educated than they were 40 years ago. Finally, a number of workers said it was labor rather than capital that is rebuilding Berlin, and so the workers should get fair wages.

The audience seemed to grow tired of the repetitious speeches. Towards 1 p.m. one worker got up and moved the session closed. The chairman was forced to call a vote, and the overwhelming majority was in favor. This put an end to the flow of speeches, but did not stop Warnke from having the last word. He admonished the audience for leaving all the work to the functionaries while they themselves go off to lunch. I found two workers who agreed to let themselves be interviewed by me. Must call Warnke for permission to attend the next meeting in the Kliems Festsäle on 23 March.

Had lunch in Gesundbrunnen and was home by 3:30. Read Doris Peel's *The Inward Journey* and found it very stimulating. Dinner in Wannsee, then to the ballet at the Städtische Oper. Syke Schulz also came. I found the dancing in Stravinsky's *Firebird* dull and clumsy except for the fighting scene with the witch doctor. *Hamlet*, however, was superb. Excellent music, clean, very rapid storytelling through numerous scenes and, above all, wonderful expression through the movement of the dancers. Ophelia drowning was just suggested by movements, so was the king's solliloquy as he is torn between throne and altar. The end was a bit too quick, but not as bad as some people had told us. ·

Had a snack at Café Paris. Sigrid was more likable than I expected, or was she just being affable? Jay tried to test her on her anti-Semitism by claiming that Berlin's cultural renown before the war had solely come from the genius of her Jewish population. Sigrid quickly retorted, yes, but there were many foreigners who also contributed to Berlin's achievement. The reference to "foreigners" was very clever because it suggested open-mindedness. I think she guessed that she was being examined for her political views.

15 March 1954

A wasted morning. I had forgotten that the SPD library doesn't open until 2 p.m. Looked for a book on German civil law for Papa. Then spent the afternoon reading secret police records of the Bezirk Weissensee dating from the 1890s. I copied, *verbatim*, a number of reports written by half-literate police sergeants who had been forced to listen to Marxist lectures they barely understood. In the evening Jay and I went to a GSG meeting in the Leuschnerhaus. Very disappointing. There were only 6-7 people, all of them officers of the club. Jay and I really were the only audience. One student read a paper in which no one was interested. People talked while he read, went out to get beer. Obviously no "Respektsperson" was in charge, and I fear this club has not been very successful so far. Had coffee with Jay before going home.

Finished Doris Peel. She has a marvelous power of describing the nuances in people's sentiments, but I wish she would let the Communists in her book express their views better.

17 -20 March 1954

Interviewed three trade union men: Kollege Herold in the Badstrasse, and Kollegen Molitor and Schulze in Charlottenburg. Only Molitor was very interesting, the others were just being kind, I'm afraid.

Schulze's apartment in Kantstrasse 71 intrigued me. It is in a dingy rear wing of a tenement house. He wouldn't tell me how much rent he paid because it was very cheap. But it truly conveyed the idea of working-class slums: muffy, narrow rooms, a grey light coming through the small window, the courtyard disconsolate. It looks as if here every day is a rainy day. Most depressing.

On Friday, I visited the training school (Institut für Bildungswesen) of the AEG works in Holländer Strasse at the corner of Aroser Allee. I was introduced to an Oberingenieur Pflug and shown around by a Herr Seifert. Direktor Schwanke had told me to see this institute because "there is nothing like it in the USA." I read the application form by one of the boys: "I want to work for AEG because my father wants me to lead a correct life filled with serious work."

On Saturday Jay called to say he wanted to go to Eichkamp (where I have never been) to look up an American student, Herbert Maylen(?), because Herb has recently been in the Russian zone. Eichkamp is in the British sector and there is an international students' camp there. It looks quite nice: open country, tall pine trees, small bungalows dotted around like models on an architect's table. Some 60 students live here very cheaply (17 marks per month plus free lunch). I was shown around by a boy called Oppermann.

Spring 1954

22 March 1954

Spring is here. The Kurfürstendamm is full of people, some without overcoats. The sidewalk cafes are opening. Somehow one feels more alone in Berlin when one sees so many more people around, and you know that no one can be an acquaintance of yours.

Interviewed Herr Doms. It was nice sitting in his room with the window open, sunlight streaming in, and radio music from the courtyard.

The other day a Chinese peddler came to the door of the Henningers'. I was alone at home. He had an open suitcase with sweaters to sell. We looked at one another full of wonderment for a long moment, then he said in a falsetto: "Call mummy" (Lufen...Mutti)!

23 March 1954

Worked at home in the morning. Went into town for lunch and then sat in the Kleist park until after 2, waiting for the SPD library to open. Finished reading the police records of Weissensee and looked throught the rest of the documents in their archive. There were letters to August Bebel dating from the 1860s, some account books of the Workingmen's Association in London and in Geneva. Only 2 sets of documents dealt with my period, but they concerned working-class problems in Bavaria and Bohemia.

Went to Kliems Festsäle where I met Jay and Carol. This time fewer people attended. Since that meeting on 4 March, which had been for *Funktionäre* only, the various district meetings had duly been held (one of them the meeting in Wedding to which I had gone). This now was the meeting of the district representatives (*Bezirksbetriebsdelegierte*). Every Bezirk sat at one table. The debate turned around the question whether to demand higher wages or not. The TU leadership (*Vorstand*) proposed cancelling all existing *Tariffverträge* at the end of the month and to demand a 20% raise, but no one seconded this motion. Most workers who spoke said 20% was unrealistic. In the end it was decided to ask for only 10 pfennig more per hour (1.54 instead of 1.44 marks).

I saw Herr Molitor among the delgates. He had brought me as a present his journeyman's certificate from the year 1901, drafted in elaborate penmanship. He told me he was 74 years old and wouldn't be able to enjoy this document much longer. He and his wife had talked about it and she had agreed that I should have it. On condition that I write them a letter from the United States.

The discussion turned to the question whether or not 17 June should become Germany's new national holiday, leaving 1 May again as purely a festival for the workers. But we left at this point, Jay was very tired. (He had slept during much of the meeting.) We had dinner and a nice chat in Wannsee. Carol is expecting another child. Jay doesn't think he can take a trip with me to Italy in the summer any more.

24 March 1954

Ha, ha! Yesterday's trade union meeting was supposed to have been secret, but a communist spy must have been there because the East German paper *Tribüne* carried a report on it in today's issue! Jürgen Eppe, whom I met in the DGB building,took me up to the library where a Kollege showed me the paper. It included the statement that "officials of the American High Commission in plain clothes also attended the meeting of district delegates, showing proper invitation cards." HICOG also has read this, and since there is an official ban on American officials attending German trade union meetings, they immediately telephoned the DGB to find out whom they had invited. The mystifying answer was: "Yesterday's guest was a Chinese, possibly a Communist Chinese, but we think not." I now explained who my companions, Jay and Carol, were, and the DGB people in turn called up HICOG with that information.

Went to the U.S. consulate to give them the New Haven police's certificate that I had no police record, but the consulate still wants the statement from the Swiss police. Called Gustav Pietsch and he asked me to come and see him. First we discussed trade union problems. Should an electrician working for the railways join the metal workers' union or the railwaymen's union? Then Pietsch talked about himself. He is 63 years old. When he retires at 65, he dreams of taking a freighter to Asia and of seeing China again. Has started life making wrought ironwork (*Kunstschmied*), later worked on the railways driving locomotives and as ticket collector. He was penalized for being a Socialist under the Kaiser and under Hitler. Under the Nazis, he was jobless for 3 years and for 1 $^1/_2$ years was kept under police surveillance. In 1936 he was allowed to take a small job again. In 1945 he had to start building a new life.

Pietsch introduced me to a Fräulein Kohn of the union of food stuff and restaurant workers (Gerwerkschaft Konsum, Genuss und Gastwirtschaft). I am to see her on Tuesday morning, when she'll let me look into the trade union files.

Kollege Modell told me that anytime I wanted to come to the Leuschnerhaus all I had to do was to call him. He also told me that metal workers have retained most of the "class-consciousness" from prewar days, which many people now consider outdated. They still refuse to celebrate May Day together with the employers.

25 March 1954

Spent the morning reading at home. It has gotten cold again. At lunchtime went to return some books to the Stein Library and had lunch at the Mensa. In the afternoon met Jay and Carol at the Schöneberg Rathaus. Darn it, it was only 3 p.m, and yet the session was already closed! So we went to see the Martin Luther film instead. I found it admirable in its restraint (no thunder and lightning scene, no grandiose Diet at Worms, no kidnapping by Elector Frederick of Saxony, nor love story with a nun). However, it did lack depth. Luther's terror at the thought of God's mercilessness remains incomprehensible to a modern viewer, his spiritual anguish is not shared by a 20th-century audience. The Worms speech falls flat— perhaps because Emperor Charles V wears such a comical hat?

Carol had brought sandwiches and fruit which we ate in the U-Bahn on the way home.

In the evening we went to RIAS to fetch Peter Herz. Then we were off again to the Jugendlager in Kladow, the boys' refugee camp that we had seen once before. It is actually run by the Arbeiterwohlfahrt (Workers' Welfare Association), and so affiliated with the SPD. As last time, Frau Bachhofer was there, and Pastor Heim. An American State Department official named Reese (?) from RIAS came too, but he left after a short while.

The boys were quieter this time. There were no protests. Peter was also in better form. A boy who called himself a *Feldsher* (medical orderly?) in the Russian manner told us in a jocular mood about his career in the Russian zone: he had learnt the trade of baker, then was "voluntarily drafted" into the Vopo. During the workers' insurrection on 17 June, he saw the parents of a small boy killed by stray shots fired by Vopos or by Soviet soldiers. The boy hit out at the Vopos, was arrested, and our Feldsher was ordered to stand guard outside his cell. Our Feldsher then saw to it that "by accident" the shutters of the cell window came loose during the night and the next morning the boy was gone. But he was not very seriously disciplined for his negligence.

Also interesting was the following question by one of the boys: "Today in West Germany the Christian Democrats are in the government. Therefore West Germany is Christian. If next the SPD get into power, will the Bundesrepublik cease to be a Christian country?"

Then we talked about Vopos again. One boy said no one with

character would serve in the Vopo. He had been asked to join several times and always refused, yet nothing had happened to him. "Da hast du Glück gehabt!" (Then you were lucky!), the other boys shouted. In their view, if one refused to join the police one usually lost one's job and had other difficulties.

Afterwards Carol and I talked to some boys. We had a stack of old *New York Times* with us and we translated political cartoons for them. They all knew about McCarthy, and appreciated the anti-McCarthy jokes. So that's freedom of the press!

Before we left someone told us that the boy who last time had been so scared to talk to me had gone back to the zone. That is the one who had served in the Vopo and whom the American CIC had asked to go back to spy for them. Frightened because he was not immediately recognized as a political refugee in Marienfelde he apparently decided to return home and risk a prison sentence there. Peter thinks the CIC is very naive compared to the British intelligence service. Having seen the boy, I cannot understand how the CIC could even have thought of offering a job to such a timid and confused youngster.

To my great surprise I met Gordon Gould from Saybrook College at Yale in the Paris Bar. He is studying for a year at Cambridge University and is now in Berlin for the vacs. But he seems to be spending all his time going to the opera only.

26 March 1954

Morning in the Landesarchiv. It seems that I'll have to comb through many issues of the *Amtsblatt der Stadt Berlin*, starting next Monday. After a lunch of beef wrapped in cabbage in a popular Steglitz restaurant, off to Reinickendorf to visit Wilhelm Glamann.

It took 2 hours to get there. The train to Reinickendorf runs along the Soviet sector boundary for a while and I could read the latest slogan on a shed at Schönholz railway station: "1935 Wehrpflicht— 4 Jahre später Krieg! 1954 Wehrgesetz— Jugend, wehrt Euch!"[1] Glamann lives in an agricultural settlement (Laubenkolonie) where some of the small cottages are apparently inhabited throughout the year. This area already lies outside the city. A heath stretches behind the colony and one sees some factories on the horizon. The colony is not big and the setting is very proletarian. The ground is unpaved and because of the rain very muddy.

The Glamann cottage was the most prosperous looking of them all, and still it was sad. The yard is filthy, old boxes and cans lie around, the fence is broken, and the mud inches high. A white "spitz" dog was locked up in the kennel and barked at me aggressively. Frau

---

[1]"Conscription in 1935 led four years later to war! Conscription in 1954? Youngsters, refuse!"

Glamann, a portly old woman with white hair, heavy eye lids, and expressive brown eyes, let me in. The cottage consists of two rooms and a kitchen. The living room was a very narrow cubicle, dark, overcorwded, airless. Glamann was lying on a sheepskin on the couch, stroking a cat. His clothes were in rags. Since there was no other chair he remained lying down while I began my interview.

He was very good as an interviewee, in spite of his 83 years. But it was hard to keep asking him systematically all my questions because his great poverty intruded on our conversation all the time. In the first years after the war the two Glamanns received only 59 marks per month; now Glamann also gets a small pension from his trade union. To survive they keep rabbits, sheep, and chicken. They use their sheep for wool and slaughter them for meat. Both of them wore home-made woollen sweaters and socks. They also grow their own fruit. They served me an awful tea which tasted like tepid water mixed with sawdust, but for them it was a luxury. The cake they offered was stale. Frau Glamann had baked it 8 days ago and when she heard I was coming to visit she had saved it up. They have only 2 cups and the teapot is broken. Nevertheless they were both of good cheer. Glamann is even quite funny. He told me that he had taught locksmithing to both Max Urich and Franz Neumann, the two trade union bosses, but had never wanted to make a career as a trade union functionary himself.

Frau Glamann is Wilhelm Glamann's third wife. He saved her life in 1939 and hid her from the Nazis throughout the war. Once upon a time, she told me proudly, she had been a great *artiste* known under the name of Irma Raabe. There were still photos on the wall showing her in various stage poses. She used to recite at concerts, and next time I come she will recite something for me. (I am supposed to come back at Easter for a rabbit lunch.) In her best years she had owned a huge flat on the Kurfürstendamm, she said, with several house-maids, and she had owned 15 watches, 50 pairs of shoes, lots of clothes and jewelry. "This is what has become of me now" (Nun bin ich hier), she said. "I have cut all my contacts to former acquain-tances." She is working hard and she loves and respects her husband even though he is "as you may have noted, my intellectual inferior." This all sounded a bit uppish, and it would have been exactly that had she not looked so much like a grand old dame with her fresh complexion and fine features. When I left she insisted on giving me three fresh eggs and some awful smoked ham to take home for supper.

27 March 1954

Yesterday the DDR was granted full sovereignty by the Soviet Union. This explains all the flags I saw flying yesterday in the East sector. In one S-Bahnhof, I had also seen the flags of other Commu-nist countries.

Worked in the archives. Talked with Herr Siewert. He fought the war in Norway, was taken prisoner by the Amis (Americans) and then handed over to the French who needed laborers. Siewert admitted that if he was treated badly by the French in his first year of captivity, the French had good reason for hating the Germans. Besides, he said, the French simply did not have the means to provide for the thousands of prisoners whom the Amis sent them in one big batch at the end of the war. In his second year in France, Siewert worked as a domestic servant to a French General Caillé (?), who now commands the northern half of the French zone of occupation in Germany. Siewert also stated that the German invasion of Czechoslovakia, Poland, etc., was a crime and that a German victory would have been a great misfortune for Europe. It is good that Germany lost the war. "A dreadful end is better than dread without end" (Ein Ende mit Schrecken und nicht ein Schrecken ohne Ende).

28-30 March 1954

Sunday was a melancholy, grey day. I settled down to work, but fortunately Jay called and I had lunch at Wannsee and a stroll with the whole Cerf family. Jay hasn't got his social science research grant yet, which is too bad. There won't be a trip to Italy, it seems. Went home at 5 p.m.

Little happened on Monday. I worked at the SPD archives in the Zietenstrasse most of the day.

But today was a better day. Went to Schlüterstrasse to see Herr Rohde of the Industriegewerkschaft Nahrung, Genuss, Gaststätten. Had a long conversation with him and Fräulein Kohn. Rohde told me he belonged to a new school of trade union officials who believe in bargaining with, rather than fighting against, the employers. He is very *en bon point* and in his three-piece suit rather looks like a capitalist businessman. Since I had a spare meal ticket from the GSG, I asked Miss Kohn to lunch with me at the Trade Union Casino. Then I hurried over to Wedding where I found Herr Behrendt waiting to take me by car (a small DKW station wagon with a two-stroke engine) to the Emergency Service of the Berlin Public Utilities (BEWAG, Abteilung Stördienst). It was a beautiful ride in spite of the heavy rain. We saw the Havel river and the barges, the huge Berlin grain store, the Rudolf Virchow hospital and the Robert Koch Institute. We passed mountains of coal accumulated by the BEWAG in case of another Berlin blockade (there is enough here for 9 months), we saw the Borsig factory (makers of railway equipment) and also the biggest flour mill in Berlin. As we passed Tegel prison, Behrendt told me its nickname: "Hotel zum hölzernen Löffel," or "The Wooden Spoon Hotel." Near lake Heiligensee (according to an old legend, there are submerged villages at the bottom) we saw— hurrah!— open fields and a farmer with a horse-drawn plough.

The Behrendts live in Hennigsdorfer Strasse in Reinickendorf, in a small, one-family house, built 33 years ago after a design drawn up by Kurt Behrendt himself. His father was a locksmith, later a TU official, who left a small fortune when he died in 1929. The house was built with that money. Now Behrendt lives here with his wife and two sons. The interior is comfortable and modern. There is an electric range, an electric icebox and coffee machine. It reminded me of the house of the Franĕks in Krč, near Prague. Behrendt told me a lot about the Freie Volksbühne, in whose organisation he is a leading official. It is "free" in comparison to the Volksbühne in the East sector and supposedly stands above party politics, though SPD men predominate in the directorship. But the membership is not confined to workers. Behrendt wants me to meet Siegfried Nestriepke, one of the theater's two cofounders back in the 1890s. Since Behrendt himself only entered the working class movement after the war, I questioned him only about his father, an old TU and party horse. His mother had much information to contribute too. I was asked to come back in the summer.

Before I returned to Berlin we went to look at the barbed wire fence 140 meters behind the Behrendt house, where the Russian zone begins. When you walk to the banks of the Havel you see fishermen on boats just inside the invisible demarcation line that runs down the middle of the river.

I took a train to Anhalter Bahnhof where I changed to the Wannsee train. It was exciting to cross into the Soviet sector again, after so many weeks. All stations looked normal enough, except Nord-Bahnhof, which swarmed with Volkspolizisten. This must have been the "special vigilance" announced in the papers because of the SED Party Congress which begins today. (One poster read: "Der 4. SED Parteitag, Angelegenheit aller Deutschen!" – "The Fourth SED Party Congress concerns every German!"). I was worried about possible identity checks. Some buildings flew German black-red-gold flags and simple red flags, but the insides of the railway stations were lavishly decorated with flags. What is confusing is that in Anhalter Bahnhof I also saw posters advertising an American jazz band at the Sportpalast (which is in West Berlin), and advertisements for Western cigarettes. At Grossgöschenstrasse Bahnhof, there were communist flags but West Berlin policemen on patrol.

31 March 1954

I went to the American Express in Dahlem to fetch my 740 dollars in traveler's checks and to inquire about student ships to New York. After that I went to the archives. Dr. Kaeber thinks I should look up the Staatsarchiv in the East sector, but Frau Dr. Täuber violently disagrees. She thinks he doesn't know how risky that is for me.

At 6 p.m. I went to the meeting of the Restaurant Workers' Union in Alt Moabit (Delegierten Konferenz der I.G. Nahrung, Genuss und Gaststätten, Berlin N.W. 87, Alt Moabit 47/48). It took place in the Hansasäle, a large and very long hall decorated in old-fashioned style with lots of stucco and mural paintings of classical scenery (Babylon and whatnot). The ceiling was painted to look like a blue sky with golden stars. There I met three old trade union horses: E. Backert (80 years old, who lives in the East zone), Wilhelm Winzer (a man with a very red face, who had been active for the trade unions in Breslau before Hitler), and another whose name I didn't get. He was a brewer. He wanted me to sketch him. When I finished he wasn't convinced that he looked like that until everyone else at the table told him that it was his spitting image. Then finally he smiled and offered me beer and cigarettes. I am to meet them all for interviews later this week.

Rohde's speech was not good. When I later talked to him I was puzzled by his political views: Field Marshal von Paulus had disobeyed the Führer's orders at Stalingrad, he asserted, and therefore he is responsible for the deaths of thousands of German soldiers. Today he is in East Germany, training Vopos. So the Communists have no reason to complain that Field Marshal Kesselring works for the new West German Wehrmacht. In fact, Rohde sounded like a Nazi, except that yesterday he had said Hitler was the cause of all Germany's troubles.

Gordon Gould called. He wants me to go with him to the Komische Oper in the Soviet sector tomorrow.

I April 1954

Went to Schlosstrasse, bought a new *Berlin in der Tasche* (my old city map is worn to pieces), and looked up the Karo As driving school in Bismarckstrasse to find out if I needed a German driver's license if I bought a car. They sent me to the police in Tempelhof, and there I was told that I can drive in Germany with my Czechoslovak driver's license if I get an official German translation for it and pass a practice test.

Looked up Winzer who lives in a small one-family house in Tempelhof with his wife, a son, and a daughter. But old Herr Winzer had little to say. He asked me to coffee and then quickly said good-bye after admonishing me to invite him to China when I have become a minister there. The son, a textile merchant, was serious and talked to me bitterly about his experience as a prisoner of war in Russia. Winzer: "The Germans who came back from Russia were horrible to behold. But will we Germans ever learn that this is how any army looks that ruthlessly invades another country and then is defeated?" While he was in Russia he worked east of the Ural mountains. For the birthday of the camp commander the other Russian officers ordered the German prisoners to make him an elaborate desk. They constructed a beautiful "Diplomatentisch," only it turned out the commander had no idea what desks are for! He filled the drawers with fuel for the oven and fodder for the horses and used it as a kitchen table on which he put pots and dishes. "He didn't even know how one sits behind a desk and gives orders!" Winzer junior complained.

I took the S-Bahn to Friedrichsstrasse. This is the first time that I have ever gone to the East sector alone, and I enjoyed it. I bought a copy of *Neues Deutschland* (the SED party newspaper) to fold around the book I was carrying, which was definitely not communist. Bought Moskva cigarettes at a stand and then went to the Komische Oper. There were many Russian officers in the street and red flags flew from all the buildings. I saw some very elegantly dressed women too— were they from the West? I wondered.

At the opera, most of the audience were evidently delegates to the current SED Party Congress. But Western autos could also be seen outside. I met Gordon with his friends (six Yalies, or former Yalies) and the proprietress of their pension, a Frau Ina Tittel. One of the boys, Jim Thomson, has lived in China for many years and seemed like an exceptionally nice person.

We saw *Die Zauberflöte*, and the stage scenery was at times really gorgeous. Unfortunately, the dialogues without singing were too long, and the acting seemed rather poor. The whole production was overly elaborate with serpents, boy-angels in the clouds, fireworks and other tricks. The theater itself was overly decorated too. But Gordon was enthusiastic. I fear I prefer a simple violin recital or chamber music to opera. There are some good violin recitals here in Berlin now. I must go to some.

We ended the evening in Café Warschau, eating *belegte Brötchen* (open-face sandwiches) and drinking Romanian wine. Gordon is leaving for Austria tomorrow. We left East Berlin after midnight. Stalinallee was deserted save for a few groups of home-bound theatergoers like us. We saw a Vopo truck followed by a small armored car silently moving down the deserted boulevard. In a side street stood a Vopo with submachine gun. We crowded into Jim's little Hillman Minx, all eight of us (Gordon had to sit on my lap) and sped home. The Vopo at the Brandenburg Gate let us through after only a quick glance at our French TX plates. The Western police, however, stopped us because one headlight was out!

2 April 1954

A truly exhausting day. There was a letter from Yale to tell me I got a Junior Sterling fellowship (hurrah!). Then a letter from the Swiss police that they needed to have all information about my person (*Personalien*) certified by the Berlin police. So I went off to Tempelhof, waited in line for a long time, and in the end was told that the Berlin police couldn't do it, I must send for it to the Chinese consulate in New York. Frustrated, I went to the Swiss delegation, but they were closed. The Swiss mission is housed in a white building, the lone survivor in what used to be a posh street of villas in the Tiergarten close to the Soviet sector. The whole area was totally destroyed in the war, there is rubble all around. A few hundred meters away you see the reddish brick buildings with their many smokestacks and towers: the Soviet sector begins there. The rain had stopped, there was some blue sky. Red flags were fluttering in the breeze from all the roofs on the Soviet side— it made me think of a Mongolian camp site. How far the Russian armies have come! And how much determination it has taken to keep them from pushing further to the West!

Last night I lost my notebook in the Hillman Minx, so I had to go to the Hotel Pension Leibniz Ecke, Kurfürstendamm 62, to fetch it. Met a little boy in the street. He was playing with an aeroplane he had made out of newspaper. At first it was supposed to be a sword. Then he had put engines and a tail on it and now it flew. In the summer he will sell aeroplanes like this to other children for 10 pfennigs each, he says.

Went to the Turbinenfabrik of AEG in Huttenstrasse, to see Herr Dörban, the head of the factory council (*Betriebsrat*). It was a huge factory with big iron monsters lying in the courtyard. In a little grimy office sat Herr Dörban, surrounded by workers. He was brief, not too enthusiastic, but he agreed to see me at 8 a.m. (!) on Tuesday.

In Dahlem I looked up Helmut Weidmüller to borrow two periodicals from him because they had articles on Germany in 1918 which he thought I might find useful. His landlord was very talkative.

Home by 7 p.m. Jay called: he's got a fellowship too, for $1,300, which is jolly good. He also said he has located a jeep that I could buy for $75. I was too tired to get very excited about anything, but I was happy about Jay's fellowship and the jeep.

3 April 1954

Worked at home in the morning. To Gesundbrunnen in the afternoon to meet Herr Gerhard and Herr Backert at a small "Berliner Kindl" pub in Graunstrasse 42. They had much more endurance than I and after 2 hours of asking them questions and scribbling down notes I was poofed. But they still continued to chat with gusto. I liked Backert especially, he had a nice smile and vaguely looked like the first Czech president, Tomas Masaryk. The pub we were in is the regular meeting place of the union of construction workers (*Bauge-werbeverein*). It also is the rendez-vous for all sorts of people from the Soviet zone or the Soviet sector of Berlin, such as Backert and Gerhard. Gerhard is 73 years old, he was formerly the chairman of the brewers' union of Berlin. He gets his subscription of *Welt der*

𝕬𝕬alterchens 𝕭allhaus

BERLIN W 35, BÜLOWSTRASSE 37

WEINKARTE

MOSEL-WEINE   **DM**

Guest at a Widows' Ball (22 May, 1954)

Dancing at Musikverein "Echo"
(1 March, 1954)

Two women dancing the
"Schiebertanz" (6 May, 1954)

Arbeit clandestinely here. Backert lives in the DDR. It was awfully kind of them to come from so far and to give me so much of their time. But they did ask me not to publish their names for fear they might be punished by the SED for having talked to me.

Got home at 7:30 when Jay called. He proposed that we should go and inspect the jeep, and he would bring along a young auto mechanic he knew. We met at the Platz der Luftbrücke, where Jay walked into the U.S. Army building to talk to a sergeant. The mechanic and I had to wait in the guard room at the entry because we were not U.S. citizens. The guard was handing out penicillin pills to all the GIs who were returning from a spree in town and thought they needed it. The jeep is beautiful (black with bright red wheels) and I'd love to buy it.

4 April 1954

Walked in the morning through pouring rain down to the Schlosstheater to queue up for three tickets for the play *The Love of Four Colonels*. Got home, had breakfast, and shortly afterwards went to have southern fried chicken with Jay and Carol to celebrate our two fellowships. After that I went to the Kaeber's for tea and supper. It was a bit boring, I'm afraid. The other guests were a professor with his wife and sister. On the ride home around 11 p.m., the train was full of Germans in dark blue overcoats made of rough material and wearing ski caps and American Army boots. They all carried bulging briefcases and an American steel helmet in a cloth sack. They looked like men from a training unit. No badges.

5 April 1954

Went to the Swiss delegation and found the staff so delightfully courteous. A young M. Lambacher received me immediately and gave me the required attestation. We had a nice chat about Switzerland and the few years I had lived there. He even took me to the visa section personally to see whether I could visit Onkel Müller in Berne with my Chinese Nationalist passport. But when I later went to the post office to send the required fee of Frs. 4.- to the Berne police, I found that the post office here has no international post coupons! "What do you expect? They threw us out, didn't they?" (Wir sind doch 'rausge-schmissen worden!), a gruffy old postal clerk told me in Lehrter Bahnhof. I cannot send a check either because that requires special permission from the German central bank. I called Lambacher and he laughed and simply advised me to write to the Berne police and ask them to waive the four franks. (All this circus turned out to have been unnecessary. When I got home I found a letter from the Eidgenössisches Politisches Departement with a very polite *attestation* in French.)

Lambacher said there are still thousands of Swiss citizens living in the DDR. The East German authorities won't allow them to go home to Switzerland. The older ones are immune to communist indoctrination, but not their children.

Worked a little at the SPD archives but the day was gloomy and rainy and I didn't get much done. Left early, had a badly needed haircut, and went home. Sergeant Gardner called on the telephone and more or less bawled me out for wanting to buy an army jeep when a German car would be cheaper. Then Jay called to tell me that I was invited with them for dinner at Hartel's. Hartel is just back from a trip to North Africa. He leads a lonely bachelor's life in a villa in Forststrasse, Zehlendorf, surrounded by oriental treasures, some of them most beautiful. It was a delightful evening. There was some talk about travel, a little about philosophy, and very much about food. (He spontaneously ordered his maid to buy him some fresh eels for dinner next week.) Then he showed us photos he's taken and played us some Spanish and Arab records. Jay wants to marry him off to one of the secretaries in the commission for foreign students (*Aussenkommission*) at the FU. Poor Hartel! – Got home around midnight.

7 April 1954

Got up at 6 to rush to the AEG Turbinenfabrik in Huttenstrasse. It was a cold and rainy day with only occasional sunshine. I interviewed the Betriebsrat (factory council) between 8 a.m. and 12:30 p.m. Dörban, the chairman was ill, but a 56-year-old member of the Betriebsrat, Erich Tschentscher, talked with me very willingly— for 4 1/2 hours! I was given coffee, sandwiches, and cigarettes. The younger members of the Betriebsrat, wearing smocks, were busy coming and going but sometimes they stopped and joined in the conversation. The whole session was very animated and friendly. Tschentscher impressed me. He was in the German Resistance and complained that people outside Germany often underestimate the opposition to the Nazis inside Germany. For instance at the funeral of trade union or SPD members great crowds often turned out in spite of Nazi warnings to stay away. "The Nazis never found out how we were able to get so many people together without visible organization."

At one point Tschentscher referred to the "Dolchstosslegende" (the myth of the stab in the back of 1918) as total nonsense. He was then serving with the Air Force in Flanders. It was the German Army and Navy that broke down, not the home front. The soldiers and the sailors were hungry and war weary. In 1917 sailors had greeted the Kaiser with shouts of "hunger!" instead of with "hurrah!"

In the afternoon to RIAS where Hartel was waiting for me. Alas, Mr. Ewing, the director, had left town suddenly so I couldn't see him. We sat in Hartel's office while he telephoned around and proofread some programs. I sat at another desk and read Klimoff's *Berliner Kreml*, the memoirs of a Soviet officer who had defected in Berlin. On the desk was a list of telephone numbers beginning with Conant, Timberman and Parkman and going through HICOG and all newspapers offices and radio stations. Walter Sullivan's number was there too.

We had a bite at the casino. At a neighboring table, the members of the Stachelschweine cabaret were just finishing a quick meal too. Then we went with them to the studio where they recorded their number (7:30 p.m., Studio 7). They performed in a big wood panneled room filled with some 300 guests. The performance was good though not outstanding. One skit: "We'll join the new Wehrmacht, but only if it has a trade union." Maybe the problem was that this performance was just too short— they only had 30 minutes. Hartel was in a hurry to get to an appointment in Zehlendorf and took me in his taxi as far as Rathaus Steglitz.

8 April 1954

Tried to work at home. Dropped in at the Automobil Klub in Podbielskiallee, where I was told that my Czechoslovak driver's licence is valid in Germany, France, Switzerland, and Italy. Good show!

The SED Party Congress in East Berlin is over. Ulbricht is secretary general again.

9 April 1954

Went to see Herr Hammer of the Neue Berliner Bühne at SPD party headquarters. He is a student of Frau Dr. Pischel's and writing a thesis on the mentality (*Geistesart*) of Berlin workers today. We had a stimulating talk. The Neue Berliner Bühne is a students' and workers' theater, showing tendentious political plays under the auspices of the SDS (Sozialistischer Deutscher Studentenbund). The SDS will hold a conference next week and I am invited. Thursday they will show a Communist-made film on Thälmann, the communist leader of the 1920s, and he said I would love it. (I later asked Peter Herz about the Neue Berliner Bühne and he said it was too Marxist. It is true, when I asked Hammer how he defined "workers," he said he accepted Marx's economic definition of the proletariat.)

Went to the Schlüterstrasse to make contact with the trade union of workers in chemical, paper, and ceramics factories (IG Chemie, Papier und Keramik). Then went to Moabit to attend the meeting of the works' council (*Betriebsversammlung*) of the AEG Turbinenfabrik in Huttenstrasse. The directors came a little late. No one greeted them and they in turn never said a word. The session was opened at 2 p.m. and I believe that most of the workers and employees were present. The meeting was held on a gallery overlooking the main construction hall; there were only a few chairs and most people sat on benches, boxes, or on the railing. The roof was grimy, the windows dirty. Galle, the chairman of IG Metall, made a speech, so did Herr Müller and some members of the Betriebsrat. The audience was not very interested. The topic was the higher cost of living in Berlin compared to West Germany and what to do about it. Wages are said to be 10 to 15% lower in Berlin than over there. However, the public seemed to me completely apathetic, except when the talk turned to the yearly company outings. The overwhelming majority voted in favor of abolishing them. They all rather wanted a bonus of 10 marks to spend on their holidays. Why? Workers don't like organized activities, I was told. Similarly, they are not very happy living in the workers' settlements where your neighbors are the same people you see during work hours. Also, this factory employs mostly men. In order to have mixed company on their factory outings the workers would have to bring their wives and sweethearts and pay extra for them. Who can afford this?— At the end of the meeting the workers left hurriedly. All this surprised me because this factory is said to be 90% organized! On the other hand, one young worker told me that he would never think of opening a small workshop to become an entrepreneur in his own right. That would be against his socialist convictions!

After the meeting, I stayed to have coffee and sandwiches and some liquor with the Betriebsrat. One of the young workers showed me through the entire Turbinenfabrik. He let me operate one of the huge punching machines and I was thrilled to feel its enormous power.

IO April 1954

Saturday. Called on Herr Reimann, the head of the Berlin branch of IG Chemie, Papier und Keramik. He gave me a lot of old printed brochures. Then went to Tempelhof to check with the police regarding taxes on a jeep. I may have to pay an import duty because I am transferring a piece of Allied war equipment into the German civil economy.

Went to Jay and Carol for coffee. Then accompanied them to visit Peter Herz at his home in Hanne Nüte 89, Berlin-Britz, which turned out to be a very pleasant, semirural part of Berlin. We had a very cozy evening with Peter and his parents. Hartel had come too. Peter's mother rather reminded me of a Viennese lady in her out-going warmth and "neckisch" humor. Peter drove us home in his car. In spite of the late hour, Hartel asked Peter and me in for a "Cuba Libre" (Coca-Cola with rum and lemon). It was 1:30 by the time I got home.

II April 1954

Sunday lunch with the Cerfs. Hartel and Miss Edith Adamski of the FU Aussenkommission came for a fried chicken dinner. Jay wants to play matchmaker for Hartel and Adamski. When we went for a walk after lunch, Adamski to my surprise confided to me that she had wanted to get married for a long time but had come to doubt whether she would ever find the right husband in Berlin. All the men in Berlin are only interested in themselves. But she cannot leave Berlin because she has her parents here and her job. She is very pessimistic about her chances of marriage now, though I shouldn't think that she is much more than 30. I even tried to cheer her up with a pep talk!

We ended the walk with coffee at a shore-side cafe where we stayed until about 7 p.m. Then Hartel, Adamski and I went to his home in Forststrasse, where Hartel made a quick "Chinese fried rice" dinner for us and kept us till close to midnight with records and looking at pictures and just some good talking. All very agreeable, but I should really have spent this weekend working.

12 April 1954

Saw the West Berlin police in Steglitz today roaring by in a truck convoy like an army. All the cops were armed with rifles and one had a machine gun. Each truck had a shortwave radio.

Stayed at home, using Carol's typewriter to type out— at long last— my interview notes with retired Siemens workers. As I reread my notes, I was struck once more by the modesty of all these "little people" when it comes to questions of politics and public affairs. "The people in the government have better heads than we," they often say. Or: "This is high politics. We cannot do anything about that, we don't understand it." I don't think this is how the common people think in England or America. Could this be why in England and America people are less likely to believe in "conspiracy theories" involving intrigues by Freemasons or Jews? Maybe this is also why there are so few readers' letters in the *Neue Zeitung*: 3 or 4 letters once a week is about all you'll ever find. And the readers do not discuss the future of EVG, or the DDR's attainment of sovereignty, but rather questions concerning traffic regulations and the philological origin of a German word.

13-14 April 1954

Went to attend the evening session of the the Studenten- und Arbeiter-Tagung (Conference of Students and Workers) organized by the GSG in Leuschnerhaus. This afternoon's topic was: "Are young people interested in politics?" A worker, an employee, and a student spoke, followed by a lively discussion. Jay joined us for dinner and to see the play *Eskapade*, (which was so-so), in the "Tribüne" theater on Ernst Reuter Platz.

Today Jay and I joined the discussion on "jazz and film as new cultural ideals." After lunch, I phoned Sgt. Gardner. He'll show us the jeep tomorrow. And so home. Rainy, miserable day. Didn't get too much work done.

A postscript on the conference: the discussion was not well organized. There was no way for members of the audience to ask for the floor, so people just heckled and these interruptions (which were often puerile) were annoying. What was remarkable was that the workers' representative, a Kollege Hase from the Siemens works, and also the white collar employees, talked much better than the students. According to Hase, one reason why young workers do not attend more concerts and plays is that there aren't enough older and better-schooled people with whom they can discuss what they have seen or heard. In the old days the young people were introduced to the classical works of German culture through their families.

Interesting also was a discussion with the representative of the police union. He attacked jazz and cheap films as alien to the soul of the "deutscher Mensch." Later we sat opposite him at lunch, and Christine Häker started a hot argument with him. She told him the Berlin police was too arrogant and uncivil in its behavior towards the public, that they were bloated with a sense of power and that, alas, the German people is too much accustomed to being cowed down. The policeman hotly defended the police by saying a brusque tone was required when you deal with an unruly mob. He also said we should understand that a policeman who issues court summons (*Strafanzeigen*) is also trying to advance his career. The poor man felt very nervous as all us students around him took Christine's side.

15 April 1954

Went with Jay to inspect the jeep in Tempelhof once more. We found Sergeant Joe M. Gardner was still in bed following a night of CQ ("in charge of quarters") duty, so we sat waiting for him in the Silver Wing Club, which is the Air Force cafeteria. Gardner only came towards noon, a huge fellow with reddish hair, double chin, but a nice boyish face. In the course of the day we got quite friendly. Gardner astonished us by saying he's written a book, 200 pages long, on the teaching of elementary science in German schools and that he hopes to publish it with Colliers. He had taken 3 years to write it. Good for him! – The jeep's OK, though the clutch is much softer than I had expected. We negotiated the purchase in Gardner's workroom, which is also the arsenal of this barracks, stacked with rows and rows of rifles, pistols, bayonets, flamethrowers, heavy and light machine guns and bazookas. We saw his room, which he shares with another buddy and found it clean, airy, and neat, rather like a hotel room. Gardner says "du" to everyone. At the Cerfs', where we met Hartwich, he said: "Bist du Deutscher?" At the cafe where I invited him for a snack, he asked the waiter: "Hast du keine Butter?" We went to the McNair Barracks to complete the legal transfer, then to

Wannsee where I bought a second-hand battery in a garage. We dropped in at the Cerfs' to give them a ride to their dinner party with the Sullivans. (Jay has received a 6-month extension on his Fulbright!) Finally, Gardner drove me to the Leuschnerhaus, where the SDS had their Easter conference.

The Easter conference was much more impressive than the recent GSG Tagung. Lots of foreign students attended, many from Yugoslavia. A Herr Brandler entertained me. He is a slight, young man, very thin, with dark hair, and was released from a communist penitentiary (*Zuchthaus*) only a year ago. His great-uncle was a KPD leader in the 1920s who now lives in West Germany.

We went by bus to the Philosophische Fakultät of the FU to see a German communist film on women in the new society. Title: *Frauenschicksale*. It is the story of three young girls living in the American sector of Berlin who are suffering the hardships of capitalist exploitation. They are all poor. Two of them finally pack up and move to the "Demokratischer Sektor." The third one, Renate, however falls victim to a seducer, a dissolute baron. This girl, in order to please the baron, buys an expensive blue dress (which the saleswoman almost refused to sell her because she had come into the shop looking so shabby), only to discover that the baron's interest in her had been just a momentary fancy. The trouble is, she had stolen the money for the dress from her mother, and her little brother had seen her. In her attempt to stop his shouts, she accidentally suffocates him. The Vopo arrest her. Very beautiful prison in East Berlin. Lenient sentence: only 2 $^1/_2$ years. And while serving her sentence, Renate is allowed to work in a steel mill. She's happy there, drives a locomotive, and falls in love with a steelworker. When she is released from prison, the steelworker waits for her in a gaily decorated lorry. In the last scene they drive through the streets of East Berlin. The World Youth Festival is on, and FDJ boys and girls are out on parade. There is sunshine and throngs of well-dressed workers and their families walking around, happily laughing. The steelworker then takes the heroine to a HO clothing store and buys her a blue dress just as nice as the one she had bought with stolen money in the American sector. Happy end.

I was astonished that no Russians and no Americans were shown in this film. The picture is even sparing with red flags. The decadent West is pictured like this: endless queues in government offices where food rations are distributed. The civil servants are arrogant. Lots of nightclubs. Right at the sector boundary lurk black marketeers who whisper, "Kaffee? Schokolade?" Many prostitutes in the streets. The upper classes are dressed in the fashion of the twenties. Garish checkered sports coats, long feathers in the women's hats. When the dissolute baron visits Friedrichsstrasse in East Berlin, an FDJ girl asks him to sign a peace petition. His natural response is to try to seduce her.

Technically, the film is very good. The macabre dancing scene of the upper classes in the U.S. sector is excellent. The vivid colors reminded me of an illuminated church window: red, blue, green. Decadent revelers with green faces. The sound track was less good. Interesting background music: where in Western films you would hear sentimental schmalz, here you get popular marches and polkas.

16 April 1954

Good Friday. All the shops are closed. I did some work at home during the day. At 7 o'clock went back to the Leuschnerhaus. Jay was there too. We talked to some students over supper. Then we went to see the movie *Die Unbesiegbaren*, the German socialist workers under the Bismarck Empire being the "invincibles." This was really a first-rate picture, historically convincing and remarkably free of heavy communist propaganda. It tells the story of the Social Democrats during the period of the antisocialist law from 1878 to 1890. You see such well-known figures as Wilhelm II, Bismarck, Herrfurth, Bebel, and Liebknecht. There are army officers, estate owners, industrial captains like Krupp and members of the Reichstag. You see the interior of a workers' tenement (*Mietskaserne*), the home of the worker Schulz and his family. The policeman lives in the same house. Neighbors spy on one another. One worker becomes a police spy. When the other workers discover this, he is treated with contempt— but no more. A secret printing press operates in a pub and secret SPD meetings are held in back rooms. Police supervision is defeated by ruses rather than revolutionary defiance, and the Bismarck regime is portrayed as far more tolerant than a modern police state. Marvelous glimpses of working-class life: frugal suppers of potatoes and herrings. As you eat, you peel the potatoes and put the peels on the table. Kerosene lamps and enamel washbowls. Streetcars pulled by horses. Here are some lines from the dialogue that I remember:

Worker Schulz to his wife: "What I mean by a better world? Eight-hour day, more free time, Sunday rest..."

August Bebel to Wilhelm Liebknecht: "We must always be revolutionary until the socialist state has been set up..."

Girl to police spy: "I much prefer Franz to you. He may always remain a proletarian, but that is much better than being a white collar proletarian (*Stehkragenproletarier*) like you."

Frau Schulz to policeman: "Don't talk to me about insulting officialdom. Don't you officials insult us too?" (Von wegen Beamtenbeleidigung. Beleidigen Sie uns etwa nicht?)

Went to Harnack Haus for a hamburger and milk shake. There was a small orchestra, but very few guests. By the time we left there were no more tramways running, and I had to walk all the way home.

17 April 1954

Went to Tempelhof to see Herr Hartung of the Württembergische insurance company. He helped me to get temporary number plates (KB 040-679) for my jeep. By noon, after getting Sgt. Gardner out to fix the battery, I drove the jeep back to Steglitz. Discovered that the steering is loose and that the jeep sways left and right at 40 mph. Also the brakes seem weak. Gave a test drive to the Henningers.

Dinner with the Cerfs in Steglitz. Afterwards we all went to see the play *Love of the Four Colonels*, by Ustinov. Hartel was there too. It was really rather good. Four colonels of the occupying powers come upon Sleeping Beauty in a magic castle, whereupon they take turns waking the sleeping princess, each one in his idealized vision of himself. The Frenchman imagines himself a 17th-century cavalier; the Englishman a sort of Sir Tobias out of *Twelfth Night*; the American is a family father in shirt sleeves rescuing a young maiden; and the Russian sees himself as a Tsarist officer in the time of Chekhov. Only the Russian is skeptical of success and makes no effort to win the princess— is he the most perceptive of the four? There is also a good fairy and a bad fairy. Morale? Man's always got to make yet another choice.

18 April 1954

Birthday party for me at the Cerfs. Hartel came also later in the afternoon. Carol had baked a delicious chocolate cake.

19 April 1954

Attended the SDS meeting in Leuschnerhaus. Pietsch was there too and he introduced me to Kollege Scharnowski, the chairman of the DGB in West Berlin. The meeting lasted from 10:30 to 1:30 and became quite stormy. Mr. Leithauser, a journalist from the periodical *Der Monat*, gave a rather emotional account of the uprising on 17 June last year. He wanted to move his audience by conjuring up pictures of unarmed men hurling themselves against Russian tanks, and clouds of teargas causing panic among hapless pedestrians, but the audience reacted unfavorably to his emotional style. One boy afterwards got up and protested against this kind of "idealized mythmaking" (*Weihrauchbeschreibung*). He said the uprising was too serious an event to be romanticized in this way. Scharnowski got up and criticized the West German and the Allied authorities for not having offered active help to the East Berliners during the uprising. On 17 June, he said, he had had the greatest difficulty getting the Americans to allow him to broadcast messages of support to the East Berliners over RIAS. As to the only other radio station, NWDR, it had even remained neutral throughout the uprising. Had the West actively intervened, he declared, the communist regime would have been brought down. He ended, rather dramatically, by shouting, "Freedom or death! No peace without freedom!" (Freiheit oder Tod! Kein Friede ohne Freiheit!).

The audience, however,reacted very strongly to Scharnowski's speech. The majority rejected the idea that active intervention on 17 June would have done any good. They loudly applauded one boy who said that Western style freedom was not worth the price of a third world war. "As long as the Western powers remain in West Germany, the Russians have the right to be in East Germany," he went on. The Russians can only be made to leave through diplomatic negotiations. Scharnowski's contention that a general strike would never bring down a communist regime was countered with the argument that a general strike had put an end to the Kapp putsch in 1920. In any event, strikes cost less lives than full-scale war. Scharnowski did not reply.

Late in the evening, Jay called and suggested we go and attend the social evening of the Socialist Student Conference. I took the jeep and met Jay at S-Bahnhof Steglitz. It turned out to be very interesting. First I met Egon Müller, the author of the book *Stürmt die Festung Wissenschaft*, which describes education in East Germany, but I admit I found him a bit pompous. Then we sat down with a Yugoslav boy named Uros, a Yugoslav girl whose last name was Petrovich, and a Herr Schindler. I am still unused to meeting people like Uros who say, "Of course I belong to the Communist party!" and the girl who wanted me to assure her that I am "a Socialist too." We gave them a ride back to their youth hostel in Wannsee. Jay said we might travel to Yugoslavia in the summer and asked whether they would have trouble if Americans visited them in their homes. They did not reply. When we drew close to the Russian zone just before Wannsee, I joked: "Did nobody warn you never to ride in cars with strangers in Berlin?" It was a bad joke, because they really became fearful that we would take them across the boundary. Jay says that according to Herr Schindler Petrovitch has bloomed since coming to West Berlin. Life in Yugoslavia must be as strictly regimentated as in the other Soviet bloc countries.

Jay has contacted a boy from the "Aktionsgruppe Freie Deutsche Jugend," whose headquarters is in the Jebensstrasse near Bahnhof Zoo. This is a group of ex-FDJ boys who try to undermine the morale of the FDJ by broadcasting songs and mailing pamphlets to the Soviet zone, trying to shake the faith of the FDJ leaders in communist doctrine.

21 April 1954

My jeep didn't pass inspection at the Technische Prüfstelle of the TH because it doesn't meet German traffic regulations. Its exhaust pipe must not point towards the sidewalk. Did some work at the Stein

Bibliothek. In the evening after dinner, I was locked out of my house because I had forgotten my keys at home. After a whole hour of knocking at windows and trying to wake the Henningers by telephone, I stopped a police patrol car to ask for help. But the policemen just shrugged their shoulders. This is none of our business, they said. "We maintain public order, that's all." I walked on before I would say something rude.

22 April 1954

The jeep passed inspection, thanks to a mechanic from a nearby garage who came along to pull the handbrake during the test ride because I am not strong enough. (He said the brake was all right, it was I who should "eat more cake.") In return I invited him to lunch. He is a refugee from East Berlin, Meister des Kraftwagengewerbe (master motor mechanic), who spent the war repairing tanks on the Russian front. He thinks the Russian tanks were pretty good (marvelous diesel engines) but that the German Tiger tanks were better due to their invulnerable armor plating. Hitler, he thinks, was destined by history to rule Germany. There was little freedom under Hitler, but under Bolshevism there is still less. Hitler according to him had not wanted war, but certain elements like Krupp had manipulated him to their own ends.— Wouldn't take his coat off during lunch because he thought his clothes were too shabby. "I have nothing to show" (Ich habe nichts zu zeigen), he explained.

Jay called in the evening. Drove over to Wannsee, where a Ben Rees and a Wilfried Kleinert were visiting the Cerfs. Ben is a Harvard student visiting Berlin. A Quaker and pacifist, he is doing refugee work in West Germany. His friend Wilfried is a journalist for United Press. According to him, newspapers in the West are no more free than their counterparts in the East, with the exception of the *New York Times*. During the Berlin conference, he charged, the Western press distorted Molotov's speeches and gave undue coverage to Secretary of State Dulles.

23 April 1954

A hectic day trying to straighten out the auto papers for the jeep. In the afternoon I finally got my license plates officially stamped and the jeep is now allowed to travel around in the streets. Worked at home. Hartel called to invite me for dinner next week.

In the evening I went for a coffee and piece of cake to Konditorei Rabien around the corner. An elderly man sat down at my table and we fell into a long conversation. He comes from Zeiz (?), which he described as a small Thuringian town with a big old castle, a moat, and cobbled streets so steep that horse-drawn wagons had to be pulled by a cable to reach the top. Then he talked of Germany and the "good old times." France, he lectured me, has made war on

Germany no less than 200 times! Therefore it was no wonder that Germany in turn attacked France when she finally was strong enough!

He also talked about his youth. Though of bourgeois family, he had admired the "Sozis" (Social Democrats). Of course he could not join the party since his father would have thrown him out of the house. Why he had liked the Socialists? Because they were a real fighting party and their cause had been just. The workers suffered gross exploitation. Besides, socialism before the First World War had not been as doctrinaire as it has become today. They may have quoted Marx, but at workers' meetings a simple turner Krause could and would still bang the table and speak his mind, and he would be listened to. With their faith in class solidarity, they believed they could force social improvements with their voting power. There was no need for bloody revolution.

Class distinctions before the First World War had been stricter than today. Children of different classes only attend the same school during the first few years. They seldom played together. Working class children were better behaved than bourgeois children because overcrowding leaves you less freedom and poverty forces children to work from an early age. The schools taught bourgeois values but working-class children never forgot what class they belonged to. To be sure, in the army the workers were taught patriotism, but when they returned to the workbench they also reverted to their socialist views.

One last piece of wisdom from my new friend was that the Germans who after the war joined the French Foreign Legion in Indochina had fought too well. They had scared the French into opposing any proposal for German rearmament.

24 April 1954

A Saturday, but I worked hard. Gorgeous weather. Bought a small Tyrolean neckerchief (*Seppeltüchlein*) for Randolph's first birthday. In the evening I was invited to the Rothschilds'. There was another guest, a pastor Makiewicz, who recounted how during the Weimar Republic the Wedding had really been a communist district. Since the war it has become petty bourgeois. Mrs. Rothschild talked about her earlier work as a hospital nurse. There was also a doctor from Dahlem and his wife, and a woman dentist from the floor above.

25 April 1954

The weather continues to be wonderful. Read at home. Got Esther and Mischa to help me wash the jeep. Then tea at the Cerfs'. The Yugoslavs did not come, to our great regret, but Christina and Horst Häker did. But the party was not relaxed. I noticed there were many little misunderstandings because of the way the Cerfs said things or the way the Häkers sat, or nodded their heads, or moved their hands. In spite of plenty of goodwill on both sides there seemed to be a strain caused by differences in national mentality. We took a short walk along the Wannsee. Went home at 10 o'clock.

Concerning the May Day that is approaching: in West Germany this is a workingmen's day, in Berlin it is "Day of Freedom." Workers and employers demonstrate together. All because, someone said recently, Berlin is supposed to be the "Bastion of Freedom, Meck Meck Meck!" (I.e.: the Berliners are tired of hearing it.)

26 April 1954

Was told at the U.S. consulate today that I probably will receive my visa next week. Very happy. Didn't get much work done at home. Went to the meeting of the GSG in Leuschnerhaus. Some chap from the Institut für Arbeiterbildung showed us what teaching methods they use. The Institut is said to be unique not only in Germany but in the world (!). The Americans have financed it since its foundation in 1950. Last month, however, they finally decided to hand it over to the Germans. Only the German government has so far refused to allocate money to it so that the Institut may have to close down. "The Americans prefer guns to education," said the Referent, Hannes Zippel. But the students disagreed with him. "We think that the Germans should pay for it themselves."

Christine Häker tried to find out what program people would like the GSG to organize in the future but she got little encouragement. People are so apathetic!

27 April 1954

Worked at home. Took little Esther along for the ride when I went to the American Express to make a reservation on the "Groote Beer" sailing to New York in October.

28 April 1954

Got up early and drove to the DGB. The IG Nahrung, Genuss und Gaststätte were paying retirement pensions to their old members. Only 10 marks for each person, and this was for quarter of a year. Fortunately, these pensioners also draw some money from the state. I was told that the trade unions had lost most of their funds when they broke with the communist FDGB and so cannot afford to pay their members any more. I circulated among the pensioners waiting in line and tried to get some of them to talk to me. But the old men and women merely smiled embarassedly and gave evasive answers. Finally, I got the man who checked the membership books at the door and Fräulein Kohn to introduce me to some people whom they knew by name. The oldsters became immediately much more friendly. I got several addresses and 2 people sat down and chatted with me on the spot. The only trouble was that they couldn't keep to the point. One of them was Herr Kretschmer, an old waiter who has traveled and worked all over Europe. He was not a convinced trade union man, I found, and would have loved to run a hotel himself. He had once been a very rich man, he said.

After lunch I went to Ziethenstrasse. Since I was early I first went into a bistro. This is a working class area and I got talking to a man at the bar as I drank my Coke. This man had been a commercial apprentice in Berlin back in 1910. He said he hated the Social Democrats and that the rise of Hitler was all their fault. Then he told me of his war experiences as a sergeant in the corps of engineers (*Festungspioniere*). How, instead of blowing up his depot at the approach of the Allies, as ordered, he distributed its contents among the population of a backward village in the Black Forest, and how in 1945 he tried to reach the Swiss frontier with his remaining 22 men but fell into French hands. During his captivity he commanded a camp of some 300 Germans whom starvation had driven insane but whom he had brought back to strict discipline thanks to his talent for organization. "Alles ging zack zack!"

At Ziethenstrasse I found a few useful books and was also told not to miss the coming May Day celebration in Berlin.

29 April 1954

Interviewed Herr Langer of the IG Papier Chemie Keramik. He is an old man with only one eye and awfully friendly. His daughter brought us coffee and sandwiches. In the afternoon I also interviewed Herr Müller, a former hors d'oeuvres cook (*Chef der kalten Küche*) at the swanky restaurant Kempinsky Weinkeller. He also was very forthcoming. He offered to take me round some of Berlin's biggest kitchens, and to a meeting of the Association of Berlin Cooks (Verein Berliner Köche).

I get much more work done now that I can race around town in my jeep. In the evening, dinner at the Cerfs'. They had guests from Frankfurt, a Florence Nelson with her husband Gil, and a friend named Harry. The Nelsons work for the U.S. government, Harry for a firm making sewing machines. The conversation turned on McCarthyism. Jay said German intellectuals see in McCarthyism as a kind of American facism, which only shows that they are still politically very naive and cannot be counted on to resist a real fascism should it recur in Germany in the near future.

SERVING THE WORKING PEOPLE

Factory inspector Trapp
(15 June 1954)

Ida Wolff, head of Workers'
Welfare (15 Sept., 1954)

Dr. Höhlmann, judge at the
labor court (15 Sept., 1954)

Dr. Ernst Umbreit, poor-law doctor
(9 Aug., 1954)

Bruno Stephan,
teacher and historian
of Berlin-Wedding
(15 May, 1954)

SERVING THE WORKING PEOPLE

Making the rounds with welfare
worker Rohde (2 June, 1954)

Juvenile delinquents on
probation (20 June 1954)

School teacher in
Berlin-Spandau (13 Jan. 1954)

Juvenile delinquents on
probation (20 June 1954)

30 April 1954

Had a very successful day at an office that runs the public schools in Berlin, the Hauptstelle für Erziehungswesen. Talked to a Herr Günther and then to the librarian, a Frau Struwe. It seems I'll be able to meet with some old elementary school teachers.

After lunch, gave Carol, Jay, and their friend Florence Nelson a ride to Spandau. We visited the same places that Jay and I had seen a few weeks ago, only this time we knew our way around better and we were also able to get inside the 13th-century Nikolaikirche and into the Juliusturm. Herr Pauknin, Siewert's friend, was in and readily chatted with us about Spandau's history. It is said people in Spandau still keep pigs in their houses like pets. Some of the side streets smelled as if that might be true.

For dinner we were invited at Al Hartel's. The Herz family was there too. Peter gave me a sticker to put on my windshield so that I can drive my jeep right into the Platz der Republik on May Day. He also told us there had been a fire at the Kladow refugee camp and five boys had fled back to the East zone. They were likely to have been saboteurs. The Herzes and I stayed till 12:30. Hartel gave me lots of American cigarettes to take home. I wonder why he is so friendly to me. When I left I found that the jeep had a flat tire and that the electric starter was stuck. Had to leave it there.

1 May 1954

Glorious weather. Got up early to see whether there was no garage that could help me get the jeep running again, but I couldn't find one that was open for repairs. Waiting for a bus in Schloss Strasse, I was picked up by Ernst Gries who happened to pass in a blue Volkswagen. He gave me a lift to Wannsee, where he wanted to pick up someone. He said he had a meeting with eight other boys at the Brandenburg Gate to shoot off rockets filled with propaganda materials into the East sector. These rockets contained hundreds of small paper doves with the inscription: "Der freie Westen grüsst die Unterdrückten in der Terrorzone. Die freischaffende westliche Welt gelobt, sich für Eure Befreiung vom bolschewistischen Joch unablässig einzusetzen!"[1] He and his friends were armed: he had a gas pistol (though it looked to me like an ordinary starter pistol used at sports events) and his friend showed me a Browning. Ernst said he was very busy now because he is leading no fewer than two underground propaganda groups.

In Wannsee I fetched Carol and Jay. I told them my car wouldn't

---

[1] "The Free West sends greetings to the oppressed people in the terror zone. The liberal West is committed to your liberation from the Bolshevik yoke!"

work and that we could get a lift with Ernst. But Jay objected. He doesn't want to have anything to do with Ernst any more. He told me that he has been to the police to inquire about Ernst. (That can be done here. All you need to say is that you are considering giving someone employment and want to check up on him and the police will tell you if he is reliable or not.) The police told Jay that Ernst was an ordinary criminal who has twice escaped from a Western prison. His last offense was assaulting a policeman. In the end we did ride in Gries's car, but we made sure to get out as soon as we reached the Platz der Republik.

First we strolled along with the crowd down the Strasse des 17. Juni towards the Platz der Republik. There was gorgeous sunshine and the Tiergarten was enchanting with its fresh green colors. Lorries with workers carrying red banners and boards (*Transparente*) drove by, mostly flying big SPD flags (which look so much like Russian flags) or the green-white flag of "United Europe." Socialist youth groups (*Falken*) were hurrying towards the rally in their uniforms. Like the Schweigemarsch, it was a very sloppy but merry procession. A band was playing. Among the crowd I discovered Direktor Zopf from the Senatsbibliothek, who waved to me gaily. The girl student whom I had seen at the Schweigemarsch was there too. At the Platz der Republik we stood or sat for about 2 hours listening to the chimes of the freedom bell ringing from the tower of the Schöneberger Rathaus. The Schöneberger Sängerknaben gave a concert, there were speeches by Lord Mayor Schreiber, Otto Suhr, and Scharnowski. (Scharnowski was very lively and demanding direct action, as usual.) In the end a loudspeaker broadcast a recording of Ernst Reuter's May Day speech from last year.

I made some drawings. Carol later told me a policeman had walked over to look over my shoulder but decided to leave me alone. 4,000 doves were released, helicopters and some ordinary airliners flew overhead and both sides sent balloons into the air with leaflets intended for those on the other side of the frontier. Close to the ground the wind blew from the East and favored the Communists, but higher up the air current was reversed and so gave our side a chance. But we didn't pick up many communist leaflets. Most of the leafets we found were Western ones blown back from across the Iron Curtain. The Reichstag building at the sector boundary was the site of a big contingent of Western motorized policemen ready to intervene at need. The Russian war memorial was cordoned off by British Military Police. The communist parade in Unter den Linden continued long after ours had ended. To prevent people from invading the East sector *en masse* from the Platz der Republik— which could have produced serious troubles— the Western police had cordoned off the Brandenburg Gate.

We took a bus to go towards the Memorial Church. On the bus were a few American Fulbright students who had just been in the East sector. They said that civilians and Vopos had busily torn up all the leaflets that were dropped by Western balloons.

Had lunch at a sidewalk restaurant on the Kudamm. It was very peaceful and quiet here downtown. A marriage took place in a side street off Hardenbergstrasse, and we waited to see the newlyweds arrive in a white horse-drawn carriage.

Carol decided she would come with us to the Wedding, where the SPD was organizing a popular festival in the Volkspark Rehberge. In the Wedding whole families were strolling around in their Sunday best, many of them carrying watering cans (probably because they owned small garden plots nearby?). Not many people we asked knew about the Volksfest. We finally found the open air theater where it took place. The stage consisted of an elevated ground of stone and sand with fir trees and thick hedges, and young people with flags formed the background. The audience sat in a semicircle as in an amphitheater. There were poems recited, an SPD man made a speech, a few comedians told dirty jokes, and there was some folk dancing and gymnastic display. Most of it was amateurish and rather bad. The worst was the gymnastic display. The audience laughed whenever one of the performers fell down. This made Carol and Jay furious. They thought an American audience would never have been that cruel. We left before the show was over. Willy Brandt is said to have organized it.

On the way to S-Bahnhof Wedding, we decided on the spur of the moment to have dinner at the French Foyer in Müllerstrasse at the corner of Seestrasse. Not very well arranged, we found, no comparison to the elegant Maison de France downtown. Yet the food was quite good. I tasted some of Jay and Carol's escargot, we had filet mignon and excellent salad. In the basement, the Foyer has a shooting range. *Très amusant.*

Went with the Cerfs to Wannsee for a cup of coffee and orange juice. On the way home, in Steglitz, saw that the pubs in Schützenstrasse had dancing to celebrate May Day. But was too tired to go and do more "research."

2 May 1954

Had to get up especially early because today was the confirmation of Frau Henninger's 14-year-old son, Mischa. It took place in the St. Annenkirche in Dahlem. The church service was simple and dignified. At the end the pastor said to each child a few words of admonishment for the future ("mit auf den Lebensweg"). Mrs. Henninger's divorced husband could be seen at a distance giving Mischa a watch. The guests who were invited to the Henningers' family celebration all looked so dreadfully boring that I excused myself and spent a few hours in the streets. Had lunch at a cheap restaurant, then went for a walk. In the Wolfstrasse, I sat down at a fence and began to sketch a quaint old house that must have dated from the time when Steglitz was still half rural until a policeman came to tell me that a neighbor had called up the precinct station because he thought I might be a communist agent making plans for a kidnapping. The policeman was very friendly, though. I showed him Professor Rudin's letter of introduction, which I think he just pretended to read. Then he looked at some sketches in my notebook, saluted, and let me finish the drawing.

Took tea with the Henningers later in the afternoon and had a lively discussion with Mrs. Henninger's sister-in-law, who admits having been a loyal supporter of Hitler. Her theory is that Hitler's promises in 1933 so appealed to the German people that the criminality of his regime was not perceived by them until it was too late. Another sister-in-law told me indignantly that a Turkish acquaintance of hers had displayed disgraceful bad manners by not bringing flowers on a first visit to a certain family. She was astonished when I told her that bringing flowers is not the custom in every country. I was glad Jay called and suggested that I should come over to their house, for I was just dying to get away.

3 May 1954

Found a very nice master craftsman of the pneumatic trade (*Meister des Vulkaniseurhandwerkes*), a Herr Adam near S-Bahn station Zehlendorf, who repaired the tire on my jeep and also fixed the starter. In his repair shop I met an inventor who let me try out his newest contraption: a bicycle without revolving pedals but with lever-like pedals which are far less tiring and produce a greater mechanical advantage. After a lunch at the Mensa, I went to the U.S. consulate. A woman doctor, Frau Dr. Misgeld, was supposed to give me a medical checkup for the American immigration authorities, but I lured her instead into a conversation about the health standard of the Berlin working people before 1914 and she promised to introduce me to an old welfare doctor (*Fürsorgearzt*). Got my visa to America at last.

Marion told me that people under 18 in Germany are not allowed on the street after 10 p.m. except under the escort of "a person qualified to exercise a tutorial function" (*eine erziehungsberechtigte Person*).

4 May 1954

Busy day. Went to see Herr Konetzky of the Hauptstelle für Erziehung und Schulwesen in Grunewaldstrasse, who promised to arrange a tour of elementary schools in Berlin's working-class districts in the near future. Konetzky wanted to be helpful, but he doesn't seem to be very bright. As a village schoolmaster before the

First World War (1909-1914), he taught as many as 105 children of all age groups in one classroom!

After a lunch in the Hauptstrasse, I was off to see Wissell, who kindly invited me to a district meeting of the SPD in Tempelhof tomorrow. He also promised to introduce me to a retired head of Berlin's factory inspectorate, a Mrs. Tabb (?), who is presently out of town.

I had to fetch my battery from Clayallee and gave Esther a ride in my jeep. On my return I found the Cerfs had called, so I had dinner with them to celebrate my getting a visa to America. They also gave me a Berlin flag as a birthday present. They think I need a rest. Maybe I should go to Italy?

5 May 1954

Worked at home until 11 a.m., then went to the Lehrergewerkschaft (Union of School Teachers) in Schlüterstrasse to interview Emil Beise, the third chairman of the Berliner Verband der Lehrer und Erzieher. He presented me with a few booklets on the history of Berlin schools. The Berliner Verband der Lehrer und Erzieher is a local branch of a larger nationwide association that is not necessarily socialist, the Arbeitsgemeinschaft Deutscher Lehrerverbände.

Read a little at home. Esther came to play in my room, so that I couldn't get too much done. Went with Jay to listen to Pastor Martin Niemöller preach in the St. Annenkirche at 8 p.m.. From what Jay had told me of Niemöller's past—a ruthless U-boat captain in the First World War and afterwards a freecorps fighter[1], but also a courageous opponent of Hitler during the Third Reich who spent nine years in Sachsenhausen and Dauchau—I was very curious to meet him.[2] The service had not been publicized in the press, so the St. Annen community hall was not very crowded. The congregation appeared to consist mostly of regular churchgoers. The service was plain. Niemöller gave a sermon on man's need for hope and on the evil of living aimlessly from day to day. After the service, Jay and I approached him. I introduced ourselves as Yale students who are interested in present-day German problems and who were delighted to meet one of Germany's leading figures today. Would he not tell us something about his ideas on the German problem?? Niemöller smiled and said he was not a leading figure at all. "But you are known the world over," I persisted. "That may be true," he admitted, "but I have no power to influence the course of events." Then he said he was

[1]Freecorps: right-wing armed units who fought against communist insurgents and Polish nationalists in Silesia after the First World War.
[2]Martin Niemöller (1892-1984), member of the Council of Evangelical Churches in Germany, became president of the German Peace Society and Pacifist League in 1957. He resigned all his church offices in 1964.

deeply concerned about the division of Germany, both personally because the German nation culturally belongs together, and also as a churchman. "The present division of Germany threatens to make all the people of West Germany Roman Catholic, and all the people in East Germany Soviet. Where would that leave the Lutherans?"

Then Niemöller suddenly launched an attack on America. He blamed America for all the international tensions in the world. "Wir Deutschen sind vielleicht blind geworden, die Amerikaner sind nie sehend gewesen!"[1] America follows a policy of provocation whereas what is needed today is sensible negotiations. "Why did Dulles confer with Eden and Bidault before coming to the Berlin conference? Do you call that negotiating if one side comes to the conference table with resolutions prepared beforehand?" At that point Gunar Hering, a German refugee student who has helped Jay with his research during the past few weeks, interjected. Niemöller's point of view, he said, reminded him of the editorials in the communist paper, *Neues Deutschland*. "*Neues Deutschland*?" Niemöller asked, "Never heard of it. If you want to condemn American foreign policy, all you need to do is read the Western papers!"

During our interview a crowd had gathered around us. Suddenly a woman stepped forward and touched Niemöller's hand. Could not what he said be "misused" by us? But Niemöller just waved her off and I turned to her and told her we were only two foreign students. When the woman merged back into the crowd I saw her shake hands with another person. She must have felt very brave, having warned the great Niemöller.

Just before he left Niemöller, however, assured us he was not anti-American. He owed them a lot, he said, especially at the end of the war when there was so little to eat. Afterwards we got into a long conversation with two men among the crowd. One was a well-dressed man who said he had been an infantryman on the Russian front but had deserted because of the German atrocities towards civilians in Russia. He is now trying to obtain compensation from the West German government. He calls himself proudly a member of the anti-Hitler resistance, but from some of the other things he said I could not help wondering whether he might not have deserted from other, less honorable motives. Like Niemöller, he is sore against the West, though mainly because he lost his fortune in the 1948 currency reform. And he is disenchanted enough to consider moving to East Berlin, where he has been offered a good job in the postal service. Furthermore, he also told us he hates Jews. (What a peculiar freedom fighter!) Meanwhile Jay talked to his friend, an elderly man who knew English very well and who, according to Jay, is a real Nazi even though he never joined the party.

Jay and I retired to a cafe in Steglitz to discuss all this.

---

[1] "We Germans may have lost perspective, but the Americans have never been able to see at all!"

7 May 1954

Today Karl Malbranc of the Hauptstelle für Erziehung und Schulwesen gave me lots of tips for my research on education for working-class children before 1914. Drove to Neukölln Rathaus to see the Bezirksschulrat, but it appears I'll have to wait till next week when he has office hours again. At 7:30 I met Max Hübner, the chairman of a workers' music club (Musikverein "Echo") in the club's regular haunt, a *Familienrestaurant*. I listened to the band rehearsing Elgar's "Liebesgruss" for several hours, again and again. Their conductor was in despair over the harsh sounds produced by his musicians: "Also, meine Herren, Musik ist kein Handwerk, das man erlernen kann. Für Musik braucht man Seele..."[1] The members all seem to be workers, most of them were rather old. Frequently they had to shake the water out of their trumpets. Mugs were constantly being passed around. One old man collected membership dues and also put down the number of beers each person ordered, entering everything neatly in a book. The playing was so-so, a little too loud and raw. The club is going to give an early-morning concert at Whitsuntide, starting in the morning at 6 a.m., which is an old Berlin tradition. I will try to go to it.

It rained hard when I drove home. The jeep works beautifully after a mechanic yesterday told me to have one of my spark plugs replaced.

Saturday and Sunday, 8 and 9 May 1954

Saturday, little happened. Tried to work. Got bored and saw the Carol Reed film *Gefährlicher Urlaub*, which is supposed to represent today's Berlin. A kidnapping story with shots of the Kudamm, Potsdamer Platz, Friedrichstrasse, and the Städtische Oper. Technically the film is good and the plot quite exciting, but this is not really Berlin today. You just don't see car chases and manhunts on the Kudamm everyday.

Sunday spent entirely at Wannsee. Gorgeous weather. I drove there for breakfast of pancakes and then took Jay, Carol, and Randolph plus two little girls from a Jugendheim (friends of Carol, one is called Brigitte, the other Christine) to the Pfaueninsel. The sun was really hot. In the afternoon various guests arrived for tea at the Cerfs': Al Hartel, a Miss Eleanor Kohler (who writes for the *Neue Zeitung*), Herr Horst Hartwich, and finally (very late) the Herz family. (Apparently in Britz, where they live, there is a festival celebrating the cherry trees in bloom, as well as the party conference of the SPD Berlin.) It was 8 o'clock by the time we broke up. Hartel, as usual, had me come into his house, this time with Miss Kohler, for supper, recorded music, and photographs. But throughout the day conver-

---

[1]"Gentlemen, music is not a trade that anyone can learn. To make music you must have a soul!"

sation never became very lively. I think everyone must be tired from too much sunshine.

Monday, IO May 1954

Today I drove to the Leuschnerhaus to attend a class given by Kollege Modell. Modell had me stand up and explain to the workers in his class the purpose of my visit. But the response to my invitation to old workers to tell me about their lives under the monarchy was very feeble. I think I'll give up the Leuschnerhaus as a source for prospective interviewees.

After a few hours of reading on a bench in the Steglitz park, I was off to the "Berliner Kindl" restaurant in the Sportpalast to attend the monthly meeting of the Association of Berlin Cooks. They met in an airy, modern dining hall on the upper floor of the restaurant. The main speech was given by the chairman of the waiters' union, Metzel. He spoke about the need to raise the prices in Berlin restaurants because this would permit paying higher wages to the cooks and so would also improve the standard of cooking. He pleaded for leniency towards Germany's young cooks who, he said, had been forced to learn their trade cooking with inferior materials right after the war: dried potatoes and other such stuff which "the foreigners sent us in order to purify [*säubern*] their own agriculture." But there were almost no young cooks present. The youngest cook seemed to be the one from the French Foyer in the Wedding, and he told me he was 40.

It is difficult to think of all these cooks or their union as part of the working-class movement. Wages seem to be less important to them than furthering their art by exchanging the recipes of their chefs d'oeuvres. Their highest goal, they said, was to please their clientèle. One man got up and complained about a new trend to demand a secondary school diploma (*Abitur*) of cooks. No, he said, let boys who want to become cooks begin their apprenticeship at fourteen. If they want to have an education as well, let them read in their own spare time. (This sentiment struck me as so old-fashioned. I felt as if I had attended a guild meeting.)

II May 1954

Going to the Wedding used to take me over one hour on foot and by tram. Today I could drive there by jeep in only 20 minutes even though I stopped several times to look at my map. I was early and sat for half an hour on the north bank of the canal near Tegeler Strasse. Watched children tumbling out of a school building and innumerable elderly people with watering cans walking towards their little plots of land. It all looked so very peaceful. In the background, a Thyssen factory was working full-steam.

Interviewed Rektor Friedrich Buchholz, the first chairman of the teachers' union, whose appartment is in a school building in Tegeler Strasse 18-20. Buchholz received me in a large study that was very tastefully arranged. He proudly showed me his large collection of fairy tales from practically all over the world. He is a kindly small man, unassuming yet fiercely independent (he said he defied the school board's attempt at regimentation under Wilhelm II and under the Nazi regime), a good storyteller and, obviously, heart and soul a schoolteacher.

Left at noon, had lunch in the Müllerstrasse and then went to Rathaus Wedding. I was received by a Bezirksschulrat Diesterbeck. He was anxious to help me and started telephoning around. He gave me the addresses of one headmaster in Utrechter Strasse and one teacher in the Heimat-Verein Wedding. When I've seen them, I am supposed to look him up again and get introduced to the health department at the Rathaus.— He explained to me that "Rektoren" administer elementary schools (*Volksschulen*), while "Direktoren" head secondary schools (*Gymnasien*).

On my way back I happened to pass a French administration building and was surprised by its inconspicuous appearance. It was just an ordinary entry in a tenement house, wedged in between shops.

Bought tickets for Circus Grock for the Cerfs and myself through the *Telegraph*.

In the evening I went with Jay to the GSG cinema show. We were first shown a film that is used for the workers' training course in the Leuschnerhaus, a very interesting picture on Berlin's social history from about 1890 to 1954 and with a wonderful commentary ostensibly by an old organ grinder. The next film was a documentary on the S-Bahn strike of 1949, but I found it too polemically anti-Russian. Finally we saw an American film on the history of the United Ladies Garment Workers' Union, which seemed to be a prewar film and was quite good. Met an English student from University College, London, who is taking a semester at the FU. Sat with Jay over coffee in my Steglitz cafe till midnight.

Poor Christine and Horst Häker. They tried to get people to join the GSG but no one signed their application list. It was partly their own fault since they could have organized all this better. For example, Christine read out a new regulation for the club, and while she read it decided that it should be changed and altered it on the spot. This gives the impression of improvisation. Not even the other GSG officials supported the Häkers.

Saturday, 15 May 1954

Lent this diary to Jay a few days ago, so I must now sum up what happened over the last few days.

On Wednesday, went to the Leuschnerhaus and interviewed a few elderly workers from this week's training course. Two of them were rather conservative. In their recollection everything had been fine under the empire. The third interviewee was younger, a man with a yellow, emaciated face and long hair. He talked bitterly about working-class life before 1914 as recounted to him by his mother and grandfather. He talked well, and he invited me to visit him and his mother and aunt in Reinickendorf.

Jay borrowed the jeep in the afternoon, and in the evening I went over to Wannsee for an egg foo yung dinner.

Thursday was a busy day. Drove early to the Wedding trying to see Rektor Stickdorn and Lehrer Stephan. Found out that this Stephan was in fact Bruno Stephan, the author of *Heimatbuch Wedding* and the founder of the Heimat-Archiv (local archive) in the Wedding. Both were unfortunately not at home.

After that I met a Mr. Brinkmann at the district school council (*Bezirksschulrat*) in Neukölln. First he took me to see a Schulrat Köpnick to get his permission to visit a few local schools. Brinkmann has just come back from a journey through the U.S.A. visiting educational institutions, including Yale, and was very cooperative. Some of his observations about America: (1) He likes the system of the "open door" which he had found there. All American offices keep their doors wide open during work hours. This discourages private conversations, nepotism, and obliges the officials always to remain calm. (2) Americans don't write letters for the sake of maintaining a correspondence with someone. They only write when they want something. (3) American schoolchildren learn much less than German children, but they get a better education. (4) Brinkmann admires the versatilty of American teachers, who, he says, all learn a practical trade as part of their training.

Went to Restaurant "Zum Sängerverein" in the evening to meet the workingmen's choir "Hoffnung" and to listen to their rehearsal. As with the Musikverein "Echo," the members consisted mostly of rather old men. The tenor section was very weak. The piano broke down. But on the whole they sang quite well. Some of the men are preparing for a singing contest in Hannover. This singing club was one of the first such clubs to resume its activities after the war. It was registered with the U.S. Military Government as a nonpolitical organization.

Yesterday was Friday. First I had a busy morning. At 9 a.m. I interviewed Rektor Stickdorn in his school, Utrechter Strasse, Wedding. A kind old fellow, though he did not have much to say. After the interview, he introduced me to the local baker, his wife and little daughter, who had come to deliver the buns which all the children get with their lunchtime cocoa. (The cocoa and buns are distributed free twice a week, on other days they get soup. To supplement this fare the children bring their own sandwiches.) Stickdorn regretted that I wasn't writing on present-day Berlin. He would have liked me to see how little the children of workers today differ from the children of the rich. For some reason he took me to look at the bowl of goldfish in the teachers' conference room. What were his politics? In the last war, he said, he doused three incendiary bombs that fell on the school in 1943, while local Nazis fearfully hid in the cellars.

I also met Bruno Stephan in the Heimat-Archiv, at Müllerstrasse, corner of Triftstrasse. The son of a small official, he became a schoolteacher and never regretted it. His interest in the local history of Wedding was spurred by his involvement in Adolf Damaschke's land reform movement back in the 1920s: this was a program of social reform inspired by the horrible housing conditions for the poor in the Wedding.

At 12 noon he had to be back in his school, a secondary school for children going into practical trades (*Oberschule Praktischer Zweig*). He teaches a class of 36 girls aged around 15 and told me to come along because the girls had asked him to bring me to school. First we had to call on the Direktor to get his permission. The girls were very noisy and Stephan had trouble keeping them quiet. Indeed, I was amused to discover that he was most uncomfortable because of my presence. He didn't dare to smile in front of his girls and kept his cap on. I also thought he was very tactless when he proceeded to ask the girls questions about their families, ostensibly for my research benefit: "How many of you share one bed with your mother? How many of you live in flats without toilets of your own?" But the girls did not mind at all. They took great pleasure in answering his questions, as if it were a special distinction not to have a private toilet. Of the 36 girls, more than half lived in flats without toilets, a few of them with only one toilet for all the families in their staircase. About one third shared a bed with their mother or sister. Health seems to be pretty good, except for some cases of scarlet fever and two cases of infantile paralysis, now completely cured. All of them seemed to have made up their mind about a career (shop girl, hairdresser, dressmaker, secretary, nurse, etc.) and all of them said they had made their decision in accordance with their own inclination rather than because their father was a barber or their uncle had a millinery shop. I then asked whether none of them wanted to become a film star? Riotous laughter. "They are sensible girls," Stephan told me, "they do not aspire to impossible heights. We once had a girl who wanted to become a newspaper reporter and she ended being a washerwoman!" (This story once more provoked riotous laughter. Why??)

Throughout the hour Stephan looked as if he were in constant fear of losing control over his class. He kept his cap on and tapped the floor with his walking stick while standing in front of the girls. He did not like my talking directly to the class, especially not when I tried to be funny. He wanted me to put my questions to him so he could transmit them to the class, which I didn't do. Maybe I felt offended by the cruelty with which he ordered a girl to tell me the wretched story of her mother's three husbands, whereupon he turned to me, remarking: "You see, we still have things of this sort going on here in the Wedding!" It seemed to me a teacher would only act this way if he wanted to show off his power over his pupils.

Finally, the girls sang songs. This was a bit embarrassing. First a song entitled "In Canton bin ich geboren…" suggested by Stephan, then a song they themselves chose and which happened to be a sailor's love song ("Not taught in school, mind you," Stephan hastily told me, "the girls learn that from the radio!") and then a few folk songs. At the end I had to say a few words in Chinese and write a few Chinese characters on the blackboard. As Stephan escorted me out to my jeep, the girls were hanging out the window and made a most frightful farewell racket.

On my way to Steglitzer Bahnhof to meet Jay and Carol, a tram ran into my back fender, causing a delay of 15 minutes. Fortunately, the tram driver readily admitted that it was his fault; he had not noticed me in time. Damage is slight and the BVG is going to pay for it. Went with the Cerfs to NAAFI in Reichskanzlerplatz where we bought BAFs from a British officer and with these Bafs Jay and I bought sandals (chupplees) and some Scottish tobacco while Carol bought marmelade and jam. We had dinner there too and afterwards went to Circus Grock. Too bad we all were so awfully tired— Carol even lay down and slept during the intermission— because the circus wasn't bad. The tent was small and we sat very close to the stage. The acrobatics were wonderful, especially two rubbery gentlemen in blue suits, and the final number with Grock himself, memorable because one can see that Grock is getting old. His face is full of lines.

Today I interviewed Dr. Gettkant, a former school doctor and welfare doctor in the district of Schöneberg, and also a former city councilor. The interview was short but pleasant and very productive. After we finished talking about the time before 1914, he also told me about the situation with tuberculosis in Germany today. Both in the East zone and in the Western zones there is a serious problem caused by tuberculosis among cattle (*Rinderpest*) whose milk is being sold without proper sterilization. In the 1920s a Jewish doctor in Berlin named Friedmann had discovered a serum that was effective against TB, but the German doctors had blocked it because (1) Friedmann was a Jew, (2) it made curing TB too easy and cheap. And yet this serum has proved very effective in Colombia. Friedmann died a poor man a few years ago and Gettkant, who is one of the executioners of his will, is fighting to get the serum finally recognized in Germany.

Went to a garage in Steglitz. The repair on my back fender will take only a few hours and cost about 20 marks, which I find most reasonable. Couldn't do much work. So sleepy. Also, my neck aches a little from the jerk of yesterday's collision.

Drove to Reichskanzlerplatz to buy George Mikes's satirical book, *Über alles* for Jay. Read it quickly and was disappointed. I find Mikes's observations on Germany and the Germans shallow and often simply wrong. His only excuse is that he wrote it after a sojourn of little more than a month, and that this was his first trip to Germany.

16 May 1954

Sunday. Went to the Cerfs'. The two little girls, Brigitte and Christa, were also there and we had sandwiches in the garden. The children played with Rascha's puppies. Jay said he had an exciting interview yesterday with a young man who was a high-ranking FDJ functionary (a member of the secretariat?) until 1951 and whom he hopes to interview at length.

I had to leave at 3:40 and made a long 1 1/2 hour trip by S-Bahn (I was too tired to drive the jeep) to Hermsdorf up in the very north of the city. A certain Oberschulrat Richard Keller lives there in Freiherr-vom-Stein Strasse 31. Keller turned out to be a good-humored, well-nourished bourgeois who on Sunday afternoons likes his television and beer. Fortunately he introduced me to old Willy Kubig, a lithographer and printer, 80 years old, and an SPD member for more than 50 years.

This very pastoral area is reminiscent of Reinickendorf. The Kellers have a small, modest house, with a garden where they mainly grow vegetables. They had kept some coffee and cakes for me and for an hour or so in the garden I had a very satisfying interview with Kubig. Keller sat there too, helping to explain whenever Kubig did not understand my question. Now and again he himself threw in a good remark. Keller also talked a little about himself. When the Nazis seized power in 1933 he had wanted to go to Sweden, but finally decided to stay. During the war he served on the Russian front. Near Kharkov he was billeted in the home of a Russian communist family and had liked these people very much— they had been nice and highly cultivated. In the Russian prisoner-of-war camp everyone including himself was ready to become Communists. But when Keller witnessed the cruel behavior of the Soviet troops and saw that they treated German Communists no better than German Nazis, he turned away from communism. Keller also mentioned the French, whom he knows well as the occupation authority in this part of Berlin. They are making a great mistake, he said, trying to get the Saar to become part of France. This will only fan German nationalism just as the Versailles treaty had after 1918, however much the Germans then had been sick of war.

The Kellers kept me for a supper of sandwiches and beer. Then I had to watch German television with them for an hour. There is only one channel for all Germany, but studios in different cities take turns going on the air. This time it was Hamburg broadcasting. The program was called "1:0 für Sie," an American-style audience show where people win prizes after performing some feat. It was very well done, I thought, with much taste and imagination.

I had to run for my train at 9:20. The train was jammed full with people returning to the city. It was so stuffy that I nearly got sick but decided better not to, since we were just then passing through the Soviet sector. In Nordbahnhof (still in the Soviet sector), a man got on the train in plainclothes and shouted: "Everyone out, please!" (Alles aussteigen bitte!). People got up, bewildered, but it was only a joke. A strange joke.

17 May 1954

Worked well at home. Around noon I went to fetch my jeep from the very grimy workshop in Steglitz. To get a written bill for the repair work I had to go to the Meister's home a few house away. I was amazed to find his home on the first floor of a new apartment building, spacious and very tastefully furnished. Big lace curtains, expensive radio in one corner, a cupboard filled with books and wine glasses. It just didn't seem to fit him with his eternally grimy hands.

In the evening I called on the secretary of the "Echo 1878" men's choir in Neukölln, a man by the name of Heinz Reck. He lives in Erlangerstrasse 11, 4th floor, a spacious flat, newly painted, but rather bare. From his window you see lots of children playing ball in the wide street below, among them his two girls Kati and Puppi. Reck is about 30 years old. For a carpenter and bricklayer I though he had strangely weak arms. He showed me the register (*Protokollbuch*) of the club which dates back to 1902, and told me I could borrow it for 2 days. Then he asked a friend of his, Klaus, to drop in and join our conversation.

Klaus Pupmann, 22 years old, was a metalworker. He was remarkably articulate, which may explain why he already is a functionary of the IG Metall. He said he distrusted all capitalists, whatever their nationality. ("Capitalists stick together like crows who won't peck at each other's eyes.") He would never trust a man who offered him something for nothing. This is why he had refused a scholarship to become an engineer. He has no ambition for himself, he said, and only became a *Mechaniker* because his father had found an apprenticeship for him. If he has any goal at all it is to further the trade union movement. He laments that most workers merely live from day to day and want no more than better wages and more comforts. "The workers must learn to engage in politics lest they be made the *object* of politics." When I asked him whether he had ever heard of the GSG, he shook his head. Students who are interested in unionism? He is suspicious of them. "The gentlemen of the FU and TU will never understand us workers." In their eyes the workers are too primitive in their thinking. And the workers in turn won't have any dealings with gentlemen.

Reck and Klaus agreed to make a tour (a *Bierreise*) of Neukölln's workers' pubs with me on Friday. Friday you can see workers drinking, and their wives come to drag them home before all their pay is spent.

When I started the jeep to drive home I saw that the headlights didn't work. A kind policeman in Karl-Marx-Strasse said to me that if I wanted to drive to a garage to have my lights repaired he'd close an eye. But no garage was open. Had to take the U-Bahn and S-Bahn home. What takes 12 minutes by jeep now took me $1^1/_2$ hours by train.

22 May 1954

Did not write for about a week. Stayed at home most of the time getting some solid reading done. On Wednesday I asked Jay out to see the French movie *Sous les toits de Paris*, which was just superb. (He came with the 12-year-old daughter of a friend of his, Sybilla.) On Thursday, Jay borrowed the jeep for the day and in the evening called Sergeant Gardner to warn him that unless I get the promised spare tire by Saturday afternoon he will go to the judge advocate general's office on Monday. The telephone booth shook as Jay unloaded a Zeus-like wrath on the sergeant.

Yesterday, Friday, was the first busy day of this week. I looked up Franz Neumann in the Hochschule für Politik (Neumann wore his usual air of indifference, so I did not stay long) and then went to Neukölln, Weigandufer 31, first floor, to look up the old restaurant waiter Burose, who together with his housekeeper treated me to coffee and pastry. But he was a poor interviewee, which is too bad because I had hoped he would also talk about his father, who used to be a local poor-law and school commissioner. Weigandufer, however, I found beautiful with its canal and the thickly leaved trees bordering the cobbled streets on both banks.

In the evening I dressed in my shabbiest clothes before leaving for Neukölln. First I met Hübner from the Musikverein "Echo" in the Sängerheim who talked to me about recreation clubs for workers in the old days. Then Heinz Reck and his friend Klaus came and we made our tour of the Neukölln pubs. We started in a pub in Herrmannstrasse at the corner of Nogatstrasse named "Rohde," which looked enormous and was cheap. I guess about 20% of the customers were women and 80% men. We saw what Reck said I would see, namely, wives coming into the pub looking for their husbands to take them home. (But I also saw a father and child looking for the mother who was out on a spree.) We started talking to a worker from a chemical factory. He was very noisy, treated the whole table to cognacs and beer and loudly announced to everyone that he was no Berliner but a Rixdorfer, born in 1902.[1] When he started to sing (very loudly and very out of tune), the waiter shook his finger at him. His wife was squeezed in a corner but she readily talked to me. They go out to drink about once a week, she said. They would visit 3 to 4 pubs and not go home until the early hours of the morning. On Sundays they work in their allotment garden (*Schrebergarten*). They never talk about politics. She likes to go to the newsreel theaters (*Aktualitätenkino*) and she regularly reads magazines like *Quick, Das grüne Blatt, Der Abend,* and *Welt am Sontag.* She likes *Quick* because of its many stories. I made a portrait of an unemployed barber who drank beer to my right and happily posed for me. Later I also had to make portraits of Reck and Klaus.

We left and went to another "Rohde" joint, this one in Kienetzer Strasse. We talked with one pimp, actually a quite nice-looking boy, and then went to a posh place for a change, the Café "Florida Bar." It is hidden in a small, dark street, but inside it has luxurious furnishing and thick carpets. A small discreet band played and the customers looked much more elegant than in the "Rhode." A quite awful dancer gave a small floorshow to the tune of Liszt's Second Hungarian Rhapsody, the prices were awfully high, and so we left. We went to "Schalenberg," Sonnenallee corner Hobrechtstrasse, but saw only old pensioners quietly drinking beer and the bartender told us they always close down by midnight because these people don't stay late.

Outside in the street under a lamp post we saw an enormously fat woman with a garish makeup talking to someone. "Dicke! plumps doch mal!" (Hey, fatso, let's see you bounce!), jeered Klaus. Someone in an upper window demanded quiet and Klaus promptly responded with insolent Berlin bons mots. Heinz and Klaus nearly died laughing when I suggested the fat lady must have eaten several pounds of sweets for breakfast. They decided there and then that I was a Berliner too.

Next we went to the "Blauer Affe," off Hermannplatz. This was a spacious but shabby-looking joint. My two companions suggested we should say "du" to one another, and I was baptized "Charlie" since my name is too difficult for them. Observed some elderly ladies sitting drinking beer by themselves, hoping to find husbands (at least that's what Reck said). This brought up the question of "widows' balls." I have read about them before— do such things still exist? Sure, Heinz said, so we jumped into the jeep and drove out to "Walterchen der Seelentröster" (Little Walter, the lonely-heart comforter), a huge set-up known as the "Resi of the little people." It is a regular night club plus dance hall. At the entry there are uniformed doormen, and you must be over 25 to get in. No "modern dancing," the doorman warned us. The entrance fee was 80 pfennigs and you are obliged to leave

---

[1]Neukölln before 1912 was called Rixdorf.

your coat in the cloakroom. Inside was a big dance hall with a garish blue roof on which "stars" (Osram electric bulbs) twinkle on and off and the walls are painted with idyllic Italian landscapes. The public looked superficially elegant, but you soon noticed the colored check-patterned shirts of the men, the cheap sandals worn with lounge suits, the 10 cent store jewelry of the women and their reddish plump hands, raw from work. On a rostrum was a band and leading it was Walterchen himself, an elderly man in a cutaway and with a thick-set, oriental face, wearing a golden chain with a golden heart round his neck. So this was "Walterchen mit dem goldenen Herzchen," a Berlin character. (He said to me I could visit him in his office on Sunday at 7 p.m.) Reck started telling everybody that I was— or rather that *we* were— conducting "social studies here for an Ameri-can university and would people please answer some questions," but only one man said yes, a fireman who was about 60 years old, drunk and lonely, and whom I didn't like. Also the waiter talked to us for a while (he told us this institution is about 40 years old, though it only moved here after the war) and one man suggested to me that I should read Zille.

I was getting sleepy and so we left for our last stop, the "Rollkrug" on Hermannplatz, corner of Hermannstrasse. I had been here with Voigt during Fasching, only this time there was more to see. It was half past 12 by now, but the place was still full. Some people danced, including a boy who should have been in bed by now. Some people stared at me with ugly, challenging grins but did nothing when I kept ignoring them. Reck said there were women of ill repute here and Klaus promptly went to speak to one. The three of us sat down at her table and started to ask her questions: why had she come? Why alone? What did she hope to find here? How long did she intend to stay? What work did she do? Did she easily trust other people? She gave very guarded answers, pretending to be amused at our curios-ity. She used to sell things in a shop, she said, but lost her job now. Her fiancé has left her, so she comes here to make new contacts and to find entertainment. Heinz and Klaus danced with her. Heinz discovered a former fiancée of his among the dancers and wanted to stay longer, so I left the two and raced the jeep home in record time.

This afternoon I went to HQ Company to look up Gardner. He drove me out in his Mercedes to get my spare wheel in Dahlem when, one after another, two of his tires blew. People on the sidewalk stopped and stared and gesticulated as Joe nonchalantly kept going, driving his car on the wheel rims until the American garage near Truman Hall.

23 May 1954

I woke up late and had to rush to keep my appointment with Malbranc, who lives in Blumenweg 14a, near the S-Bahn station

Südend. There he showed me some pictures of old Berlin and introduced me to an old printer named Prüfig who talked to me for more than 2 hours on life in Berlin when he was a young man. Had lunch in Steglitz, worked at home in the afternoon and at 7 p.m. went to interview Walter, the lonely-heart consoler. But he had already left. So I decided to leave the jeep in Schöneberg and walked around its streets. Many streets look quite fantastic, like the setting for a play. A narrow street, for instance, with old houses perched high on all sides and many quaint roofs. And suddenly, like a caterpillar, a yellow streetcar comes round the corner, a complete anachronism. And at the end of the street, sitting over the houses like a huge spider, the tower of the local gasworks. A man passed by, pulling his father home in a small cart. The two must have been in the countryside, for the old man was carrying a bunch of lilacs.

Monday and Tuesday, 24-25 May 1954

I saw Dr. Siegfried Nestriepke on Monday, the stage manager (*Intendant*) of the Theater am Kurfürstendamm and its historian.[1] A handsome old man with lots of white hair. His office is small, but cozy and well carpeted. He was polite, but didn't have much to say on the working class and their interest in the theater.

I dropped in at the DGB Haus to make contact with the transport workers' union (ÖTV). Met a Mr. Meyke, who asked me to come back on Friday. Lunch on the open-air terrace of Aschinger's, then off to Neukölln to the Schulamt. There Otto Brinkmann happily showed me 7 school chronicles dating back to the 1890s which he had asked for at last week's conference of headmasters in Neukölln. I can start working on them tomorrow, he said.

I spent all Tuesday morning in Brinkmann's office reading the school chronicles. They are quite fascinating. Fortunately Brinkmann was out most of the time, so I had the office all to myself and his secretary brought me tea as if I were the boss. When Brinkmann came in he usually started chatting about himself and then of course I couldn't work. Brinkmann says he was an anti-Nazi. His father was an officer. Otto had wanted to become a teacher but the First World War interrupted his training. He enlisted as a volunteer, served first in the Cavalry, then in the Infantry, and ended in the Air Force. He was shot down and taken prisoner in England in 1917. It was his first stay abroad. He fell in love with England, discarded his narrow Prussian upbringing and wrote a novel entitled *Romanze in England.* During the Nazi years he spoke out against them but escaped punishment by moving his home from Neukölln to Pankow. (I didn't

[1]Siegfried Nestriepke (b. 1885), city councilor and formerly head of the Berlin magistrate's office of popular education. Author of *Neues Beginnen. Die Geschichte der Freien Volksbühne Berlin, 1946 bis 1955* (1956).

BERLIN SOCIAL DEMOCRATS

Maria Reuber, Molkenbuhr
(14 July, 1954)

Meeting of SPD women
(24 June, 1954)

Anna Niemetz, Annedore
Leber (12 June, 1954)

The Wilhelm Leuschnerhaus

BERLIN'S MANY FORBIDDEN ZONES

Spandau prison: "Keep out!"

Warning sign outside S-Bahn:
Beware of East Sector!

East-west border in Berlin-Rudow (9 Aug., 1954)

quite understand how this move could have achieved that.) After the recent war, as headmaster of a school in Pankow, he ran into trouble when he said at a public meeting that though the German atrocities in Poland were abominable the Poles should nonetheless forgo all acts of retaliation for the sake of peace. The Russians accused him of being a fascist. Thereupon Brinkmann decided to escape to West Berlin. He bribed a few Vopos in 1946 and with the help of some young teachers moved all his belongings to the West. They did this by riding the S-Bahn across the French-Russian sector boundary up in the North every night for two weeks, each time carrying pieces of his household belongings. This included his furniture, which he smuggled across one chair leg at a time.

In the afternoon, drove with Carol and Jay to Reinickendorf to the home of Bruno Radeloff, whom I had met in the Leuschnerhaus. The Radeloffs live in Kühleweinstrasse 6. They have a charming flat in an apartment house, with heavy furniture, lots of carpets, many pictures, a big Gobelin, and a beautiful kitchen, which is rare in Germany. We sat on a small balcony overlooking the courtyard and the conversation soon got very warm and animated. Jay mainly talked with Bruno and a Herr Schubert, who had dropped in, while Carol and I talked to his mother. Mama Radeloff was rather nervous, fearing that the neighbors might wonder what guests she had, but she told us anything we wanted to know about her youth. Bruno also showed us an old family album. It was a scream at times. The faces! Jay liked Bruno and urged him to join the SPD.

On our way back, I took the wrong street after the victory column and so we arrived at the Brandenburg Gate quite unexpectedly. We stopped at the Russian war memorial. The Brandenburg Gate at night, seen from only 100 yards away, was grandiose to behold. It was illuminated, and the red flag on top shone brightly against a dark sky. The Russians at the nearby war memorial were just changing guards. They no longer wear the fur caps and long coats as in the winter when I last saw them. Now they have flat peaked caps and wear riding breaches. They smiled happily. Jay asked in German whether it was allowed to mount the steps and they answered with a stream of Russian in which we understood only the German words *verboten* and *morgen*. Some of their words reminded me of Czech, so I tried out my Czech on them. They understood *dobry den*, and *dobry večer*, of course. But then I pointed to the memorial and said *krasny*. "Eto prikrasnii, eto sovietskii," they replied with a grin. Jay didn't approve of my saying *da*, the only word I knew to say. There were lots of wreaths, probably to commemorate the German capitulation on 8 May 1945. The wreaths I saw were from the FDJ, the SED, and the "Gesellschaft für Deutsch-Sowjetische Freundschaft Wilmersdorf." (Wilmersdorf? Could there really be a branch of that society in West Berlin?)

27 May 1954

Ascension Day (*Himmelfahrtstag*): I left the house early and drove to Heerstrasse near Repenhorn, then walked along the bank of the Havel river through the Grunewald until Schildhorn. It was very hot and hundreds of people were camping in the forest and swimming in the Havel. Only 10% were dressed up for the traditional "stag parties" (*Herrenpartien*), and there were lots of women, although women are supposed to stay at home today. Many boats were chugging up- and downriver, and some carriages were gaily decorated. In Schildhorn were old restaurants where people sat playing cards or singing. A few men were dressed up in 19th-century clothes with tophats and acted as if they were drunk but they really were not. Everything was very reasonable, the people had obviously come mainly to have a day's rest.

By 10:30 a.m. I decided to head back for home. A quick detour to Schöneberg told me about a Herrenpartie in an allotment garden in Priesterweg because this was announced on posters, but there was nothing much to see. A tortuous narrow road led to the Laubenkolonie. There were some grimy, barefooted children and left and right acres of garden land. Otherwise everything was as quiet under the hot sun, like Mexico during the siesta hour.

28 May 1954

Went past Martin-Luther Strasse to see if I couldn't find a Zille book for Mr. Hartel, but was out of luck. Had a talk with Fritz Meyke of the ÖTV, who was very helpful indeed. He even wants to call a special conference of old TU members at which I would be free to ask as many questions as I like. Drove home through Wilmersdorf. Beautiful, quiet streets with lots of trees giving refreshing shade. The kind of streets where you should sit on a bench and dream.

29 May 1954

Read in the morning, then went to a garage to put some oil in my gear box. In the afternoon, a garden party at Al Hartel's. Lots of people were there, most of them colleagues of Al's from RIAS. I met the director, Ewing, who looks very English, and the Countess von York, whose husband was one of the conspirators of 20 July 1944.[1] Adamski was there and looked a bit lost, also the Herz family (I had to smuggle glasses of punch to Mr. Herz without letting his wife see), and a quite impossible Miss Nölle, who talked ceaselessly about wanting to do something for humanity. A surprise was meeting an American woman who now is at RIAS but formerly worked for the

[1] Peter Count York von Wartenburg was executed by the Nazis on 8 August 1944.

Chinese Air Force in Arizona. She actually had in her wallet a picture of Wolfgang Yü, the son of Defense Minister Yü Ta-wei, whom I had last seen in Chungking in 1942! Jay and Carol were there too. Jay mentioned something about a 2-day, hush-hush job for HICOG he's got, which involves the use of a staff car no less. One didn't see much of Hartel who was busy playing the good host, but he obviously was happy.

31 May 1954

Went in the morning to the Schulamt in Neukölln and finished reading the school chronicles. I was shocked to discover that in the 1890s in all the schools at least 1 to 2 schoolchildren died every year of scarlet fever or diphteria. Brinkmann tells me this is still true in some Berlin schools today. Had to get my indicators fixed in Steglitz.

In the evening went to the Bundesallee 79 where the Hagemanns live. They were throwing a wine-sampling party. A wine manufacturer named Eduard Witter from the Rhine Palatinate was there who lectured us on wine processing and on the "life careers" of wines while we slowly sipped from 4 different bottles of "Naturwein." The people who were there were mostly around 30 to 35 years old. Some were booksellers like the Hagemanns. One was a zoologist named Jürgen Brandenburg, another was an architect, one was a doctor, one a schoolteacher, and one was a chemist (*Apotheker*). It was quite romantic sitting around a table with a shaded lamp in the middle, the walls covered with lots of books, old oil portraits, and etchings. Through the open balcony door the night air smelled sweet from the lilacs in the garden, and fresh from the afternoon's rain. — I only didn't like Witter too much. His lectures went on too long and he smacked his lips in self-satisfaction. Also, he was contemptuous of Italians and French people. How could he!

I June 1954

Slept heavily after drinking all this *Naturwein*. But by 11 a.m. I was in the Schlüterstrasse to look up the carpenters' union (IG Holz), a very small trade union where the people, on reading Pietsch's letter of introduction, received me cordially. Interviewed old Neh over a cup of coffee in the Kasino (he was a good interviewee), then drove him to Neukölln where I also interviewed his wife over more coffee in the snack bar of Hertie department store. She is a kind old lady. The Nehs live in the East sector and come to West Berlin to sell their eggs (which is economic sabotage from the communist standpoint) and to buy Western goods. I spent the rest of the afternoon in the Neukölln town hall making contacts with the social welfare department and the administrative library. — It rained hard. Sat in my jeep in a side street off the Karl-Marx-Strasse sketching people coming home from work.

2 June 1954

A very full day. Drove to Neukölln early in the morning and talked with a welfare worker, Fürsorger Rohde, of the local welfare office (*Sozialamt*). Rohde is in charge of social welfare commission no. 4, controlling six out of Neukölln's 89 welfare districts. These *Sozialkommissionen* are formed of volunteers. Rohde is 39 years old, an instrument maker (*Feinmechaniker*) by trade, young-looking in his shabby brown suit, who reminded me much of Herr Siewert at the Landesarchiv. He talked to me for 2 hours about former cases. The social welfare office works hand in hand with social welfare department of the Christian Democratic Party (*Unionshilfswerk*), the SPD's Arbeiterwohlfahrt, the Innere Mission of the Evangelical Church, and the Roman Catholic Caritas. The Sozialamt is divided into (1) juvenile welfare, (2) health welfare, and (3) economic welfare. Rohde works for the third department. His department cares primarily for the old people. It gives them financial assistance, has them regularly visited by nurses, or sends them to retirement homes or hospitals.

After a snack of cocoa and a piece of black bread with dripping, we set off by jeep to call on some of Rohde's charges. First we went to see a Frau Krafft in Richardstrasse 35. This was a nasty-looking tenement house with five courtyards. Little Zille children were playing on the broken asphalt. A man in slippers greeted Rohde. (I noticed that Rohde was welcomed with much pleasure wherever he went.) Old Mrs. Krafft lived in the last courtyard, up on the 4th floor. All the toilets were on the landings of the staircase. She had a very clean kitchen plus one room. Pictures of Jesus Christ hang on the wall and 2 or 3 religious books were on the table. From the window you could see into the neighbors' apartments. Her lighting consists of a petrol lamp and candles. She was divorced from her husband 30 years ago and due to her weakness she has not been out of her flat for the past $4^1/2$ years. No one comes to visit her any more except a cleaning woman (*Hauspflegerin*) from the Sozialamt and occasionally some Jehova's Witnesses. She has two sons, one of whom even lives next door. But they never come to see her. Rohde promised her electric light at the expense of the city before the end of the year.

Next, we visited Herr und Frau Hausfeld, who live in Bertelsdorfer Strasse 2, in a damp cellar dwelling. The woman suffers from a heart disease and has not left her bed for the past 6 years. The man, a learned mechanic, is unemployed. She had a dog in the bed. Frau Hausfeld clasped my hands warmly and wished me well in my studies. Rohde promised to get her new bedsheets. The one room and kitchen were quite big but dark and musty. They did have a radio.

We also paid a short visit to an Albert Fröhlich, who was born on 15 December 1862 and is the oldest man I've met in Berlin so far. A carpenter by trade.

Our next visit was to an Emma Schiementz, who lives in a good flat with heavy, valuable furniture. One of her former roomers had been an old drunkard who had dirtied his room to the extent of using it as a toilet until the Sozialamt had called the police who took him to an asylum.

After lunch, we visited a Frau Renner. Renner lives in a real rathole of a place, the cellar of a bombed-out garden house. It was incredibly dirty. She even kept chicken under her bed. The roof leaked. On the table was an unappetizing soup made of tepid water, bread and perhaps some oil. She absolutely refuses to go to an old people's home. Like a peasant woman, she clings to her little garden plot, and to this filthy room where her husband died many years ago. She says that before he died her "Papi" told her that after his death he would go to America and would fetch her. She is still waiting for her dead Papi to come for her. When she heard that I came from America, she asked me whether I knew Papi. I mumbled something about America being a very large country with lots of people. She cried as she recited to us all the misfortunes of her life. Apparently the neighbors protect and care for her. When the Sozialamt once tried to take her to an old people's home by force, her neighbors hid her.

We also visited an 91-year-old Mrs. Fischer who lived in a Wohnküche, a combination of kitchen and bedroom. She is very lonely and welcomes anybody. We did not dare sit down for her place has bugs. I looked at some of her old pictures, one showing her at the age of 28, a very attractive and healthy woman. Unrecognizable now. Rohde promised her electric light and a cupboard. He also told her to wash her hair. On her 90th birthday, Frau Dr. Suhr had visited her here, and also a prominent American lady, but she didn't know who.

Our last visit was to Frau Hilliges in the hut of an allotment garden (*Gartenlaube*). She did not come out when we called. Rohde feared she might be dead and asked me to climb the fence. I was glad to find she was only asleep. The hut was quite clean. Rohde only told her off for not emptying her night pot. She also clings to her place, but last winter the Sozialamt transported her to a sanatorium because she nearly froze to death. She is over 85.

After dropping Rohde at the Rathaus, I drove to the Zoologisches Institut of the FU in Grunewaldstrasse to look up Jürgen Brandenburg, whom I had met at the wine sampling party. We took the S-Bahn from Schöneberg to Friedrichsstrasse. Tried to get tickets to the Russian ballet but it was all sold out. Then we walked through the streets towards Alexanderplatz. Lots of FDJ boys and girls in khaki blouses and blue shirts and dark skirts or trousers were about, also many Vopos in leather overcoats. But there were not as many slogans on display as I had expected except for the blue posters to greet the Second German Youth Jamboree. I saw an Indian couple being stopped by passersby who wanted to chat. The Indians wore communist badges. Outside the Humboldt University, a series of large political cartoons were displayed on billboards. One showed a Vopo arresting a housewife for smuggling sausages into the East sector and undermining the communist economy. In front of this poster a housewife looking very much like the one in the cartoon was laughing merrily. Was she laughing because to her mind the cartoon was so stupid or so cute?

A Vopo motorcycle patrol stopped a truck with Russian license plates for violating traffic rules. Another Vopo whom we asked to recommend a nice cafe grinned and told us he had no time to find out such pleasant things. We saw sailors making preparations for a huge parade.

3 June 1954

Got up early to drive down to Neukölln. Miss Lehmann at the Rathaus library was not too anxious that I look at the archive. When I pressed her she finally told me why: all the documents are being reclassified in the cellar. She got the *Bürochef*, Herr Zöllig, to come and explain the situation to me. That is when I discovered that Neukölln has the distinction of having saved almost all of its documents through the war intact, which is rare for a Berlin district. Next Tuesday I am to meet the local mayor, Bürgermeister Exner himself, to ask his permission to use the archive after all.

I have much asthma these days and consequently feel tired all the time. In the evening I went to the community hall (*Gemeindehaus*) of Lichterfelde-Ost to attend a meeting of the Evangelischer Jugend-Verband. There was singing and someone read two short Chekhov stories. Afterwards people went to drink Coca-Cola at the Weisses Rösslein. It was not really a wasted evening for it showed me how much of the spirit of prewar Germany is still around, preserved in the hiking songs of yore, including patriotic ones with typical staccato rhythm and shouts of "Hei Hei."

4 June 1954

Spent much of the day reading old administrative records in the Neukölln Rathaus. In the evening I telephoned Richard Gladigow, an old schoolteacher whom I want to interview. In very schoolmasterly fashion, he told me that my postcard to him was written in faultless German except for a lack of punctuation. I wonder whether he had corrected it in red ink? Received a letter from Rudolf Wissell.

5 June 1954

The Stein Bibliothek was closed today because of Whitsuntide. Went to American Express to see about a ship to the United States. Then sat in the Mensa. The main hall of the lounge has been turned into an information center (*Kontaktstelle*) for FDJ boys and girls who want to visit the West sectors. Many signs read No Photographing Allowed. But I saw no communist youths. People say the checks at the sector boundaries have become very tight. I got into conversation with a group of students waiting for jobs through the student employment office, the "Heinzelmännchen." Talking about rearmament, they expressed indignation at the prospect of becoming soldiers in a new German army when former (Nazi) Wehrmacht officers are still in jail "just for losing the war!" I asked them what they thought about the Nazi atrocities in Poland and the systematic extermination of the Jews in Eastern Europe? "The Allies have dirty hands too," was the reply. Really? I pressed, could they give me examples of Allied atrocities that compared with the Nazi concentration camps? The astonishing reply was: "No, not offhand, but the men higher up surely can!" One German girl who had grown up in Finland and has a Finnish accent, said it was incomprehensible why Japan had not attacked Russia in 1941. Why? I asked. "Then we might have won the war," she answered.

In the afternoon I was invited to the Brinkmanns' for tea. Nice modern flat. His wife is younger than he and they have a little 9-year-old daughter who seems shy but very well brought up. It was a restful, sunny afternoon. I told them something about my years in China and Brinkmann told me what he thought about the Cold War ("The West must take a strong stand! Everybody in West Berlin wants that!") and showed me pictures from his American journey. Tanked the jeep full for tomorrow's ride.

6 and 7 June 1954

Pfingsten. I don't think I've ever done so much in one day. Got up at 4:15 a.m. Had a quick bite and then drove round the corner to meet Jürgen Brandenburg in Birkbuschstrasse. The weather was gorgeous, the streets still deserted. We drove to Bundesallee to fetch Brigitte Hagemann and her mother. Stopped at Steglitz Bahnhof to meet Jay but he didn't turn up. Then drove to Britz, across ploughed fields and narrow, winding country lanes. It was a beautiful part of Britz with old rural roads covered with cobblestones and lined with grey peasant houses with big roofs but tiny windows. You'd expect a horsecart or a few cows coming round the corner any minute. Schrammer's Naturgarten was in the yard of a former farm house, with a big wooden fence around. There were barns, lots of weeds and beautiful old linden trees. Tables were set up under the trees and at one end of the garden, the musicians of Musikverein "Echo" had established themselves. Max Hübner, the chairman, was running around complaining that not enough people had come yet. Those who were there seemed to be relatives of club members, and local neighbors. But they all came in family clusters, grandfathers, aunts, nephews and nieces. All had come in their Sunday best and were on their best behavior. Still, Jürgen Brandenburg was easily spotted as an outsider with his camera, trenchcoat, and his intellectual face.

We sat down and ordered coffee. Then we strolled around, Jürgen taking pictures and I making sketches. The band began to play sentimental tunes accompanied by much percussion (*Blechmusik*): polkas and waltzes with some *Tannhäuser* thrown in, and the public got merrier and merrier, chatting loudly, gobbling down mounds of cakes they had brought along while the children played with their balloons.

At about 9, when it was slowly beginning to get hot, we left to go to the "Neue Welt" in the Hasenheide. It was full of people and we could not get a table. Here the public looked much coarser than in Schrammer's Naturgarten. The customers were dressed more fashionably but their clothing looked cheap and in poor taste. As in Schrammer's, there was a coffee kitchen and people were eating cake. On a platform that faintly looked like the Taj Mahal, a band was playing modern dance tunes and there was dancing. Two elderly ladies, enormously fat, were exhibiting the oldfashioned "shove dancing" (*Schiebertänze*) usually associated with "Apaches" in Paris in the 1920s. People gathered around them and laughed. As I began to sketch them, people also crowded around me. Everybody seemed to be in a good mood. We left and walked up the Hasenheide, past Kliems Festsäle towards the "Resi." Lots of cafes had engaged little ensembles of piano, violin, and accordion, all the tables were occupied and more people were strolling up and down the street looking at the cake eaters.

It was getting hot, so we drove to have a bite to eat at the flat of a Frau Köhler in the nearby Boddinstrasse 23, a friend of the Hagemanns who owns a collection of souvenirs of old Berlin. While we had wine, coffee, and sandwiches, Frau Köhler (who is about 65) showed us old music boxes, some 18th-century toys and original manuscripts of poetry. I was getting very tired and we all went home.

I had a nap. Then Jay called to apologize for his nonappearance this morning. I went by S-Bahn to Wannsee to have tea with the Cerfs. On the way there I noticed outside the Steglitz Bahnhof, a tent with West Berlin students waiting to give directions to any FDJ boys or girls who came to the West. A rubbish can displayed the sign: "Politischer Müllkasten," so that the visitors knew where to dump their propaganda materials.

Two days ago, Jay was given the job to write a report on these

In East Berlin

Vopo cordon at Brandenburg Gate (6 May, 1954)

Inside the German-Soviet Friendship Society (17 Feb., 1954)

At the Komische Oper

Cafe Warschau (17 Feb., 1954)

AN ILLEGAL STUDENT FRATERNITY IN WEST BERLIN
(3 AND 8 JULY, 1954)

Three students in charge of a fraternity meeting

A duellist's second

Duellists

Kontaktstellen for the public affairs director of HICOG,[1] Elmer Cox. So that was why he was provided with a staff car! Professor von Rantzau and his wife also came for tea. I had briefly met him at Yale; he will now teach at the Technische Hochschule in Berlin. There was also a Frau Wohltat and her daughter, and Sybilla with her mother. We left Sybilla to babysit for Randolph and Carol, Jay, and I went to the Ring Politischer Jugend (Steglitz, Humboldtstrasse 26) to meet the FDJ boys who had illegally come over from the East. We sat down in the parlor where a group of people were already conversing. I struck up a conversation with my neighbor, who turned out to be an FDJ in *mufti* all right. But I was also disheartened to see the house almost entirely filled with West Berlin "helpers" who sat around chatting with each other, playing ping-pong, or eating, while the few FDJ kids who had come hung around feeling rather lost.

Then, on the spur of the moment we decided to take the East German youths to see *From Here to Eternity*. The West Berlin students were discussing the film and the FDJ boys were getting curious about it. By special arrangement during the Whitsun rally all FDJ members had free entry into any movie house in West Berlin. We hopped into my jeep, other boys climbed into a Volkswagen bus, and we went to Tempelhof to the American "Columbia" movie house. Disappointment: it showed another film. After a short debate Jay had the idea of going into Tempelhof Airport to show the kids some aeroplanes. The policeman at the desk was very understanding and so was one of the Pan American Airways officials. FDJ boys? Of course they could see anything. And so our group was allowed onto the airport runway to inspect a PAA clipper and to watch some other aircaft come in for a landing.

We left rather late. We were with two FDJ boys and two FDJ girls. The boys promised to be back the following evening to see the Burt Lancaster film. We picked up some anticommunist leaflets issued by the Free Democratic Party. I found them rather badly designed. Wulf and Ulrich, two of Jay's Berlin friends, say that this poor draftsmanship shows that both the East and the West are getting sick of their propaganda war and even their artists are running out of ideas.

On Monday, 7 June, I drove to Neukölln to see the inauguration of Rixdorfer Höhe, an artificial hill made from the rubble of Neukölln which we were told is 2 meters higher than the Kreuzberg, for centuries the highest point in Berlin. Otto Suhr talked over the loudspeaker and actually managed to attribute a "strategic importance in the Cold War" to this little molehill. It was a rainy day, chilly and drab aside of a band playing a newly composed "Marsch zur Rixdorfer Höhe."

After lunch in Steglitz, I again went with Jürgen Brandenburg to the East sector. This was the last day of the Pfingsttreffen, and the

[1]HICOG: Office of the U.S. High Commissioner for Germany.

temptation to see more of East Berlin while foreigners are less likely to be checked was too great. We got out of the S-Bahn at Unter den Linden and walked to the Brandenburger Tor. Over in the West sector you could discern a row of dark-blue police vans. According to Jay, DGB loudspeaker vans were positioned there to induce the FDJ boys to come over to the West. Here on the east side stood a crowd of FDJ boys recognizable by their black trousers, khaki ski vests and blue shirts, but they were kept back by Vopos and FDJ leaders who kept saying: "Go away, you've seen enough!" (Nun los Freunde, geht doch schon fort, ihr habt genug gesehen). The FDJ youngsters did not seem to mind too much; they nonchalantly turned round and strolled back towards the center of town. We passed the Soviet embassy, where people were queuing up for conducted tours. I was told that anybody could go in but when I saw that identity cards were checked at the entrance, I decided I had better not.

It seems that all of East Berlin was turned into a giant fairgrounds for the young. Next to the embassy, the "Gesellschaft für Sport und Technik" had opened an open air exhibition (field telephones, shortwave radios, an old aeroplane dating from 1909). At the Humboldt University a number of people in training suits were receiving medals from communist functionaries while a band played a marching tune. The audience began to clap their hands over their heads in accompaniment, "Freundschaft" fashion. At the Marx-Engels Platz, a huge trapeze had been erected in front of the Dom and some high-wire artists were descending from its tower hanging by the neck, others raced motorcycles up to the Dom on tight ropes. (Today's *Neue Zeitung* reports that just at this moment two FU students from West Berlin were arrested by East German police before the Dom— but we didn't notice anything). We next walked to the Alexanderplatz. Great crowds. All the FDJ'lers, I noticed, had a very filthy appearance. Their clothing looked coarse and dusty, their hair uncombed, and their skins had a very brown color, only it was not a healthy suntan, but plain dirt. The only cars driving around were FDJ buses, or cars with communist officials in them (these were decorated with red and blue flags and pictures of white doves) and a few West Berlin cars. Lots of hot-sausage stands and lemonade stands provided refreshment. Mobile post offices allowed you to send greetings with special commemorative stamps, and there were even lottery tickets to buy.

We took the S-Bahn (oh, so crowded!) to Stalinallee and walked to Café Warschau. I had never been to the eastern end of Stalinallee before and now discovered how shabby indeed this boulevard is, once you leave downtown. This, after all, used to be the very proletarian Frankfurter Allee. Back in the posh part of Stalinallee, an activist was leaning out the window and, seeing in me a foreigner, beckoned me to come in and see him. I waved back and pointed to my watch, meaning I had no time. Later I regretted having refused his invitation; it was a unique opportunity to meet a successful communist worker. A few steps later I met to my surprise one of the two FDJ boys from last night. He told me he and his friend had safely returned to the East sector yesterday but that trying another trip tonight was too dangerous. Two FDJ boys were shot and wounded by the Vopo yesterday as they tried slipping into West Berlin. We shook hands with them and I had to autograph his FDJ membership book. It made me feel like Charlie Chaplin or Grock.

On the little square between Café Budapest and Café Warschau, a small orchestra played music while FDJ youths danced. We watched from the terrace of the Café Warschau, drinking mocca. Two FDJ boys at our table said that tonight all streets would be full of dancing. Outside the House of Sports (on our way to the U-Bahn) we passed a girls' choir singing Hungarian folk songs while a man beat measure with a long whip.

We took the U-Bahn to S-Bahnhof Stalinallee and returned to Schöneberg by city train. At the sector boundary Treptower Park all Vopos and FDJ'lers in the car got out, except for one boy who hid in one corner pretending to be asleep. An FDJ *Ordner* with a long baton came through the carriage, prodded him and threw him out. Back in the West sector there was a blissful silence. In the East sector the loudspeaker music had been blasting nonstop, though, curiously enough, often American dance music.

I dashed over to the Ring Politischer Jugend, where I met Jay. Jay went into a room upstairs and asked me to join him as interpreter. There we both talked to FDJ boys about America: Jay as a native American, I as a foreigner living in America. The talk mainly centered around the racial problem in the U.S., American policy towards Germany, atomic bombs, and above all the American standard of living. Unfortunately there were many disturbances. Some FDJ boys left to go to the movies while more and more West Berlin students came in. They were all far more articulate than the FDJ boys and began to monopolize the talk. Worse, they began arguing among themselves and quite forgot that the meeting was primarily meant to benefit the boys from the East. Jay had a hard time to keep them quiet. By 10 o'clock the housekeeper threw us out.

Jay said that Elmer Cox had tried to get hold of him during the day, so we drove out to HICOG to see him. We found him sitting behind his big desk, with nothing to do and nothing much to say to Jay either. Finally, we got into his State Department car and drove to the sector boundary at Potsdamer Platz. It was past eleven o'clock by then. On the brick wall of a ruined house a movie projector was showing the film *Shane* (in German: *Mein Freund Shane*) and lots of people stood on the rubble watching it, among them some FDJ boys for whom this show was actually meant. A few hundred yards away in the Soviet sector, the beams of anti-aircraft searchlights were constantly moving in a circle through the night sky, throwing into stark relief the silhouettes of the ruins in this badly damaged section of Berlin, a spectacle that reminded some people of the bombing nights during the war. At any rate, it was quite a grotesque situation.

After the movie we returned to HICOG to pick up our jeep. Had a gulash soup with Jay in Steglitz and talked with him until 2 p.m. Jay went home in my jeep since there were no more city trains running at that hour.

8 June 1954

Met Bürgermeister Kurt Exner in the Neukölln Rathaus. He looked so friendly and self-effacing you'd never guess he is said to be "the busiest Bezirksbürgermeister in all Berlin!" He readily allowed me to use any materials that I can find in the Rathaus for my studies.

In the afternoon, Jay called to ask whether I wanted to go with him to a youth hostel (*Jugendheim*) in Prinzenstrasse, Berlin-Wedding, where many FDJ people were reported to have called over the past two days. Prinzenstrasse, we found, is a really shabby-looking street, and the house we went to, no. 8, very ugly. The Jugendheim was on the first floor of this old Mietskaserne built at the turn of the century. The wooden floor boards helped to make it stifling hot. There was nothing going on when we arrived. FDJ people sat around bored, drinking orange juice and glancing listlessly over the propaganda materials laid out on the tables. When we got there and Jay explained that he was an American who would be glad to answer any questions about America there was quite a lot of enthusiasm and we began a session like the one yesterday in the Humboldtstrasse. But, alas, once again the Western "helpers" proved to be rather unhelpful because they quickly dominated the conversation. One West Berlin student began to attack U.S. foreign policy and called the Viet Minh and Red Chinese governments the legitimate, popularly elected governments of Indochina and China, while another man, this one a Bonn government official sent here to observe the Whitsuntide events in Berlin, got up and launched into an anticommunist speech which I found very unpleasant since his attacks sounded like a personal reproach to the FDJ boys. In any case he talked too vehemently, almost hysterically. It was not a successful session. I wished those Western "intellectuals" would go away since the boys from the East seemed rather pleasant and I suspect they were not that interested in politics.

While we talked, a West Berlin policeman came to join us. He had noticed two foreigners arriving in a jeep and thought it best to investigate. Jay told the FDJ boys that this was one of the "faschistische Stummpolizei,"[1] which the cop acknowldeged with a tolerant

---

[1] A derogatory term used in East Germany for the West Berlin police, whose president was Johannes Stumm.

grin. He also allowed a West Berlin student to pull his leather helmet off and hang it on a hook to indicate he was here only as a guest. He stayed for a while, then left.

We left too at 7:45. I dropped Jay in Steglitz and went on to have supper with Jürgen Brandenburg. He showed me pictures that he had taken on a trip to France, and we talked about travels. I was astonished to hear he is a friend of Klaus Schulz.

9 June 1954

The *Neue Zeitung* today brought the shocking news that the West Berlin criminal police has arrested "our" Ernst Gries as a communist agent. It said Gries had come to West Berlin as a "refugee" last September and had then returned to the Soviet zone in May. He had come to West Berlin a second time not long ago and tried, first, to recruit a refugee in Sandwerder to spy for the East German secret police, then to kidnap an anticommunist political fugitive. When the West Berlin Kripo (criminal police) seized him at Lehrter Bahnhof yesterday, he tried to resist and had to be subdued by force.

In the morning I interviewed the teacher Gladigow, who lives in Boddinstrasse 23. Did not like him very much. Since I was already in the neighborhood I called Frau Köhler, who had promised me some materials on Berlin local history. She asked me to drop in at 3 p.m. I walked for two hours through the side streets of Neukölln and enjoyed its rural appearance. I even saw a horse-dealer's yard. Good old Frau Köhler turned out to have only items of antiquarian interest to show me, like mementos of everyday life in the 19th century, but I was glad to sit with her and her 88-year-old mother, sipping coffee, and eating cake with strawberries.

Later I also interviewed a teacher named Emil Wedding. It was a short interview. All his answers to my questions were negative: no, there were no problems with working-class children and no, he doesn't remember any parents who held socialist views. Unreliable too.

II June 1954

Read at home. In the afternoon Jürgen Brandenburg suggested going to a movie, *Bitter Rice*, at the Filmbühne am Steinplatz, after which we had dinner at the Café Paris with bouillabaisse, filet mignon, pommes frites. I was invited to this scrumptious meal by Frau Hagemann, who, together with Frau Köhler, happened to meet us in this cafe. We drove Frau Hagemann home. After that, because I had told Jürgen about my excursions into working-class pubs, we decided to visit some beer houses in Schöneberg. We found one that is really the most depressing dive I have seen in all Berlin. It was very small. The people in it looked very coarse. One customer was always holding my hand and gibbering nonsense, another with a deeply tanned face and a sinister look in his face tried to approach me but was held back by another man, a waiter, who was a bit more humorous but equally suspicious of us both. We had been spotted as "students" right away and I as a foreigner to boot. One old gardner, who said he spends every night here because he can't get along with his wife at home, proved very nice, however, and so did the proprietress, an old woman with a very delicate face.

We also dropped in at a bigger pub in Neukölln. A small ensemble of guitars and violins was playing dance music and people were dancing, playing billiards and the gambling machines.

It was past midnight. I was sketching some people. Jürgen was talking to someone else. There was a little girl of 8 who was still up, playing the gambling machines. She was pale and thin.

12 June 1954

Was tired all morning because of a night of asthma. Drove to the Technische Hochschule in Hardenbergstrasse where the llth Social Democratic Party Congress for Berlin (SPD Landesparteitag Berlin) was being held. The event took place in a huge modern hall, filled with several thousand people. I was met here by Mrs. Trapp, the former head of the Prussian factory inspectorate who is very English looking in her short-cut white hair and reddish complexion. She introduced me to everyone around her, among them the party chairman, Willy Brandt, the deputy chairman, Willy Braun, Annedore Leber (the widow of the famous socialist Resistance fighter), and Paul Löbe (former Reichstag president under the Weimar Republic). Among the crowd I recognized Glamann, the Häkers, Otto Suhr, Mayor Exner, Eberhard Hesse, and the professor whom I had met at the home of Ernst Kaeber not long ago. The Häkers pointed out Jürgen Gerull to me, the leader of the socialist "Falken" youth organization. Two years ago he voluntarily went to East Berlin to give evidence in favor of a number of Falken boys who were caught distributing anticommunist leaflets. Gerull himself was arrested in court and spent 2 years in an East German jail.

The meeting itself was not too interesting except for Willy Brandt's excellent speech. The debate turned on various propositions whose text, however, was known only to the delegates so that most comments were incomprehensible for us guests.

I left at about 7 p.m., had a bite at Aschinger's, and went for a short stroll on the Kudamm. Since I mostly meet students and workers it's been a long time since I've seen so many well-dressed people about. Glancing at our old embassy building at Kurfürstendamm 218, I suddenly noticed someone unlocking the iron gate and walking in. I raced after that person and it turned out to be Brigitte, the youngest daughter of our old porter Rollke. I went in with her and there, sitting at a table having supper, was 73-year-old Rollke himself. I had last seen him as a young boy in the time of the Munich crisis in 1938! They called the second eldest daughter, Doris, from another room (she had worked in the embassy as a secretary for some years and still sometimes cooks Chinese meals), and shortly afterwards came Ulla, the eldest daughter, with her husband Werner Hoffmann. Hoffmann had been chauffeur for the Chinese military mission after the war. We were all soon in a jolly mood. They told me a lot about the Chinese embassy staff before the war and during the military mission after 1945. The whole family including Hoffmann are presently out of work but nevertheless seemed very cheerful. (Brigitte, who is 31, works occasionally in a fur shop. She has a small daughter.) In the basement flat which they occupy only one piece of Chinese tapestry and one porcelain lamp remind them of the old days of glory when this house represented the Chinese empire. They also had a photograph of me as a little boy with my brother and sister and Mama. The embassy has stood empty since 1949 except for an old Maybach 1936 automobile that still stands in the garage (it hasn't run since 1939), a few typewriters and precious vases, and a ghost which I am told periodically haunts the fourth floor ever since an attaché committed suicide there around 1937.

I got home shortly before 10. Jay had called, so I called back. He wanted me to come out for a cup of coffee and meet Ulrich Morgenschein and Wolf Müller, two German students from the "Aktionsgruppe der FDJ." It was indeed an interesting conversation. The two believe that the recent Pfingsttreffen should be regarded as the first major political success of the FDJ. Very few FDJ boys had come to the West and very few had wanted to come. Ever since the proclamation of the Neue Kurs (the "new political direction" on 17 June last year) the FDJ has leaned towards de-emphasizing politics. There were no long political harangues to endure at this most recent event, they said, nor were the boys made to carry rifles. Instead there had been entertainment, free distribution of nonpolitical literature, plenty of food, and— except for an obligatory parade before DDR President Wilhelm Pieck— the boys and girls were given much free time. The result? No one was interested to read Western leaflets and the Kontaktstellen in West Berlin had done poor business. Müller thinks that if the Neue Kurs also succeeds in improving the supply of consumer goods, it will win the Communists many new adherents. In another two years the Reds may have progressed far enough to risk holding free elections.

13 and 14 June 1954

I'm still terribly sleepy. On Sunday, which was a rainy day, I stayed mostly at home to work. Called Jürgen and asked him to tea in a

Lichterfelde pastry shop nearby. He in turn invited me to dinner at the Canton Restaurant on Stuttgarter Platz, a posh place but frightfully expensive. Jürgen does not think much of the SPD. "A party without a sense of realities and too dogmatic," he says. Thinks well of Adenauer, even though the chancellor tends to be autocratic. He also disagrees with me about the Schmidts: they are not necessarily Nazis, he said, because you can have social contacts to the Ribbentrops and not agree with their politics. He also thinks the Allies made a great mistake when they imprisoned German war criminals after the war.

Today worked in the Rathaus Neukölln and finished reading the old administrative reports from the 1890s. Still sleepy. The transmission in the jeep broke down and I had to drive home all the way from the Karl-Marx-Strasse using my 4-wheel drive. It was like driving a tractor: it roared loudly and proceeded at a snail's pace.

15 June 1954

The jeep is repaired. I had to pay 41 marks for a new rear axle. Uff! The mechanic who performed the job is called Bischof and he said he might want to buy the jeep when I leave Berlin. Went to Neukölln, first to the Britzer Damm to check whether the "Kürbisranke" allotment garden will have a traditional summer festival or not, complete with Onkel Pelle, a torchlight parade, and so on. It will. It's a wonderful Laubenkolonie, not too big, not too pretty, and surrounded by old houses belonging to the historical part of Neukölln. It had a wonderful smell of vegetables, rabbits, sunshine and flowers. I am supposed to come back tomorrow to see the 2. Vorsitzender of the allotment garden. (The Germans have *Vorsitzende* for practically everything.)

Then I visited an old school headmistress, Schulleiterin Elisabeth Rothe in Neukölln, Bouchéstrasse 68. By accident I nearly drove into the Russian sector. The second part of Bouchéstrasse where Rothe lives is already in the Russian sector, but the houses on her side of the street are still in the American sector. I left the jeep in the American part of Bouchéstrasse and walked through the "Russian" street to enter her— again "American"— house. She told me that on 17 June last year the Soviets had placed tanks at her house door, which forced her to use only her American backdoor. She offered me cider and biscuits and talked to me about school discipline before 1914. Curiously, she didn't understand why I found what she told me awfully harsh. She obviously took great pride in the strict order that she had maintained in her schools. Two girls who missed school regularly were "of course" reported to the police, whereupon the police not only had fetched the two children but also given them a good whacking at the police station.

At 7 p.m. I was invited to supper by Miss Margarete Trapp, the former head of the Prussian Gewerbeaufsichtsamt (factory inspectorate). She received me rather grandly in a black evening gown. Her flat was very modern and elegant. I was ready to be very impressed except for one story she told about her experience in the war, which I thought snobbish. In 1944 she was bombed out. But because of her title as *Regierungsrat* she was given new quarters in a beautiful house in Potsdam which formerly had belonged to a Hohenzollern prince. A Nazi officer already lived there and he was glad that "people of culture" (*gebildete Leute*) were moved into the house. But in the same year Hitler also ordered the repatriation of Germans (*Volksdeutsche*) from the Ukraine. And so it happened that not long after she had moved into the house in Potsdam a woman arrived with 7 children, armed also with an order to be put up in that house. She was a simple peasant who barely spoke German! "Und das in diesem Hause mit dem wunderbaren Parkett! *Das* haben uns die Nazis gemacht!!"[1]

Trapp had entered the service of the Prussian Gewerbeaufsichtsamt in 1913. Before then she had been the *directrice* of a large Berlin house of fashions. She chatted quite amusingly throughout the evening though she kept losing the thread of her thoughts. I did not learn very much about factory conditions before the First World War but she gave me an introduction to the present factory inspectorate in Berlin which, she hoped, would allow me to visit some old Berlin factories.

Coffee at my Stammcafé and then home. Started to review the progress of my research so far.

Sunday, 20 June 1954

Haven't written for several days. Was exhausted. Must have been the sun. On Wednesday, 16 June, the eve of "Tag der Freiheit," Jay called and I went down to Wannsee to join a torchlight procession from Wannsee to the Russian war memorial on Potsdamer Chaussee just short of the Soviet zone. A memorial stone was being unveiled to the memory of 21 Russian officers and men who, it was said, on 17 June 1953, refused to shoot at the demonstrators and were executed because of it. There were speeches by Senator Bach and by a Russian émigrée woman who heads the Human Rights League (Liga für Menschenrechte). One speaker said Germany would have been spared some of her national shame today had more German soldiers during the last war behaved as these Russians had. Finally, the crowd sang the old soldiers' song, "Ich hatt' einen Kameraden." (Afterwards Jay told me that Walter Sullivan, the *New York Times* correspondent, doubts that the story about the Russian officers' disobedience is true. For one thing, on 17 June last year, the

---

[1]"In that house with its magnificent parquet floor? That's what we owe to these Nazis!"

Russians were under strict orders *not* to fire on the people, and for another, discipline in the Red Army was much too good.)

On Friday afternoon I interviewed an old social welfare doctor, Friedrich Lorentz, also nicknamed "Gesundheits-Lorentz," who lives with and his wife in an old-fashioned big flat in Bochumer Strasse 11, Berlin-Moabit. Lorentz had his wife first announce me before he came out from a back room in old-fashioned dark clothes. He looks like an old aristocrat who has seen better days. Sitting in his alcove he told me many incidental things about the health of schoolchildren at the beginning of this century, which seemed to have been pretty dismal.

Saturday I went sailing on the Wannsee with Jay. It was wonderful, only the sun was too hot. Because there was no wind we couldn't return until almost 2 in the afternoon, which worried Carol.

In the evening the three of us went to the allotment garden "Kolonie Kürbisranke" in Britz to attend their summer festival. The chairman, Köller, and the treasurer, Bergwitz (who was drunk), treated us like guests of honor. The people who took part in the festivities were mainly the young, the older ones prefered staying in their own little garden plots. There was dancing and beer drinking. A clown-like figure, "Onkel Pelle," gathered all the children around himself to sing songs. They got some sweets and we got some eggnog, and then we joined the children's lampion parade through the colony and back before taking our leave.

Summer/Fall 1954

Wjderstraße, Berlin-
Neukölln

21 June 1954

American Express called in the morning to tell me that they've got me a berth on a boat sailing from Rotterdam to New York on 11 September.

Awfully hot weather; we are told this is the hottest June since 1909. At 8:30 I was invited to the home of an FU student called Dietrich Herrmann who lives with his parents and 4 brothers in a small house in Zehlendorf, Onkel Tom Strasse 136a. His father is a natural scientist, a research chemist who works for an institute in Putlitzstrasse. It was a "homey" evening. The mother was darning shirts and also mended my jacket while the rest of us sat sipping red wine and eating biscuits. We mainly talked about different countries and their customs, including of course the Germans. Unfortunately I did most of the talking so I didn't learn too much except that to people like the Herrmanns, who seem to belong to the solid bourgeois milieu, the working-class districts like Neukölln and Gesundbrunnen (which they nickname "Plumpe") are dreadful places that one shuns.

22 June 1954

Tuesday, and an exhausting but very rewarding day. Drove early in the morning to Puttkammer Strasse 14–16 in Kreuzberg, near Anhalter Bahnhof, to the Gewerbeaufsichtsamt, where I met a 28-year-old factory inspector (*Sachverständiger*) named Bindel. Bindel had been instructed to guide me through some of Berlin's typical factories. I owe this courtesy to Mrs. Trapp, who has phoned the head of the Berlin Gewerbeaufsichtsamt, Oberregierungsrat Fietz, for me with a nice recommendation. Fietz kept me waiting for a long time before I could see him. I don't think he is popular among his subordinates. Though he was courteous towards me, I could see that he was a rude boss and his staff fears his temper. Fietz said his office had no old reports on file, and that they knew of no retired inspectors whom I might interview. But he would have Bindel show me a dozen of Berlin's oldest factories during the next few days.

Bindel is a badly mutilated war veteran. A former Hitler Youth leader, he drove tanks on the Russian front. He lost an eye and both his lower arms as a prisoner-of-war clearing minefields for the French. After his demobilization he became a welfare worker. "Hitler was very popular in his time," he said, "let us be honest about that. No one realized where all this would end until it was too late." Today he is a bitter man without any illusions. During the many hours that we spent together over the next few days he never understood my delight in encountering so many original characters among the working people.

Bindel told me that the Gewerbeaufsichtsamt concentrates primarily on visiting large factories because by doing so it can show in its year reports far more worker's working conditions as having been inspected than if it visited an equal number (or even a larger number) of small enterprises. The small workshops are therefore treated like stepchildren. Accidents there are more serious. For every 2 of West Berlin's 12 districts, Bindel told me, there is one factory inspector. (Before the war, there had been local inspectorates for the several districts.) Bindel is for Wedding and Reinickendorf. To control factory accidents, there are *Berufsgenossenschaften*, which are not state-run, and I must look them up, he said (Bundesallee, Friedrich-Wilhelm Platz).

We first drove way north to Heiligensee to visit a cardboard factory, the Pappenfabrik Berpa. Berpa was a small enterprise. It is situated on the Havel river in very rural surroundings. It consists of only one big shed, which formerly had been a dry cleaner's and a shop for rug cleaning (*Teppichklopfanstalt*). The yard was full of weeds and bushes, everything lay around in disorder. Big bundles of old paper were stacked near the gate. We were received by the owner, a Herr Bergmann, who let us in. He and his brother together inherited this factory from their father who founded it some 20 years earlier in what today is the East sector. When they moved here after Berlin became divided into East and West, they changed the firm's name to avoid trouble when sending goods through the zone to West Germany. The Berpa work room was noisy, hot and grimy. What a difference from the clean and supermodern factories I have seen in the electrical industry! The shower room and the dressing room looked depressing. These had wooden walls covered with crude paint and a few rough tables with benches. It was hot and stuffy and smelled like the changing rooms you get on the beach. Women worked here too, mechanically passing piece after piece of cardboard through large steamrollers. There are some 20 work people in this factory which makes it a medium sized plant. (Under 5 is considered "small," over 50 is considered "large.") One worker sat in a corner spreading butter on a piece of bread: this was his lunch. There is a recreation room but we were told no one uses it except for changing clothes. Bergmann, rather surprisingly, looked very aristocratic and out of place in these surroundings. I asked him about discipline and learned that for most offenses, especially stealing, the workers are warned the first time and sacked the second time. Smoking is forbidden, but workers smoke anyhow and it is better to let them break the rule than to have them smoke secretly.

Bindel was always careful to obtain the permission not only of the owners but also of the workers' representatives before we asked any questions. The workers' representatives (mostly the chairman of the factory council) would otherwise have felt offended.

After Berpa we went to the sawmill (Holzbau) of Leo Poblotzki, Holzbau, which was next door. It was founded in 1932 but moved to this address in Heiligensee during the war. Today it employs 21 men. Poblotzki himself, a man with a big belly and no shirt on, readily showed us through his domain. Everything— the mill as well as the shacks which housed the administration and Poblotzki's own bungalow— was made of wood. "Very dangerous," grumbled Bindel, "should anything here ever catch fire." In one section carpenters were making window frames. "Carpenters are very conservative people," Poblotzki told me by way of explaining the absence of washing facilities. "They *don't* wash after work and don't want a room to change clothes." They had little iron cages in the workroom in which they put their street clothes while they worked, even though the room was filled with sawdust. Underneath the floor boards of the sawmill, in the basement, workers were filling sacks with sawdust. I found the constant dust in the air most uncomfortable.

Poblotzki said he doesn't care whether his workers are organized in a trade union or not. They may even agitate for their trade union inside the workshop for all he cares. He does not know about their private lives, doesn't want to know about their activities after hours, and offers them no days off at the company's expense (*Betriebsfeiern*). He gave himself the appearance of unconcern but it could have been a pose, I thought, since this way he could answer some of my questions about his men with an indifferent shrug. For as we parted Poblotzki told me that he would rather be a workman than an entrepreneur, which puzzled me.

The road to our next destination led through the beautiful countryside of Heiligensee. It must be wonderful to live here in one of the many delightful bungalows outside the city. In Reinickendorf we stopped at a mill, once famous as the Humboldt Mühle, but now called Viktoria Mühle. This is a large enterprise, more than a century old, with an iron gate, imposing brick buildings (one of its wings was the first major structure built in Berlin after the fighting stopped in 1945), a canal of its own, a huge grain store, and private railroad tracks. Lots of trucks and vans passed in and out of the gate. A porter asked us to wait until the master miller, Obermüller Buick, came, accompanied by an *Untermüller* named Fischer. Both wore long white gowns and looked like scientists. Buick was suspicious and asked to see our identity cards before grudgingly ordering Fischer to lead us around. But he did instruct the porter to give each of us two little sample bags of flour as a gift before we left. He apparently was upset because he had not expected an inspection and, so he admitted, the mill was not in perfect order today. Not that I would have known. The whole mill reminded me of a wooden ship. Wherever you looked there was very clean panneled wood, but the entire edifice was filled with noise and it was in constant vibration. There were huge wooden cases, called *Mehlsieben* (flour sieves) that shook violently all the time. We were joined by the vice chairman of the works' council, Herr Neumann, who was very friendly when he found that I knew the chief officials of IG Nahrung, Genuss und Gaststätte, including Herr Neh. Neumann impressed me as a tough person to bargain with, because he is calm, logical, and matter-of-fact. He told us that most of the improvements in the mill (such as the very good washing and shower facilities) were brought about through union pressure. The mill employs about 170 people who work in three 8-hour shifts. 85% of the men belong to the union. They receive Christmas bonuses and twice a month 2-pound sacks of flour. "The management could not abolish these benefits without a very good explanation," Neumann grinned. "After all, we know the exact economic situation of the mill."

It was good to breathe some fresh air after leaving the Viktoria Mühle. We made a quick dash over to a smithy (*Hammer- und Gesenkschmiede*), still in Reinickendorf, belonging to Fritz und Erich Hanemann. It looked like the cardboard factory we had seen in the morning. Work had already stopped. During the hottest part of summer they work from 5 a.m. to 2 p.m. The nephew of the proprietress let us look through the now deserted workrooms. I was glad that the men had gone because it allowed me to look quietly at the immense furnace, to examine the soot and dirt everywhere, to poke around the heavy iron prongs and lead pipes, and all in all to take in this symphony of brown mud floor, slimy green windows, red rusted iron. "Smithies are coarse. They are a hard and crude people," Hanemann said. "They have no cultural aspirations. Their one sport is to drink [*saufen*]. When they fall into their beds at night after a heavy day's work— so long as they had a lot to drink too— they think they've had a great day." This factory is quite old, more than 60 years. There are still no washrooms, only buckets of water. The men throw red-hot pieces of iron into the pails when they want their water warm.

We drove a little through the Wedding. We stopped the jeep and walked into some of the fascinating buildings in the Gerichtstrasse. These were tenements with many courtyards just as Heinrich Zille painted them half a century earlier, with the workers' homes facing the street and workshops in the back. Near the Panke river the streets were full of the most curious-looking people. We saw a crowd gathered around a yellow-skinned old man with a big moustache and a dwarf-sized white-haired woman, and everyone was laughing at them. Bindel also took me to the bizarre Versöhnungs-Privat Strasse, a street designed in the 1890s to encourage the intermingling of the classes through the physical proximity of their dwellings. A "social reconciliation" between rich and poor on the private level was to result from this layout, hence the name of the street. But Bindel was not really interested in social history, so I will have to come back on my own another day. The Wedding is exciting in the summer!

23 June 1954

Wednesday, and a comparatively restful day. Called on Eberhard Hesse in the morning. He gave me the addresses of several old SPD men whom I am supposed to look up. Stopped on the Kudamm on the way home to look at the crowds outside the Filmbühne Wien and the Hotel am Zoo next door, who were hoping to glimpse some of the film stars who are in town for the yearly Berlin Film Festival. An Italian actress named Gina Lollobrigida posed on the balcony of the Hotel am Zoo for one minute and there were sighs of "ah!" and "oh!" Had lunch at Aschinger's and sat in the jeep for a while to make a sketch of our old embassy.

Did some work at home in the afternoon. In the evening went with Jay and Carol to see a Japanese film, *Einmal wirklich leben*, which was three hours long and very exhausing because the same gloomy mood prevailed in every single scene.

24 June 1954

Drove to Attila Platz in Tempelhof to pick up Herr Bindel at 8:30 a.m. to see more factories in the Wedding. I think we had better results this time. First we went to the Sauerstoff Fabrik Berlin (founded 1889) in the Tegeler Strasse 15, makers of oxygen tanks. The manager, Herr Hummel, who began here as an employee 49 years ago, at first didn't want to show us the factory because it is undergoing reconstruction and is very dirty. It is situated, like so many other factories, in the backyard of a tenement house, hidden from the street. The yard looks depressing, though it is clean. But Hummel talked to me readily in his office for one hour and in the end gave me a prospectus of this firm from the year 1914 as a present.

Next we went to the *Sandbläserei* (sand blasting works) Starke & Co., Berlin-Wedding, Müller Strasse 72, a very small workshop and one of only a very few such enterprises in Berlin. It was founded in 1912 and is situated in one corner of an inner courtyard (*dritter Hof*) quite far from the street. We talked to Frau Thiele, who is the present owner, to an old draftsman, and to the sandblaster himself. There doesn't seem to be much need for "factory discipline" in this small setup. The whole shop came to a standstill while we sat in the office to talk about the unusual and dangerous profession of sandblasting.

Sandblasting is used to roughen iron articles and to decorate window panes. Later Herr Tantow, the sandblaster, put on his helmet and continued his work while I was allowed to watch through a small glass window from outside. There was lots of dust, but Bindel told me the dust you can see is not as dangerous as the dust you cannot see. The average sandblaster dies at 35 or 36. Officially no one is allowed to practice this trade for more than two years, but Tantow has been a sandblaster for 15 years already and his skin looks grey and flabby. He lives in the East sector. He won't give up his job for he knows he wouldn't find another job in West Berlin once he is unemployed. He is also comparatively well paid. The shop, in turn, is anxious to keep him because sandblasters are difficult to find nowadays. We also inspected the sanitary facilities. The toilet was very dirty and the shower consisted merely of a water hose. — Later we were to see more toilets without doors. Bindel explained that the privacy of workers had to be cut to a minimum to prevent them from loafing during work hours.

From Starke we went on to Trinks & Co., Normenlager Gesellschaft, makers of nuts, bolts, and screws, in Berlin N 20, Hochstrasse, an outfit that formerly used some 40 to 50 men, but now stands idle owing to lack of orders. We found a lone woman sitting in the office counting screws into a box, and she gave us a quick tour of the factory. The main workshop is in a souterrain 2 meters below the surface of the street. (This is against modern police regulations, but this factory was built long before such prohibitions.) The machines stood crowded close together, each of them connected by belts to a main rod (*Welle*) near the ceiling. The whole factory was situated in this one cellar. There were some wooden toilets in the courtyard, and a washroom in the cellar of a neighboring house. The entrance to this washroom was a very low iron door leading down a steep stone stair case. There, in the half darkness you could see a row of rusty iron stands holding a few grimy washbowls made of tin.

Our next visit was to the Hebezeug Fabrik (crane and pulley factory) of the Brothers Bolzani G.m.b.H., founded in 1880. Again we were lucky to encounter a talkative group of people. A Herr Becker, who seemed to be the manager, and an old workman who headed the works council talked, with us for nearly an hour, comparing the social customs of workers before the First World War and today. Bindel only cautioned me later to take some of Becker's statements with a grain of salt since he too obviously had represented the view of the management. After our long talk, Becker had come to trust our intentions and gave us a tour through the factory. The factory disposes over comparatively much open space around the main workshop. It has a courtyard with fresh green weeds and some iron girders and chains to sit on. The workshop, built of yellow brick, is big and airy and looks almost like an aeroplane hangar, especially when all the doors are open. The lavatory is in a separate wooden shack. It has no door.

Finally, we called on the Leder Fabrik und Färberei Knoell & Co., Berlin N 20, Prinzenallee, a leather tannery and so a relic of a very traditional trade. Only the main office looked modern and this is where we were received by Frau Dittmar, the head of the firm, wearing a white overall. I think she mistakenly thought our visit would provide her shop with some welcome publicity; in any event she happily invited me to come back on Wednesday to interview old workers who had formerly been employed here.

A Herr Schmidt showed us through the workshop. He was a very chatty old man and got on my nerves— or was I simply irritated by the overpowering smell throughout the factory? There were large pools of water everywhere. The clerks had standup desks to discourage laziness. I seized the first opportunity to talk to some workers, including the chairman of the works council. He turned out to be very friendly. The factory is very old-fashioned— one of its two buildings looks like a horse stable built in the 19th century. We were shown the separate stages of tanning and dyeing and left around 4 p.m. I dropped Bindel off at the Kudamm and raced home for a quick rest before my next engagement.

My next engagement was driving with Mrs. Trapp to an evening meeting of socialist women, the SPD Arbeitsgemeinschaft der Frauen, in the Wedding. Trapp herself could not stay but she wanted to introduce me to this gathering where she thought I would surely find many a good witness to tell me about life among the poor in Berlin before 1914. Indeed, most of the women at the meeting were white-haired and looked well over 60. I met a Genossin Lotte Biener, who is the head of the office for women's questions (*Frauensekretariat*) in the Zietenstrasse, and a Frau Rutz, who wants to put me in touch with a welfare office for young delinquents. I was also introduced to Maria Reuber, who is one of the four party leaders (*Landesvorsitzende*) of the SPD Berlin. By the end of the evening I had lots of names and addresses of old women who were willing to be asked about their life. When I first entered the hall I overheard people whispering about a mysterious foreigner who was looking for old *Genossinnen*, which had made me feel quite uncomfortable, but I was quickly put at my ease by the friendliness of the people I spoke to. The meeting ended with a violin and piano concert that was astonishingly good.

P.S. Here are some observations about the factories I have visited, which I want to note down while my impressions are still fresh: (1) The workers work hard. I saw no one loitering or chatting anywhere. (2) The representatives of the workers are fine fellows. Serious, attractive personalities. The workers choose their best men to speak for them. They are polite, but feel equal to the employers in affairs where they can speak up in their official capacity. When the employer is not listening, they will also cautiously say something critical about them. (3) The workers vary greatly from one industry to the next. Can one speak about "workers" when a miller is so different from a turner? (4) Few workshops that are over 40 years old still look as they did before the First World War. Many enterprises closed down between 1914 and 1945, or were moved and modernized during the past generation.

25 June 1954

Didn't get much accomplished. Wrote some letters, transcribed yesterday's interview notes from shorthand into plain text. Lunch at Wertheim's restaurant (very good), dinner at Mrs. Sullivan's with Carol and Jay. The Cerfs are going to move into the Sullivan house next month while Mary and Walter return to the States for 3 months, so the talk centered around domestic arrangements. Mary Sullivan worked with the U.S. Information Service in Shanghai from 1945 to 1949 and had many nice things to say about China.

26 June 1954

Saturday. It rained all day. In the afternoon Mischa offered me a ticket to the Hebbel Theater to see *Der 35. Mai*, a play adapted from Erich Kästner's children's story, and so I went with him. The play was short but entertaining and included some good dancing numbers. I invited Mischa for a quick meal at the Café Paris afterwards. He had one interesting story to tell: he was recently at the Polizeipräsidium at Alexanderplatz in East Berlin to apply for a permit to travel through the Russian zone. A Vopo searched him and took away his scout knife (*Fahrtenmesser*). He was then asked in a derisive tone whether he also wore "Ringelsöckchen"— for some reason the Communists have a cliché about multicolored socks as the trademark of American decadence— and whether he read trash literature. They finally advised him to have a look at life for young people in the East when he travels in the Democratic Republic, and to note how they differed from the youth in the West.

27 June 1954

Worked in the morning. In the afternoon, tea with Gladigow. I was surprised how nice it was there. Gladigow's wife was kind and motherly. They suggested that I give a lecture on China in their son's school. After that I went to the Kudamm to visit the Rollkes. Rollke was in bed, lying in a room without any windows at all. He has suffered a stroke recently and didn't look well at all. He was very pleased about the bottle of red wine I had brought. Then Brigitte took me on an extended tour of the embassy. It was like exploring a

haunted castle. Beyond the shuttered windows the Kurfürstendamm was alive with motor cars and pedestrians flocking to the
Fourth Berlin Film Festival, but inside the embassy there was dead
silence. Layers of dust had settled over the half-empty rooms on the
upper floors. The apartment where our family lived in the 1930s is
still intact. But the *Handelsabteilung* (the trade department, which
was a cover for the office of the military attaché) was hit during the
bombing and the floors have only been patched very hastily. In the
big reception rooms and the chancellery there were still precious
items of Chinese furniture such as a huge carved chest, big Chinese
carpets with lion designs, carved ivory, vases, and lamps with silk
shades. All this in sharp contrast to the porter's lodge in the
basement where the Rollkes still live and which is moist and in
perpetually darkness, the typical picture of working-class housing
as designed by the class-conscious architects of the Wilhelmine
period. I was given a detailed account of how the Rollkes fared during
the war and what happened to the various embassy staff. Got home
rather late. The Kudamm was all deserted except for— to my horror—
droves of dubious looking women.

28 June 1954

Went to Reinickendorf in the early morning to interview Frau
Bertha Kolasinski, a former housemaid. The interview was scheduled for 11 a.m., so I went on to Tegel for a walk. It was gorgeous out
there. Reinickendorf with its ploughed fields and forests nearby
looked like a small provincial town. I even saw some old peasant
houses dating back to the early 19th Century. I got to the banks of
Lake Tegel. Around the Humboldt Castle were pretty villas hidden in
spacious gardens. Someone was softly practicing the piano.

Frau Kolasinski lives in Kleiststrasse and I met her in the street
outside her flat, just as she was coming home from shopping with her
dog. She had bought fish. We sat down in her living room (quite
spacious and well furnished) and she told me about her life under the
reign of Wilhelm II. I was a bit surprised when, at one point, she called
herself "middle class." But upon reflection, it seems to me that house
servants in middle-class homes really belong to that culture.

I made a small tour of the Gerichtstrasse in Wedding, hoping to
find a really proletarian restaurant but without success. Worked at
home in the afternoon. In the evening on the Gobenwiesen, a meadow
just behind our apartment, there was a solstice festival (*Son-
nenwendfest*) organized by the local newspaper, the *Steglitzer
Lokalanzeiger*. It was not very good. The fire brigade supplied
amplifiers which distorted the singing. There was the usual amateur
gymnastic display. An awful speech by Stadtrat Nikolai, who said
that "bonfires still frighten the grown ups because they remind them
of the horrible bombing nights, but young people see in a brazier the

symbol of a better future," etc., etc. A choir sang "Flamme, empor!" and "Heil dir mein Vaterland" and other old patriotic songs.

29 June 1954

Today was a long day. At 10 a.m. I was in the Zietenstrasse where two old women were waiting to be interviewed by me: Frau Hubert (a former factory girl at the Manoli Zigarettenfabrik), and Frau Grossler (a former cook and housemaid). After we talked for an hour we were joined by Lotte Biener, the head of the SPD Frauensekretariat, by her chairwoman Grete Stenzler, and finally by Maria Reuber from the Berlin office (*Landesvorstand*) of the SPD. I got quite a lot of information. We stopped at noon. Hubert, Grossler, and Biener still lingered for a while. Hubert reported that downstairs in the porter's lodge this morning, she had observed a refugee family waiting to see someone of the SPD. She happens to know that these people are not genuine political fugitives, they were only behind with their rent in East Berlin.

I had lunch at Aschinger's on their outdoor terrace. Then I went to the Wasmuth bookstore to have a cup of "Muckefuk" which Frau Hagemann had long promised me. This is substitute coffee for the poor, but perhaps less often used today than before 1914. Actually it didn't taste too bad, though more like bitter tea than coffee. After that, off to the Wedding to see a parole officer for juvenile delinquents, Bewahrungsfürsorger Jabs at the Haus der Jugend, Reinickendorfer Strasse corner of Schulstrasse. Since I was a little early, I stopped the car and made some sketches of the houses around here. Jabs was sitting in the winter garden of this modern superduper Haus der Jugend (built mostly with American money but unfortunately not much used). Fifty-three years old and balding, Jabs rather resembles General Eisenhower. I sat down and we waited together for his probationers to come and see him, juvenile delinquents who had to report to him regularly every fortnight. First we talked a little about my work, then he talked to me about social problems in this district. Before long his first protégé arrived: Gerd Barsch. Very dark skin, long hair, ill-fitting loud clothes. Gerd had wanted to become a tailor but had found no apprenticeship at the end of the war. Because he was the youngest in a family of 10, his mother had neglected his professional training. Now he is 20 and too old to learn a trade. His mother died a few days ago. Jabs, to my horror, pointed his finger at him and said to me: "You see, he is now condemned to perform unskilled work for the rest of his life." Gerd works on emergency labor projects (*Notstandsarbeiten*) for 1.40 marks an hour, digging ditches mostly. His only interest is going to the movies as often as he can.

He was followed by another boy, Gerd Fischer. Fischer is learning to be a metalworker at AEG. Some time ago he was given a prison sentence that lasts till 1958, but is now out on parole. His mother and father also work at AEG. On Sundays he plays football. There seems to be more hope for him than for the first Gerd, though he did not appear to me as trustworthy as Barsch. Jabs suggested that Fischer should show me around the Wedding, so I loaded him and his bicycle on the jeep and off we went. First, we saw some new 14-story high apartment houses under construction in the Acker-strasse. I can see that the appearance of the Wedding will be radically changed if this sort of building continues. We saw the new Ernst Reuter Oberschule (Praktischer Zweig), a new school building designed with imagination and good taste. Finally, we went to Hussitenstrasse no. 40, an old Mietshaus with five dingy courtyards full of children and youngsters hanging around. Older people looked out of the windows. Jabs had given me the name of the superintendant, Hausverwalterin Schönbrodt, and suggested that I look her up. I rang the bell and Schönbrodt, a 60-year old woman, looked at me inquisitively. When I told her that I was studying "the Berlin of 40 years ago" and could I please talk to her, she narrowed her eyes and raised her finger: "Ha! Say what you want, I know you are from the press! Oh, but the press won't get anything more out of me!" Apparently the press had been here recently, on what account I didn't find out. Perhaps some murder? At any rate, the good old lady pretended to read Professor Rudin's letter of introduction which I showed her, and let me inside. She had just been enjoying an afternoon coffee with her sister and another woman. I saw a spacious living room with a big radio. A delicate looking child was doing home work at a little table in a corner. Soon I had the three old women chatting merrily about the good old times under Kaiser Wilhelm II and was hard pressed keeping up with my shorthand notes. From time to time Frau Schönbrodt, who by now was beaming, raised her finger and screamed: "Young man! One word to the newspapers and I'll kill you!" We left the best of friends.

I drove back to the Haus der Jugend to make a date with Jabs so we could continue our conversation when he would have more time. Had a plate of noodle soup with a sausage at a good proletarian restaurant in Müller Strasse, stopped to look at a children's fair where a delightful old man was running a merry-go-round, and was off to the Steinplatz where I met Jay to see Jean Cocteau's film *Les parents terribles*. The acting (with Jean Marais) was first rate; however, it was more a play than a movie. It lacked the superb street scenes of Paris and its inhabitants which I like in French films. After the movie we had a snack at Aschinger's, watching the crowds. Among the crowd was a Fulbright student from Fordham University named Ray Mc(something) who overheard us speaking English and joined us at out table. After the snack the three of us strolled down the Kudamm and finally went inside the burnt-out synagogue in Fasanenstrasse, destroyed in the infamous Kristallnacht of 1938.

We climbed over boulders and across pit holes into the centre of the immense aisle and looked with admiration at the slim, long columns and arches which once supported the rims of the cupolas (the cupolas themselves were no longer there). It was almost completely dark in the synagogue. Jay and I climbed up the stone stairs in the darkness till we reached the top landing where the choir must have sung. At places there were holes in the floor and if you weren't careful you'd have a very long fall. When we came down again, Ray had disappeared. He must have thought that we had ditched him.

As we were walking past the Café Paris towards my jeep in the Kantstrasse, a man accosted us and nearly collapsed. He was crying, he smelled strongly of beer, and he didn't talk distinctly. I heard him mumbling something about nervous breakdown, so we seized him under the arms and rushed to the intersection, looking for a policeman. Jay gave him a cigarette. He said he was a butcher with a shop of his own in Dresden in the Russian zone, that he had once been condemned to death and had sat in a concentration camp, and that he suffered from trichinosis and would soon die. Someone had now brought him to Berlin and ditched him here. When he had begged for a drink someone had brought him a glass of beer in the street. "I was treated like a dog!" he wailed, "like a dog!" He didn't seem to know that he was in West Berlin rather than in the East sector. So we tried to cheer him up by telling him that he was in the British sector— without concentration camps— and that there were people here who would help him.

We took him to the Red Cross station opposite Bahnhof Zoo. An old nurse and an old Red Cross officer were there. The Red Cross station itself looked neat, clean, and well equipped. At first the Red Cross officer shook his head skeptically and said there was nothing he could do for our man. Our protégé, whose name turned out to be Walther Putzke, wanted to go to a hospital but again the old man shook his head. "I am going to die of trichinosis," cried Putzke and pointed to some sores on his palms. "I have tried to commit suicide!" he continued. But the Red Cross man just waved his hand and said, "Who on earth would hang himself for that, it's all nonsense!" However he was becoming embarrassed and no longer sounded so sure of himself. He and I sat down to go through Putzke's papers. He had a torn letter stating that Putzke had been condemned to death in 1944 for desertion from the German Army. (The Red Cross man seemed to take a dim view of this.) In the end I think it was due to our pressure that the nurse and he decided that they could not ignore Putzke completely. The nurse stayed behind while the three of us took Putzke to the police station on the other side of the railway station. As we entered, a few cops were just taking a couple of young men in. I explained the case to the officer in charge, who seemed competent enough. Jay sat down on the desk of the officer in charge to give him his name and address. I tried to assure Putzke that the

Churchmen in Berlin

A socialist clergyman,
Pastor Bleier (10 Sept., 1954)

Arthur Rackwitz, Berlin's only
Communist pastor (8 Sept., 1954)

The Lange-Schucke Foundation
in Berlin-Wedding

Peter Klausner (17 Sept., 1954)

Vikar Mundt, Harald Pölchau
(10 and 11 Sept., 1954)

Martin Niemöller (5 May, 1954)

WAR RELICS AND COLD WAR

RIAS, radio station and intelligence agency

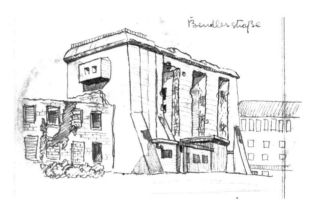

Bendlerstrasse, formerly Wehrmacht headquarters

Potsdamer Platz, now a no-man's land

West Berlin police was quite different from the Vopo. When Putzke said he was afraid because everyone was looking at him, a young policeman asked us all to look away. It just so happened that an ambulance driver of the West End Hospital was at the police station. He was very kind, assured Putzke that he would not be taken to an insane asylum, and simply loaded Putzke in his van. We then left too. It was already past midnight. We told the policemen that we had promised to telegraph Putzke's wife, but they told us that would be uncautious. The best thing to do, they said, is to mail her an anonymous letter from East Berlin. It was very late when I got home.

30 June 1954

Got up and wrote a letter to Mrs. Putzke telling her of her husband's fate. I signed the letter "Heinrich Janusch, Johannis-strasse 3, Berlin." Then I drove to the Wedding, Prinzenallee 60, back to the leather factory of Knoell & Co. I had a brief talk with Dr. Volkenborn, one of the owners, and also got to speak to old Knoell himself. After that I was led to the mess hall (if one can call it so) of the factory, where 4 old men were already waiting for me. We sat down at a long table, I at the head, and started our session. It was like a Yale Graduate School seminar, with myself as the professor questioning each man in turn as point after point was brought up. At noon, workers came in to sit at the other end of our table to eat their bread and drink their beer. They listened to our seminar with much astonishment. Herr Schmidt also came in to say hello. I didn't like the way he came in and just shook hands with me, completely ignoring the 4 old men. (Later I also found out the 4 men had merely been told to be here today at 10:45 without first being asked whether they would allow themselves to be interviewed or not.) This all seemed to me rather highhanded on the part of the management. They dispose of their old workers as they dispose of their machinery. You want to see the factory? Have a look! You want to talk to old workers? We'll tell them to come on Wednesday! No wonder none of the 4 expressed any fondness for the factory management.

Had lunch at a delightful little proletarian restaurant called Schlecht (hence their motto, "Man isst gut bei Schlecht")[1] in Prinzenal-lee. Had a sweet-sour lentil soup for 60 pfennigs. Outside the air was blueish because of today's eclipse of the sun. I drove to the SPD headquarters to see Genossin Reps, who first took me to the roof to look at the eclipse through a piece of camera film and then readily agreed to mail the letter for Mrs. Putzke for me when she returns to the East sector tonight. Then I went to Schöneberg, Eythstrasse 24, to meet a Mrs. Jeschke and her daughter Hanne Jeschke. Miss Jeschke was introduced to me by Frau Rutz since she, too, is a

---

[1] A pun on the word *schlecht*, meaning "poor" or "poorly": "You eat well at Poorly."

probation officer. Her mother is a real working-class woman, hard, proud, and cheeky, and with a sense of humor. She straight-facedly told me she got beaten by her teachers in school because she bit them and stuck needles into their cushions.

When I left it was getting towards 6 pm. Frau Jeschke had mentioned a "Schwarzer Adler" as one of the places where she used to dance as a young girl before 1914. Since it was not far I went to have a look but was disappointed. It was just a renovated restaurant with a dance floor. I had a plate of pig's head with sauerkraut for 90 pfennigs and went home. I was so tired I immediately fell on the bed and slept like a log.

l July 1954

Thursday, and a rainy, windy day. No engagements today. Wrote a series of letters to people whom I want to interview, and then telephoned Paul Löbe and Willy Brandt to ask for appointments with them. Late in the afternoon went to the petrol station to fill up the jeep for tomorrow's long drive through the Wedding. When I left the station I suddenly didn't feel like going home. I drove on and eventually found myself at Potsdamer Platz. I got out before the sector boundary and walked to the square. On the Western side very close to the border were cinemas showing bad, sensational films, snack bars, and many little shops selling food parcels for the East zone. Everything looked shabby here, and the few people who stood around were poorly clad and didn't look too trustworthy. A few people with large suitcases (refugees? black marketeers?) tramped past. One feels like standing at the end of the world. For the Western tramways this is the last stop. On the opposite side of the square, the communist tramways also go no further. I could not see any Vopos from where I stood, but also no shops, no movie posters, only brick walls and rubble and a poster attacking the Allied plans for a European defense community.

I entered a house on the Western side of the square where, according to a notice at the door, pictures of Berlin after the collapse of the Third Reich were on show. They were photographs taken by a staff of six cameramen under the direction of Hugo Welle, a producer of cultural films before the war. He was there himself, explaining that this was his personal contribution to the recovery of Germany.

The pictures were good. They showed the awful ruins of Berlin after the capitulation in May 1945— Berlin completely burnt out and seemingly deserted, with German and Russian tanks half buried under the rubble. Other pictures told stories: the blowing up of the big bunker in the Tiergarten together with its splendid hospital while old women were freezing to death in cellars and medical help was in short supply. One woman had to undergo surgery without anesthetics and her doctor had no rubber gloves. War victims in mass graves, their names hastily written on pieces of paper stuck into the soil. A 70-year-old woman who cleared rubble was also taking care of 2 little grandchildren. "Where are they while you work?" Welle had asked her. "One is in a basket, the other one I have tied fast with a piece of string," she replied.

Had coffee, then drove to Hallesches Tor in Kreuzberg, a region of Berlin I have so far not yet visited. At Hallesches Tor, I looked at the new American Memorial Library, which is superb, then walked through some real working-class streets. They look as drab as those in the Wedding, but the cosy light behind some of the windows, the old-fashioned iron gates and other details give it less harsh a look. Maybe here you feel closer to the heart of the city with its gay boulevards than you do far up in the North. I noticed quite a number of young toughs (*Halbstarke*) hanging around.

2 July 1954

Met Bindel at 8 a.m. in Attila Platz. He said there had been a fire in a factory up in Reinickendorf yesterday, so we drove there first. The enterprise was called Erich Wilde & Co., in Borsigwalde. The owner, a Herr Will, and 2 workers and a boy stood around. Bindel called his office and they said they would send out some investigators. Half an hour later they came: Herr Jantz, Herr Dr. Lüdtke, and Herr Wayamenkov. Soon the police came too, a Herr Michaelis and a Herr Peters from the arson division (*Branddezernat*) of the Friesenstrasse (where the criminal police has its headquarters). A few men from the Berlin city government came also, but they left soon. It was interesting to see how the story changed considerably during the investigation. At first Herr Will put the primary responsibility on the firemen, who he said took more than 20 minutes to come and another 30 minutes before going into action. But persistent questioning and an examination of the account books also revealed that there were no safety devices on the boilers to prevent their overflowing, that the fire extinguishers had not been used (had they been serviceable at all?), and that the factory had used the cheapest and hence most dangerous oil.

Two hours went by in discussion. The factory inspectors would have liked to order the installation of more safety devices, but who in Berlin had so much money to invest? One thing puzzled me: the factory inspectorate asked the police for copies of the photos they took. The police in return wanted copies of the technical reports which the factory inspectors were writing up. And— each side said no to the other's request!

Bindel and I went to the old machine concern Schwartzkopff in the Scheringstrasse, Wedding, where we saw a Direktor Kleinhaus, but he could not help me much in my research. He showed me a jubilee brochure published in 1927 and allowed me to take a quick look into the foundry. To judge from the old photographs in the 1927 brochure, the workrooms have changed very little since before the war. Then we went to a factory making electrical cables (*Viacowerke*, or *Vereinigte Isolatorenwerke*) in Wollanckstrasse, but no one of the management was there to receive us.

Our last stop was at the chocolate factory Hildebrand. Direktor Hildebrand was away attending a funeral, so all we could do was interview the old porter, Otto Witte. The result of this trip was therefore pretty negative. I drove Bindel home and said good-bye to him. He had to get some rest because tonight he was supposed to inspect bakeries to make sure none of them start work before 4 a.m.

Jürgen Brandenburg called in the evening and we went to see the German picture *Weg ohne Umkehr*. Excellent, almost as good as *Die letzte Brücke*. It portrays Russian officers and men in East Berlin. The cossack chauffeur, the MWD officer, the Russian secretary— all of them were played so convincingly. In one scene the secretary, an affected Russian girl, screams at the German hotel manager because she has no mirror, no carpet, and no potted plants in her room. The manager is speechless but the other Russians merely laugh and bring her mirrors, carpets, and plants from the lounge downstairs. An ironic sally at the way Russians in occupied Germany are concerned about their prestige and at the way Germans feel uncomfortable with any improvisation, and be it just the rearrangement of furniture.

After the movie Jürgen and I drove to Potsdamer Platz to look at the East sector lying so calm and lifeless only a few yards away. Had a strong mocca and went home.

3 July 1954

Worked a little at home, then decided to drive to Kreuzberg to get acquainted with that part of Berlin. I parked the car at Kottbuser Tor and then walked for a solid three hours. I am not sure I can already describe this part of Berlin, I'll have to visit it several more times. But it has a certain fascination and strikes me as distinctly different from the Wedding and Neukölln. Saw an old Hinterhof where chickens are kept and which had cow stables dating back to 1818. A house was painted completely green. I found really proletarian streets near the Moritzplatz, and had lunch at the "Max u. Moritz" Restaurant in Oranienstrasse, which looked quite funny on the outside. One part of Kreuzberg is completely destroyed. You can stand in the middle on this square mile of rubble and fancy yourself in the Sahara. There is not a soul around and you can only see some houses on the horizon. I talked with a tobacconist and a young musician who gave me the address of an old Berlin Kapellmeister who may have some things to tell about the Berlin before 1914.

In Kreuzberg you seem to bump into the East-West sector boundary at every corner. In one street stood the usual two wooden boards, the bigger one announcing in four languages that you were leaving the American sector, the other telling you that this was the beginning of the "Democratic Sector." But on the Western side there was an additional big poster showing a human face behind barbed wire and, in German: "Watch out! Only ten more meters!" (Gib acht! Noch 10 Meter!). The Communists had responded with a poster carrying a political rhyme: "EVG bringt Tod, Friedensvertrag bringt Brot, Westberliner denkt daran, Auch auf Eure Stimme kommt es an!"[1]

Jay phoned in the evening to ask whether I'd join him on a visit to an outlawed student fraternity (Burschenschaft) tonight. Of course I said yes. The event took place in a big villa in the Grunewald, Lynarstrasse 21. A uniformed butler and maid answered the door. This place is a sort of clubhouse for several Burschenschaften or Landsmannschaften. Ours, the Landsmannschaft Altmark (founded 80 years ago), was having one of its regular *Kneipen* (beer evenings) in a basement room. The room was not large. Oakpaneled, it had two rows of wooden tables and one smaller table for its three presiding officials, the Erster Chargierter, Zweiter Chargierter, and Dritter Chargierter. (I think the second is in charge of fencing, the third acts as secretary.) We shook hands with the trio and sat down at one of the tables and were given beer. Jay was talking with a neighbor, Siegfried Klaue, to pump him for information and I was doing the same with another man, an elderly law student (who still held the rank of *Bursche*). I didn't get his name.

Some basic rules were quickly learned. When you first enter the Landsmannschaft you are a Fuchs and you are supervised by the "Fuchs Major." When, next, you are made a Bursche, you belong to the *Aktiven.* Finally (usually towards the end of your university studies) you are promoted to "Alter Herr." The Aktiven and the Alte Herren have their respective meetings. Then there are joint sessions to decide on matters regarding the entire fraternity. Hence the claim of the Landsmannschaft that they are "most democratic."

Soon after our arrival, a "Salamander" (or toast) was given. The chairman jumped up, loudly crashed his sabre on the table and yelled: "Silentium!" He then announced the death of a 90-year-old *Bruderbursche* named Luther (hence the three candles burning on the table), and asked everybody to get ready to sing a certain song. (The Fuchs Major repeats every order from the other end of the room to show the chairman that he has been heard.) "Silentium Ex!" came the next order of the chairman, and "Silentium Ex!" repeated the Fuchs Major. We all began to thumb through our *Kommersbücher* for the particular song, while someone played the tune on the piano.

---

[1]"EDC means death. Peace treaty means bread. West Berliners, remember your vote also counts!"

(Every Kommersbuch has studs in its leather cover so it won't get soaked by spilled beer.) "Silentium! Das Lied steigt! Akt Eins!" After we sang the first three stanzas, an old man got up to say a few words of eulogy for the dead man. He had been director of a university library somewhere. "This shows," said the speaker, "that Waffen-studenten are not poor scholars as some people claim. On the contrary, they have achieved great things in public life." We then all had to gobble down our beer and bang the empty glasses on the table. The man who had spoken smashed his glass on the floor. Then we were ordered to sing the rest of the song. "Das Lied fällt!" (which means: sing the last stanza.) "Silentium Ex!" At last we could talk again.

I questioned the elderly law student on the organization and purpose of the Landsmannschaft. He didn't tell me much about dueling, only about the organization. *Anybody* could join it, he assured me, even foreigners (though this has never happened so far). Of course the candidate must have certain qualities of character because Bruderburschen must be able to trust one another com-pletely. The purpose of this society is to foster the spirit of comrade-ship, discipline, and self-control and to find friends for life. Some students are young men who have left home for the first time and who need to be given a firm hold. Another law student who sat close by, was also a guest who had come here for the first time. He said to me that though he was an admirer of Erich Kästner and Kurt Tucholski, and had serious socialist leanings, he also felt a need for more discipline (*Manneszucht*) than he found in social satire and liberal teachings. He had therefore come in order to see whether he wouldn't like to join. I am sorry I didn't have the opportunity to tell him how much I wanted him to keep out of it. Because I joined in the singing he may even have thought that I myself was favorably disposed towards the fraternities.

When my law student neighbor was made chairman, he first proposed a toast to his predecessor, which was a traditional cour-tesy. In unison, everybody said: "Prost! Denn— das— ist— Deine— Pflicht— denn— so — will— es— der— Kommers!" It sounded like "Ein Volk, ein Reich, ein Führer."

At about 10 p.m. Jay got up to thank the Landsmannschaft for having allowed us to come tonight. He said that he'll never forget this evening. The chairman (by this time my law student) replied that he hoped we had liked what we had seen. The "much maligned" Waffenstudenten were not really nationalistic and desired peaceful relations with all nations in the world.

We had a snack first at the American PX and then at my Stammcafé. My primary impression is that these are people I certainly wouldn't want to have as friends. Their thinking is alien and at the same time so familiar to me. It is the old spirit I had found in German schools before the war, with all its attachment to national honor, combat, and comradeship to death. These people enjoy giving orders and receiving orders. There was an old man who was made chairman for a while. Did *he* like bossing us around! When some of us sang badly he screamed: "Silentium!! I thought I had told everyone to get ready to sing. Once again: Akt eins!" Some of us didn't sing or bang the table: worse still, I was seen looking through the *Vereinsbuch* instead of paying attention. He had us all stand up. It made me furious. Apparently these Burschenschaften and Landsmannschaften are again becoming powerful in German society, including in the Bonn government. Jay said that according to Siegfried Klaue, the greatest enemies of these societies are the Jews and the SPD. Hooray for the Jews and the Socialists!

4 July 1954

Sunday. Stayed at home most of the day. Esther came to play in my room, and to satisfy her I took her out and bought her an ice cream. In the evening fell into a long coversation with Mrs. Henninger. She also admires Manneszucht, Treue zum Vaterland, alter Preussengeist, even the Führerprinzip (the virtue of leadership, so long as you get a good leader). While she acknowledges that Hitler was evil and that Germany should not have tried to conquer all Europe ("that was a mistake!"), she insists on blaming the Allies for imposing Versailles on Germany and thereby provoking the Nazi movement. The Americans are also blamed by her for failing to remove Hitler in 1943 or 1944. I was aghast when I heard this. Apparently she never asked herself how the Americans could have removed Hitler, she only insists that for the Germans to overthrow him from below was "impossible." She also said that Hitler never married the better to exert his magic hold over German womanhood. (Did he also bewitch Mrs. Henninger?) She obviously is sincere, but she does not know what democracy means. She also heartily dislikes the SPD and the working class.

5 July 1954

A long, exhausting day, as my Mondays usually are. Got up early to drive to Puttkammerstrasse, where I visited Herr Ufermann, the head of the Berlin government's department for arbitrating labor disputes (Senatsverwaltung für Arbeit, Abteilung Schlichtungswesen). His job is to settle disputes between employers' associations and trade unions. In other words, he is not concerned with disputes between individual employers and workers. That is the job of the labor court (*Arbeitsgericht*). But he has no power to compel the disputing parties to appear before him— they must come to him on their own free will.

Dropped in to thank Oberregierungsrat Fietz for having arranged my tour with Bindel. I also wanted to say hello to Bindel but he was not in. Drove over to the IG Metall where a Herr Erich David gave me lots of protocol booklets from the pre-1914 period to look at. He said he remembers me from previous TU meetings but I must confess I have completely forgotten him. Herr Molitor was there too. I left rather overwhelmed: how am I to read all this by next week?

Met Brigitte Hagemann when I returned to town. We went together for lunch in Kreuzberg (it was difficult to find a cheap eating place!) and I told her about my evening at the Burschenschaften. Brigitte also disapproves of the student fraternities as arrogant, devoid of finer feelings, and brutal.

Then I went to the Zietenstrasse where I met the head of the SPD in Berlin, Willy Brandt. An impressive person. With his high forehead and dermined jaw he conveys the feeling of a man of action. His table was clear of all bric-à-brac. He speaks with a strong foreign accent (is it Swedish?) and rolls his r's. Brandt unfortunately did not make any significant pronouncements about the state of the world for my benefit. But he gave me a few names of people whom I should meet, including one Harry Hurwitz, an American sociologist who is doing research for Brandt for a book on Ernst Reuter. (He called Hurwitz on the phone, and I am to see him on Wednesday.) He also instructed a Frau Keil in the office on the first floor to make me a list of old SPD veterans whom I might want to interview. I am also to attend a meeting of SPD veterans next week.[1]

Happy with my success, I was off to Tegel. Since I had a meeting in nearby Reinickendorf at 6 p.m. and did not want to waste gas by first going home, I decided to have a good look at Tegel. From Tegelort I walked east along the highway and was enchanted by the shaded lanes lined with trees, the elegant Konditoreien and the small country houses. On a bridge, in front of a correctional school for difficult children, I started talking to a rotund policeman who obviously was not averse to a conversation with a stranger to relieve his boredom. We stood there and talked for a whole hour: about Tegel, about traffic accidents during rush hours, the problem of drunkenness on Fridays and Saturdays, and the number of shiftless refugees in nearby camps — at least *he* thought they were shiftless. We also talked about the policemen's lot: the low pensions they receive and their exhausting hours of work. Policemen have 12 hours of duty every day with one day's rest only every 10 days, which gives them no more than 3 Sundays per month. On the other hand, Tegel is a quiet beat, he said. At the most sometimes flowers are stolen in the park and occasionally there are problems with young rowdies. He is a native of Tegel and quite proud of its old history. He told me to

[1]Willy Brandt (b. 1913), was deputy chairman of the SPD in Berlin, 1949-57. Elected Governing Mayor of Berlin, 1957-66. West German foreign minister, 1966-69. Chancellor of West Germany, 1969-74. Won Nobel Peace Prize, 1971.

go to the Restaurant "Zum Alten Fritz" nearby, so named because King Frederick II once ate there, and to tell the innkeeper I was sent by "der dicke Wachtmeister von Tegel." Talking of innkeepers: the owner of the Schultheiss Quelle in Tegel Ort, I was told, is known as "Hunde Gustav" and is an enormously fat man with a little dog who weighs over 300 kilos.

The interview with Frau Clara Hoffmann and her son lasted 2 full hours and was most profitable. In the evening at home, Marion came to ask my help with her French homework.

7 July 1954

Went to see Harry Hurwitz, who lives with his German wife and a sweet little daughter above a shop in Zehlendorf, Waltraut Strasse 38. Hurwitz is a sociologist from Columbia University and translates film dialogue for Metro-Goldwyn-Mayer. He is 30, the descendant of Russian Jews. He didn't know very much about working-class life before 1914, but he once made a study of the 1918 revolution in Bavaria. Presently he is preparing a doctoral thesis in which he compares the social background of *Spiegel* readers in the Soviet zone and in the West. Talking about my research, he suggested that when I interview people I should ask them for old family letters. I thought that was a good idea. He kept me for lunch and then showed me his little Renault car.

Had my brakes fixed in Steglitz (no more brake fluid!) and then went to see Paul Löbe, the former Reichstagspräsident, who has an office in the building of the newspaper *Telegraf* on Bismarck Platz in the Grunewald.[1] You walk into an impressive lobby. Since it was already after office hours the whole building was quiet. The porter first phoned to see whether "der Herr" was at home and then took me upstairs. Löbe had a wonderful big office, very well furnished. He was already waiting for me. Now 80 years old, he has served in the labor movement for 60 years and just published a new book. His demeanor was both friendly and modest. "Ich bin nur ein Volksschüler" (I never went beyond elementary school), he explained to me. But working in the book printer's trade enabled him to pick up much knowledge through proofreading, including knowledge about China. So while I asked him questions about the Berlin workers, he asked me various questions about China. As we talked, an 80-year-old Genosse came in with his family, refugees, came in to ask Löbe to vouch for his political integrity, so I took my leave and went to Steglitz for dinner.

---

[1]Paul Löbe (1875-1967), SPD politician and Reichstag president (1924-32). Imprisoned by the Nazis, member of West German parliament (1949-53). He published *Der Weg war lang*, an autobiography, in 1954.

8 July 1954

Stormy weather. Stayed at home writing to my teacher at Yale, Mr. Holborn. At 2:15 p.m. I went to look up Frau Lier in Tempelhof, Arnulfstrasse 71. She and her daughter Hildegard (who is 49 years old) were waiting for me. The interview lasted over 2 hours. I was exhausted but they kept on talking merrily. Frau Lier ran a trade union and also an SPD beer *Lokal* in Kreuzberg for 40 years, located in Naunynstrasse 9, and she wanted me to inspect the place provided I keep in mind that the place was much better run when she was the owner. Frau Lier who once weighed 200 kilos, engaged in long lamentations about the treatment she and her daughter receive from the welfare authorities of West Berlin, who fail to give the needy their due.

After I left them, around 5 p.m., I went for a stroll in Tempelhof. At 6:24 I met Jay at S-Bahnhof Steglitz and drove with him to fetch Walter Sullivan, who wanted to come with us to see the Mensur (the student duel) at the fraternity tonight. We had a cup of coffee and biscuits in Sullivan's home while we debated on the best way to introduce Sullivan. Obviously he could not be identified as the *New York Times* correspondent in Berlin. So he became "Mr. Walter," a member of the Byrd Expedition to the Antarctic and presently engaged in writing a book on German polar expeditions. Walter drove his Morris close to the Lynarstrasse and then got into my jeep. (He thought it was better not to show his "U.S. Mission to Germany" license plates.) We arrived there at exactly 7 p.m. My law student friend of last time was there and didn't seem at all pleased at seeing us again, though he pretended to be. I also saw the vicious old man again. This time the house was crowded with people from the Landsmannschaften Alt-Mark, Alemania, and Spandovia. The first fight was between Alt-Mark and Alemania. It was not a duel, we were told, but a fight between 2 members of different Bünde each of whom was designated by his Bund to undergo this test of fortitude. A fight is called "Partie" and consists of 30 rounds (*Gänge*) of 4 blows each. The distance between the fighters is the length of one sword. The 2 seconds shout: "Mensur— fertig— los!" and interrupt the fighting with "aus!" either after the 4 blows have been exchanged or when one of the duellists (*Paukanten*) has broken some rule. The swords are very sharp and with each blow bushels of hair fly around. After each round the 2 Testanten wipe the swords of the Paukanten with cotton wool dipped in disinfectant and rebend them if they were crooked. The *Sekundanten* can demand *Verbandspause* if one of the fighters needs bandaging. The fighters can also take a break after the first 15 rounds. The fight is terminated either after all the 30 rounds have been fought or when one of the doctors decides that the wounds of his client demand that he withdraw from the fight. The Paukanten are not allowed to flinch or to duck, not even instinctively when they are hit. They may lose the fight, for that is regarded as no more than a misfortune, but they must prove their steadiness, their physical courage, their self-discipline. Getting hit also has the advantage that you collect scars in your face (*Schmisse*) which you can show off for the rest of your life. In short, the only requirement is that the Paukant fight in a morally fair manner, or courageously. All eyes are watching him very carefully, friends and opponents alike.

As soon as the fight is over, the M.C. takes place. This is the "Mensur Convent" of the Landsmannschaften which criticize the performance of their respective Bundesbruder. I got into the M.C. of the Alt-Mark, although guests are usually excluded from these conferences. They strongly criticized the performance of their man, a Fuchs named Birkner, who got a bad gash over his skull. They mercilessly analyzed his bearing throughout the fight and hotly debated whether or not he was ready for his *Rezeptionsprüfung* to become a Bursche next week. His Sekundant, who was present, introduced a motion to accept his performance as satisfactory ("Bitte, die Partie als zulässig zu erkennen"). This motion was passed by a narrow majority.

I later talked to an old man of the Spandovia and asked him how it felt being a Paukant who is closely scrutinized by his own comrades. "Oh, it is all done in a comradely spirit," he assured me. "So long as you fight courageously you are a hero. If you don't, you're given a chance to try again...against a more formidable opponent! If you live through that ordeal without flinching, all is forgiven. You lose your colored band during this period of 'disgrace,' but you can still attend beer evenings while waiting to rehabilitate yourself."

We saw about 4 fights. After each fight a charwoman came in and mopped the blood from the floor. No one took notice of her. During the fights there was "Silentium," but afterwards there were animated discussions among those present. One fight between a left-handed and a right-handed man drove the "vicious old man" of last time into ecstasy: "The best fight of this kind in the last ten years," he said. There were, by the way, lots of vicious-looking old men around, proudly exhibiting the scars of their own days of glory. In the hall hung a picture of Bismarck, in another room a picture of Frederick the Great. The chairman of the "Alte Herren" kept me company most of the time. He was good at explaining the fights to me but I got angry when he started talking politics. The U.S. "liberators" had forbidden fencing duels, he complained. They have destroyed Prussia. Yet only a strong and vigorous Prussia can keep order in Europe. The U.S. should have fought Russia on the side of Germany. After the victory a way would have been found to remove Hitler. War is the only solution for the present political situation in Europe and Germany will see to it that in the next war she is fighting on the winning side. He is a former Wehrmacht officer.

There were two other Americans there. They were introduced as

Mr. Slide and a Mr. Bernard. They said they worked for an Army commission in Heidelberg. Jay thinks they were CIC agents in disguise. They did look like cops.

Sullivan left early to go to a dinner engagement. I left with Jay and we had a plate of goulash soup in Steglitz. I felt upset, almost physically sick, after watching all this ugliness, this brutish hacking away at someone's head, the diabolic faces of the older spectators, the inscrutable mien of the younger ones. At this moment I wanted to be at a symphony concert, in an art gallery, talk with lots of pleasant people. Jay had to go home so I went for a long walk along the Schloss Strasse. In a jeweler's window I saw an exhibit of old German iron crosses and other war medals. A sign read: Bald wird man wieder Orden tragen! (The time is coming when medals will be worn again!).

9 July 1954

A wasted day. The iron stove in my room is being replaced by a new tile stove so that I must sleep in the Henningers' living room. I didn't want to be in their way so I went into town. First to Neukölln, to the Naunynstrasse (popularly called "Naunynritze") to visit Mrs. Lier's former joint. Not too bad, only very small and Frau Lier was right: the street *is* ugly, and it *is* swarming with street urchins. Had lunch in Kreuzberg, strolled through the Wedding and finally called on Herr Jabs in the Haus der Jugend. Jabs spoke bitterly about the injustice of Bonn and West Berlin, who give the widows of former (Nazi) officials 1,000 marks per month and the widows of workers 50 to 70 marks. While some of Jabs's juvenile delinquents (this time they were girls) came to see him, I was shown around the house by a secretary who asked me to tell her something about China because she is scheduled to give a lecture on the Mao revolution and has no idea what she could say.

One girl for whom Jabs is responsible works in a factory. She is forced to do overtime every day, including Saturdays and Sundays, and this without receiving overtime pay. There is nothing to be done about this, Jabs said, because there is no trade union and no wage contract.

IO July 1954

After working in the morning I went to the FU library. Met Christine Häker and promised her to attend the next session of the GSG. In the afternoon I went to see the film *Schicksalswende* in which Emil Jannings plays Chancellor Bismarck. The film contains good portraits of Wilhelm II as the arrogant playboy without tact and finer feelings, Holstein as the unscrupulous plotter, Eulenburg as the effeminate flatterer, and Böttiger as the cowardly office hunter. It was more a history lesson on film than entertainment but very useful for me because of the faithful reconstruction of Berlin society in 1890.

In the evening went to visit Dr. Alinge in Telramundweg 1, Steglitz. It was pleasant to talk about China and as I left he lent me a Chinese novel to read.

II July 1954

Stayed at home in the morning, then drove to Potsdamer Platz for lunch. Stood there looking at the square (it still rained today) comparing it with the picture of Potsdamer Platz in 1937 which I found in an old *Illustrirte* yesterday. Not far from me two Western cops with binoculars watched a group of tourists in the East sector who were taking pictures of the West sector. In the courtyard of Potsdamer Strasse 24 I found to my great surprise a huge stone fountain, richly ornamented. The walls of the courtyard were also covered with mosaics, and there were elaborately wrought iron gates and heraldic shields. This is the former house of Lepsius & Fischer (an antique dealer?), I was told this afternoon by Frau Krüger.

Had a very pleasant time this afternoon with the Krügers, who are friends of the Cerfs. The mother is a gardener and lives in a large room above a commercial nursery together with her daughter Sybilla and grandmother Bahl. Their one room looks like a mansarde belonging to an artist. Jay and Carol were there too, and Randolph who now can walk very well by himself and is very proud of it. Had dinner at Steglitz. A man at my table, who seemed to be one of the querulous, self-pitying type of former Wehrmacht officers, tried to talk to me, but I was not in the mood and left as soon as I had finished dessert.

13 July 1954

Went to the Landesarchiv in the morning to check through its roster of old police records. Discovered they have a very large stock of censored theatrical plays from the late 19th century. The archivists let me go into the "Magazin" where the documents are kept. This is a damp and cold vault, and I fear these documents won't withstand this temperature and moisture very long.

In the late afternoon drove to Rudow to interview Emil Wutzki. Rudow is quite a bit away from Berlin. You reach it after a long ride past meadows and ploughed fields. It is a small village, with a parish church and two windmills, a few farms, and with cows and geese in the streets. The people in the shops were talkative and curious. I was told to go and see the castle (which turned out to be a biggish house with deer antlers outside) and talked to a woman who was painting the wooden fence of her farm. This woman was called Frau Peschke and she is the descendant of an old Huguenot family called Masante (originally "ma santé," meaning "my health"). The Masantes and some other Huguenot families gave the church in Rudow its burial ground in the 17th century. In return, all their descendants to this day have the right to a free burial plot. To Frau Peschke's distress, however, her family papers were destroyed in the war—not in the Hitler war but in the Thirty Years' War! The Hitler war for her was only yesterday, for she still keeps her Nazi *Ahnenpass* (Aryan certificate) under her bed pillow every night.

Emil Wutzki lives in Neuköllner Strasse 299, Berlin-Rudow. He was not very useful as a source of information, unfortunately. He had an unexpected engagement that night, so that we only talked about his early life. However, I am supposed to come back in order to continue this conversation.[1]

At 7:30 I went to the GSG meeting in Leuschnerhaus. Pietsch, Modell, and other trade union officials appeared (including Waldemar Jenny, a Swiss citizen who heads the textile union in Berlin), Jürgen Molkenthien-Bohm, and others. Christine asked me to take shorthand notes of the proceedings. A very lively and really searching discussion ensued on the question of workers and their relationship to "Kultur." Pietsch spoke well but was sharply attacked for saying that trade unions should restrict themselves to bread-and-butter issues and leave cultural instruction to the schools. I will have a busy time drawing up the report for Christine.

14 July 1954

Continued to work on police censorship of theatrical plays in the archive. Before lunch went to American Express to fill out a form for my passage on the "Liberté." Had lunch in the Mensa where I met the Häkers by chance and gave them a ride into town. Then I drove to the Möckernstrasse 69, the headquarters of the Arbeiterwohlfahrt (the SPD welfare organization), where the quarterly meeting of the SPD veterans was taking place.

Around 300 people, men and some women, were sitting at two long tables, smoking and chatting. The chairman, Molkenbuhr, made me sit at the Vorstandstisch on the podium, and introduced me to the audience with a request for volunteers to tell me their recollections of life before 1914. In the course of the afternoon, I got together quite a good number of names and addresses. Maria Reuber was the guest speaker this afternoon, and she gave a talk on the program and the significance of the SPD party conference next week. The discussion that followed turned unexpectedly violent. First, my old friend Glamann got up and furiously attacked some *Parteigenossen* who had aroused his ire (he called them "Parteibonzen"), but he was later rebuked by other comrades who thought that he should have been

---

[1] Emil Wutzky (1870-1963) earned the title of city elder of Berlin in 1950 for his services to the city administration.

more restrained. Someone got up to defend Maria Reuber against a current rumor that she is a former Communist party official who only joined the SPD in 1945. (Maria later got up and publicly denied any former communist affiliation.) Someone else complained that party members had too little voice in policy making, unlike "in the good old days of Wilhelm Liebknecht, who used to sit in cafes with simple workers to find out what they wanted and to tell them what they should know." At 5 p.m. Reuber made the closing speech. She lamented the insignificant role of Berlin in national and international politics ever since the SPD lost the Berlin government. The late Ernst Reuter, she said, would never have allowed the Berliners to remain so indifferent during the four-power conference which, after all, concerned their immediate future. She admonished the audience for criticizing "Zehlendorf Sozialdemokraten" (Zehlendorf being an affluent district), forgetting that in a bourgeois district Socialists have a much tougher job to do than in a workers' district like Wedding. She also criticized West Germany for its easy-going enjoyment of prosperity and its diminishing interest in reunification. This year the West Germans actually celebrated the German Day of Unity on 16 June instead of 17 June, just so that it wouldn't interfere with Corpus Christi day.

Molkenbuhr announced that Rudolf Wissel recently suffered a stroke. His doctors have forbidden him to smoke. A general exclamation of dismay went through the hall.

Went home to read. Called Jay. It is still raining. Unbelievable.

17 July 1954

Haven't been writing for the last 2 days. On Thursday, the 15th, paid for my ship ticket at American Express. I had been working in the archives in the morning, digging in the police documents though without much result. At the American Express office, where I stopped to pay for my ship ticket, I overheard the girl at the desk instructing a German chauffeur to pick up a distinguished Japanese visitor outside the Kempinski Hotel at 2 p.m. So, since I happened to be on the Kudamm at 2 o'clock, I posted myself outside the Kempinski smoking a cigarette, pretending to wait for a limousine. It didn't come.

Yesterday morning I interviewed Georg Rinkowski in Neukölln, Wipperstrasse 25. We talked from 10:30 until noon. He is the first of the volunteers from the SPD meeting I visited. His wife is charming, but the poor woman has been paralyzed since 1928. Rinkowski was a very willing informer and smiled often at my ignorance and curiosity. He got into my jeep and showed me parts of Neukölln that I had not seen before. He said he regretted that he could not show me the former Scheunenviertel where he was born, a slum whose misery has been notorious since the mid-19th century. We agreed that I should come back to finish the interview today. Then I called Carol. Jay is in Frankfurt to visit a Professor Adorno and I was to take Carol out. Unfortunately the concert by the Berliner Mozart Orchester in the Lichterfelde Castle was canceled because of rain, so we toured through the southern parts of Berlin between Potsdamer Platz, Kreuzberg, and the Bohemian Village (Böhmisches Dorf) in Neukölln. We had dinner at the Café Paris and saw *Gefährlicher Urlaub* in a small Charlottenburg movie theater where the owner says "good night" to you when you leave.

This morning it still rained— veritable monsoon weather. Rena, the maid, starts her holiday today and Mischa will also leave tomorrow. I spent the morning finishing my interview with Rinkowski and then drove to Frohnau in the uppermost north of Berlin to interview August Schmitz in Nibelungen Strasse 57. I came a bit early in the hope of exploring this region but it poured so much I could not walk around. (I wore my sandals, what a fool!) But I still saw enough to recognize the elegance of Frohnau, which was laid out before 1914 as a new, fashionable "garden city." You reach Frohnau by driving through what looks almost like mountains and forests. The hills are not steep and the trees not very numerous, but since they grow close to the road and the road itself is so winding, you can fancy yourself driving through the Berner Oberland. When you reach Frohnau with its carefully tended parks, its small, dainty shops and cafes, you feel you are in a spa. No vegetables can be grown by Frohnau residents except behind the houses. Formerly this place was exclusively for the well-to-do, now some houses are shared by several families, some of whom are on public pensions (*Sozialrentner*). The French at first billeted many of their officers here, but now they have built their own military quarters in Reinickendorf, and all the villas have been returned to their German owners.

I had lunch and set off to visit Europe's one and only Buddhist temple here in Frohnau, built by Dr. Dahlke in 1923. It strongly reminded me of China (the pagoda behind Kwang-I School in Chungking) when I started climbing the stone steps up the steep hill. The garden looks untended, here and there the stone steps and the walls have crumbled. It looked all so decadent and yet very peaceful. I met a woman with mud-splattered feet like a Chinese coolie who got someone to open the temple door so I could look inside. Both said they were Buddhists and both spoke in high-pitched and very gentle voices. They told me Berlin has about 200 to 300 Buddhists and that 5 or 6 Tibetan priests hold services here on Sunday afternoons.

Had a coffee in Frohnau, then drove to Schmitz's little villa. He lives a few meters away from the zone boundary. The road had become such a quagmire after the continuous downpour of the last weeks, that I had to use my 4-wheel drive to reach his house. He was already waiting for me with lots of printed brochures from before 1914. Since this included a short autobiography that he wrote not too long ago,

Hanne Hiob, a daughter of
Bert Brecht
(21 July, and 1 Aug., 1954)

At a party given by Hartel (29 May, 1954)

The actor Horst Buchholz (21 July, 1954)

Dr. Walter Gaede, a friend of
Ernst Reuter (13 Aug., 1954)

Harry Hurwitz, a friend of Willy Brandt
(7 and 31 July, 1954)

Caught eating
Schlagsahne
A German
Bürgersfrau

I did not ask him too many questions about his life. This was perhaps just as well because he is getting on in age (82) and has difficulty concentrating.

I left at 5 p.m. The Kudamm was decorated with flags and garlands in honor of Theodor Heuss. The presidential elections take place today. The Festhalle at the Funkturm was also decorated by the Senate for this occasion. This makes the SPD happy because they want to use the same hall for their party conference next week and now they don't have to spend much money on decorations.[1]

Wednesday, 21 July 1954

I have to recapitulate the last four days because I lent this diary to Walter Sullivan who wanted to borrow information for an article he is writing for the *New York Times* on the illegal Burschenschaften in Berlin.

On Sunday there was a tea party at the Cerfs'. For once I arrived late. A very interesting Mr. Krebs was holding forth on Germany's economic development and a Mr. Fritz Stern from Columbia University (who is presently teaching at the FU) was engaging him in debate. Interesting comment by Stern: the German industrialists did not need to rebuild their cartels after the war. Why? "There are telephones, no?"[2] – Stayed for dinner at the Cerfs.

Monday was again a busy day. Went to the carpenters' union in the Schlüter Strasse to interview the chairman, Karl Fubel. He was friendly and generously gave me some books, but not too easy to interview. In the afternoon (it rained in torrents), went to interview Paul Löber, an old SPD veteran in his home at Weserstrasse 34a, Neukölln. He is now head of a welfare commission (*Sozialkommission*) that looks after poor people in this part of Berlin. Office hours are twice a week. This was a very good interview. He and his wife treated me to coffee and cakes with whipped cream. His wife is very lively. Though she is over 70, she only looks like 50. They are both happy, which seems to be a rarity here in Berlin. Standing on their modest little balcony, with its few geraniums and two tomato plants, Mrs. Löber exclaimed: "Haven't we got it wonderful?" She insisted that if I ever came to Berlin again I should take a room with her. I am invited to lunch on Friday. I am so glad, I had wanted to be invited by a working-class family for a long time.

At 5:30 I was waiting for Herr Stieder to come and meet me outside the Neukölln Rathaus. He lives in Treptow, in the Russian sector, some 15 minutes walk away, and today came to the West specially

---

[1]Theodor Heuss was reelected president of West Germany on 17 July 1954.
[2]Fritz R. Stern (b. 1926), now Seth Low Professor of History at Columbia University, gave a commemorative lecture on the uprising of 17 June 1953 in East Berlin before the West German parliament in Bonn, 1987.

to be interviewed by me. Unfortunately he was sick and I couldn't talk to him very long. We sat in the hall of the Rathaüs until the porter became suspicious because it was after office hours and we could not possibly be waiting to see someone. (Stieder to the porter, calmly: "Wir wollten uns nicht in eine Kneipe setzen. — We didn't want to go to a pub.") Went home to the empty apartment of the Henningers and cooked myself a handful of rice for dinner.

Tuesday— yesterday— I went to Tempelhof to pay the vehicle tax on my jeep for another 2 months. Getting some money at the bank on Mehring Damm, I met a little boy of 12, Manfred Göldner, who was just exchanging some West German marks for East German marks. He is a real Berlin urchin (*Gassenjunge*), very much alive, curious, cheeky, street wise and touchingly affectionate towards his mother. He refused a 20-(East) mark banknote at the bank and asked for smaller change because the 20-mark note was torn. He told me he is saving money to buy his mother a pair of nylon stockings for her birthday. Since it was his own birthday today, I offered to buy him an ice cream cone or some sweets. First he hesitated. He'd much rather have the money, he said. Then we compromised: I went into a shop and put a mark on the counter and he got 50 pfennigs' worth of chocolate and pocketed the change. We then went to his flat. There were bundles of newspapers on the floor everywhere for his father works in the print shop of Ullstein, the publishing house. There was a little girl, 3-year-old Rosemarie, who was promptly sent to bed because there was too little room for all of us. The air was foul. I thought I would suffocate. This is the first time I've been inside a worker's flat without previous announcement. It was past 10 in the morning but everything was untidy: the room, the bed, the woman's dress. The mother was at first suspicious of me until I told her that I lived in West Berlin and was a student at an American university. But it was touching to see little Manfred feeding chocolate to his little sister and then trying the same with his mother, except that she told him that this was bad manners and that he should offer the whole paper bag, and to the guest first. She seemed a bit apologetic because Manfred next proceeded to find out how much he could exploit his new acquaintance. Thus he told me that the family bicycle needed a new back tire for 5 marks, and that his mother had to go to the youth agency and couldn't I give her a lift? At the same time I could see he was truly trying to help his family and that I found interesting and good. I invited Manfred for lunch on Sunday. Not without a selfish reason: I believe he can tell me a lot about working-class life.

In the afternoon I went to see Klaus von Wahl, who had called me in the morning. He lives in Im Schwarzen Grund no. 4, Berlin-Dahlem. The reason why he called me was that he is producing a Chinese play, S. I. Hsiung's *Lady Precious Stream*, at the British Centre in a few weeks and wants me to give the actors some tips on Chinese customs and manners. We sat in the room of Geske, the dancer, and talked about Chinese things. The actress Hanne Hiob was also there. She is the daughter of Bert Brecht by his first marriage and will play Lady Precious Stream, while Geske will play Hsieh, the gardner. She said she'll introduce me to her father so I can ask him his views on workers before the First World War. Brecht is a red-hot Communist now, she said, producing plays in the Schiffbauerdamm Theater. He won't come to the West, so I would have to visit him in the East sector. I am to read Hsiung's play and meet Klaus again in a few days.

We then went to the Renaissance Theater, where Klaus was on duty as stage manager for the evening performance of a play called *Mein Sohn der Herr Minister*. He got me a good seat for only 2.50 marks. The play was superbly funny. I sat next to an Englishman named Williams who is the Bonn correspondent for the *Christian Science Monitor* and whose daughter, he said, was studying at Girton College in Cambridge. After the play Klaus and I went to the Theater Klause to meet a young film actor by the name of Horst Buchholz who had just received a major role in a new film, *Schmerzliche Arkadie*.[1] He is only 20 years old and so far has mainly appeared in small roles in films for U.S. television programs. (Many American films are made in Germany because production costs are lower here.) In the next hour Horst and Klaus tried to educate me about the theater world of Berlin which I found fascinating though I promptly forgot all the names of the personalities they mentioned to me. From the distance they pointed out to me a famous *comédienne* named Grete Weiser. Had an espresso at the Petit Palais on the Kudamm before going home.

22 July 1954

Yesterday I went to the archives in the morning. Got into a discussion with Herr Schumacher, Herr Ilbich, and a third archivist who, during the breakfast recess, lashed out against British imperialism with the wildest of accusations. It sounded as if England was the cause of all the world's troubles in the last two hundred years. I drove to the Stein Bibliothek to return books (in passing I saw the new library of the FU, which is splendid), then to American Express to pick up steamship tickets for Jay and myself. I called Jay from there and we agreed to have lunch at the Mensa. On the spur of the moment I decided to ask Mrs. Lewandowski (the lady at the counter of American Express) to join us, since she told me she always just ate sandwiches in the park and she has been very helpful. Unfortunately it turned out Jay was expecting Krebs for lunch, so I ate alone with Lewandowsky at a separate table. Lewandowsky told me her grandmother was Chinese, which accounts for her partly Chinese looks.

---

[1] Horst Buchholz (b. 1933) subsequently starred in a Billy Wilder movie on the Berlin of the 1950s entitled *One, Two, Three*.

Today I got up early to pick up Mrs. Trapp and her friend Frau Dr. Lüdtke (the SPD representative from Lübeck) to drive to the SPD party meeting in the Funkturm. The conference was in the same huge hall where Adenauer spoke in the winter, but the loudspeaker system was so poor I could hardly understand any of the speeches. Mrs. Trapp kept on chatting away, which did not improve matters. I was introduced to Ludwig Preller, now teaching in the Akademie der Arbeit in Frankfurt a.M. Mrs. Trapp asked him to give me a few good tips for my thesis.[1] I also saw Scharnowski, who invited me to look him up some day.

I left at noon. Drove to Schlüterstrasse to see Fubel again. He had asked his secretary to copy for me the statute of an old union of apprentices (1905-1911) and accompanied me downstairs to the conference room, where I spent the next 4 hours reading back numbers of the union paper *Die Holzarbeiter Zeitung* from the year 1905.

Called Jürgen Brandenburg and we went out for a cup of coffee. He told me that half a year ago, according to newspaper reports, the student representative of the FU had informed Rektor Hirsch that Mensuren were being fought somewhere in the Grunewald (Lynarstrasse?). Hirsch had immediately gone there to see for himself and was literally thrown out of the house. And the matter had ended there. My word!

Friday, 23 July 1954

Fetched Fritz Stern, the young guest teacher at the FU, at his home in Thielallee 60. We sat sipping an espresso at the Petit Palais on the Kudamm. He admonished me for going to the East sector so often and thought it immoral to give the Reds even the illusion of sympathy by talking and smiling to them. I think he has a point but is making too much of it. I am sure that I benefit far more than they when I go to gather impressions on conditions behind the Iron Curtain.

Went to Mr. and Mrs. Löber's for lunch. It was a wonderful lunch, with Sauerbraten, potatoes, carrots, salad, and berries as dessert. I helped old mother Löber wash the dishes and she got a big kick out of it. Afterwards Herr Löber drove to Kreuzberg to a side street parallel to Naunynstrasse. First we went into a Mietshaus where a cousin of Löber lives with her husband, a former cutter in the underwear industry and later a tobacco shop owner. Their name is Zimmermann. In the courtyard of this tenement house is a dairy with 40 cows. The animals live in 2 sheds and never leave them again until they are slaughtered for meat. There was a farmhand in the yard unloading hay from a lorry. He talked to us for a while.

[1] Ludwig Preller was known to me as the author of *Sozialpolitik in der Weimarer Republik* (1949).

According to him, to have cows in Kreuzberg is an old tradition. The disadvantage, of course, is that the smell of cow dung penetrates all the apartments of the neighborhood, and that there are lot of rats in the cowsheds.

We went up to the Zimmermanns' on the 4th floor. It turned out to be quite a nice, old-fashioned flat. The husband seemed like a real Spiesser. When he saw his cousin Löber come in with me he exclaimed: "Ja wie kommst denn Du zu *diesem* Herrn?"[1] We stayed for some coffee and chatted for a while, but when we left Zimmermann was still perplexed about my provenance. Löber wanted to show me the condition of the apartments below ground which, he said, were far worse than upstairs. When we came a young housewife from one of the basement dwellings, pale and thin, was about to go to her neighbor's to fetch some tap water in a jug— she has no running water in her own flat. Löber said he was the district superintendant (*Bezirksvorsteher*, which was not quite true) and that he was showing "an American student" through some Berlin cellars for a study of Berlin housing conditions and so she readily let us in. It was cold and musty down there. There was just one room with a bed for the husband, a couch where she herself slept, and a cot for their 3-year-old daughter. They moved here when they got married 4 years ago and have so far been unable to find another apartment. The previous tenant died of tuberculosis. No wonder, for there is hardly ever any sunshine down here. We went to several other places too, most of them somewhat better because their tenants had the means to make some improvements. But it was all most depressing nevertheless. One cellar was a grocery store. Children had drawn a Chinaman on a blackboard and written underneath: "Fu Man Chu." So I took a piece of chalk and put the name in Chinese next to it. Outside in the street a man with a hand-drawn cart was going from door to door to exchange potato peels for bundles of firewood. Apparently this is an old institution also. The potato peels are used as pig food.

Saturday, 24 July 1954

Went to see Klaus von Wahl over lunch to discuss the Chinese play with him. He is very amusing to talk to. We also talked about the disappearance into the East sector of Dr. Otto John a few days ago, the chief of the German Federal Political Police (Amt für Verfassungsschutz). Klaus was very upset about this affair. His sister is married to a Justus Delbrück and through this connection Klaus knew most of the people who were involved in the 20 July affair such as the Harnacks and the Bonhoeffers. When his father died, Claus Bonhoeffer, who had a leading post in the Lufthansa airline, had become Klaus von Wahl's guardian, and Klaus had been very fond of

---

[1]"How on earth did you find that man?"

him.[1] After the failure of the coup of 20 July 1944, Bonhoeffer offered Dr. John the only remaining seat on a plane to Madrid and chose to remain in Berlin himself. He paid with his life for the chance he gave John to escape to Spain. Klaus von Wahl is now bitter at the thought that 10 years later this same man would run over to the Communists and betray to them the whole Western intelligence network in East Germany. The communist SSD is said to have started a large-scale wave of arrest.[2]

I went with Klaus to the Kudamm and showed him the furniture in our old embassy building to give him an idea of Chinese interiors. Then I went to Wannsee to have tea with the Cerfs. Carol said that Walter Sullivan may use one of my drawings of students fighting a Mensur for his *New York Times* article! Wow! The Radeloffs were also there. Bruno Radeloff talked almost without pause, mainly about the social inequalities in postwar Germany and the favors bestowed by the Bonn government on officials who were prominent in the Nazi period. In this conjunction he also shed a new light on the Otto John case. According to Radeloff, John left his post out of disgust at the sight of old Nazi bosses returning to positions of power in West Germany, unreformed and as ambitious as ever. John also had reason to fear that his own job as head of the West German Intelligence Service was about to be given to a Dr. Gerhard Schröder, a former SS official and big Nazi. One can surely sympathize with John's mental depression if this story is true, but that does not justify his running away to the East.

Sunday, 25 July 1954

To my great consternation, little Manfred Göldner did not come alone to have lunch with me. His mother came with him and she chatted on and on, never letting her son say anything at all. On top of all this she was so terribly vulgar. She ordered an enormous lunch for herself, which she then proceeded to eat in the most abominable way, scratching her chicken bones with knife, teeth, and fingers, while telling me with her mouth full that she was socially "better" than her husband and reprimanding Manfred for speaking in Berlin dialect. I discovered that I am very bourgeois in my insistence on good table manners and so I got rid of the two as fast as possible.

---

[1]Otto John (b. 1909), president of the West German Office for the Protection of the Constitution, went over to East Berlin in the night of 20 July 1954. He escaped back to the West in 1955, was tried for treason, and sentenced to four years in prison.

[2]Claus Bonhoeffer (1901-45) was legal counsel to the German airline and a prominent participant in the conspiracy to overthrow Hitler in 1944.

27 July 1954

Yesterday the newspapers reported much panic among East German officials, many of whom have collaborated with West German agents and now fear exposure by Dr. John. Today I got up late and had to hurry to keep my breakfast appointment with the Schmidts. There was sunshine for the first time in many weeks. I admit feeling really decadent spending a workday morning in the wintergarten of a Dahlem villa imbibing a huge breakfast of tea and a variety of breads with cheese, eggs, fish, and ham, and topping it off with dessert. Mrs. Schmidt lamented that the cups and saucers of her breakfast service were not real Meissen (so presumably the *plates* were) and Sigrid had a new hairdo. I didn't regret coming, indeed I enjoyed it, since this was the most animated and interesting conversation with the Schmidt family that I've had so far. This time we didn't just talk politely, as we had on previous occasions. Mrs. Schmidt of course immediately brought up the Otto John case. She and her husband, she said, were sure that this was a classical case of "once a traitor, always a traitor." John is the kind of man who will always oppose the existing regime, a habitual malcontent, a man of low moral character. So I asked her about the theory that John was disgusted by the return of old Nazis to positions of influence in the Bonn government and about this old SS man Schröder who was about to replace him in his post. I noticed both Mrs. Schmidt's and Sigrid's mouth tightened in anger. Nazi elements in the Bonn government? "Nonsense," was their reply. "This is just a rumor spread by the press which, alas, is completely in Jewish hands again. And even if this Schröder was an SS man," Mrs. Schmidt continued, "so what? The SS recruited the best people in Germany, they enlisted the best blood in the country before the Wehrmacht could draft them. As a result, some of the nicest young men were in the SS. French people during the German occupation spoke highly of the courage and orderliness of the SS, and often preferred them to the common German soldiers. The French civil population admired the SS men who so selflessly rescued them during Allied bombing raids. Only a small number of SS committed the atrocities during the war."

Mrs. Schmidt's opinion of the German Resistance fighters was in keeping with her admiration for the SS. Many of them emigrated from Germany because they thought it safer to store their assets in Switzerland or in England. At my persistent questioning she admitted some of them may have acted from idealistic motives. But she was sure most of them just went abroad for reasons of comfort, among them Otto John.

In short, Mrs. Schmidt wanted me to realize that the Third Reich had had its positive sides too. The German people unfortunately cannot live without strict discipline. Goethe himself has said that the individual German is a wonderful *Mensch*, but *en masse* he is intolerable. (Which reminds me of a story told by Klaus von Wahl. Mrs. Schmidt once exclaimed to him, triumphantly: "Oh, Herr von Wahl, I am so happy! It has definitely been established now that Goethe had *no* Jewish blood!" To which Klaus said he answered: "So what?") In any case, according to Mrs. Schmidt, Germans cannot exist without a well-organized society. Before Hitler came, the people were rude, selfish, and narrow-minded, and she was molested on the streets of Berlin. This changed overnight when Hitler came. His social reforms worked a miracle. Suddenly everyone knew his place again and people once more cooperated with one another ("Einer für alle, alle für einen"). The beggars disappeared from the streets, and the people were polite and orderly. If a girl misbehaved, her superior would tactfully take her aside and talk to her about comportment. All this is gone today, and people are rude, selfish, and egoistic once more. Her husband had said, back in the thirties, that if communism is the wave of the future, nazism is the mildest form of communism we are ever going to have, so we might as well support it. I didn't ask her whether Mr. Schmidt had been in the party. They kept Carl and Sigrid, their two children, from joining the Hitler Youth, so that Sigrid and one foreign girl were the only two in her school who were not in the BDM (Bund deutscher Mädel). Carl was exempted because of delicate health, Sigrid because she was a dancer. But I suspect keeping their children out of these mass organizations had a certain snob appeal and does not mean that the Schmidts did not think nazism quite wonderful.

Mrs. Schmidt and Sigrid also told me something about Storm Troop Leader Lutze, who lived across the road from them. Formerly prominent in the Reichswehr, after 1934 the leader of the SA, he was a splendid man except that his wife was very common (*ordinär*), the daughter of a butcher, and very uppish to compensate for her lowly origin. She once stopped Sigrid in the street and told her she must salute her though Sigrid had never met her before. As to the Himmlers, who lived in a nearby villa, they were horrible people. The Herr Reichsminister had cold, cruel eyes, his daughter was haughty and was accorded privileged treatment in school (she went to school with Syke). And Mrs. Himmler was not only haughty, she was also stingy. At a birthday party given by the Himmlers during the war, there was only tea and biscuits. And when the children got thirsty from playing in the garden, they were given tap water. Mrs. Schmidt, during the war, collected contributions for the German Red Cross from house to house in this neighborhood. Mrs. Himmler was the only one who always refused to give money under the pretext that she already supported other charitable organizations. The SS guards in front of her house sometimes felt so embarrassed that they gave Mrs. Schmidt a few marks out of their own pockets.

I left shortly after midday to fetch Fritz and Peggy Stern for a tour of working-class Berlin housing. Among other places we went to the exhibition of Berlin photos from the year 1945 at Potsdamer Platz, then to the dairy in Kreuzberg in the Waldemar Strasse. The 40 cows in the sheds were listening to radio music from RIAS! It was very enjoyable to be with the Sterns. Interestingly enough, they thought that the working class houses that I showed them were quite good and the dairy with its perpetually imprisoned cows very well run. They invited me to look them up in New York (440 Riverside Drive) and promised to show me the slums of New York.

In the evening Harry Hurwitz called to ask me to come and visit him and his wife on Saturday evening.

Wednesday to Friday, 28, 29, 30 July 1954

Three days spent almost entirely with the Cerfs. On Wednesday, I helped the Cerfs move into their new house, Am Hirschsprung 35, Tel. 76 56 21. At the end of the day, I accompanied Jay to Brandenburgische Strasse 34, near the Kudamm, where he went to see a Mr. Gordon of the ETG (Europäische Television Gesellschaft), who wanted to try Jay out for a role in a short television film to be shown in the States. Gordon is a naturalized U.S. citizen of Hungarian origin. The story is about an American couple who are adopting a German war orphan. Jay did his part very well. The studio itself, and Mr. Gordon, were most resplendent. One could fancy oneself in the home of a wealthy art collector. Before returning home Jay and I endulged in a "Komm' morgen wieder" (a kind of Latvian cannelloni) and some coffee in a snack bar on the Kudamm. On Thursday I had intended to go to the Landesarchiv but ended up going shopping with the Cerfs now that they have a big American refrigerator to put food in, and in the evening I cooked some rice with pork and beans.

Today I spent the morning at the archives. Read through some manuscripts of the Berlin insurance office from around 1910. I found nothing very interesting for my thesis, alas. It is laughable to think that in these vaults reams of documents are being preserved that only concern petty details such as "Who left the main office door 2 inches open after office hours on a certain day last week?" or "Why did the porter not answer the door bell on a particular afternoon?" I asked Frau Dr. Täuber what she thinks about the Otto John case. Like Frau Schmidt Täuber was anti-John, but only because she hates the Communists to whom John has defected, not because she likes old Nazis. "People ought to have been suspicious of him long before now," she said. "He was known to be friendly with that Communist, Dr. Wohlgemuth."

3l July 1954

In the morning Rena came back from her vacation. I worked at home until noon and went shopping in Steglitz at lunch time. In the evening I was invited to dinner by Harold Hurwitz and his wife Grete. It was interesting to listen to their talk of Berlin "in the good old days," which for them were the years immediately after the war. Then it was a city of grey rubble over which people climbed to go to the theater, the most wonderful theater in the world precisely because you wanted to go there despite hunger and cold. He told me the story of his friend Pinske, an idealistic communist (*Edelkommunist*) since back in the 1920s, who originally was a worker and under the Hitler regime ran a second-hand bookstore. His shop was in Friedrichsstrasse, underneath the railway bridge. In a little cellar beneath the shop, he had a couch for his customers to sit on and shelves full of forbidden books: a meeting place for anti-Nazi underground fighters of whatever brand, Communists, Liberals, Social Democrats, everybody thrown together. Pinske enjoyed this period best, for among the anti-Nazi groups there existed a spirit of real cooperation and mutual confidence. After the war, the shop became the center of FDJ leaders who wanted to educate themselves beyond what official party propaganda offered them. Pinske encouraged their quest for knowledge for he still believed in a future Communist society founded on the liberal spirit of toleration. He gave away good books to whoever liked to read. In the evenings, after closing hours, he carried books in a heavy knapsack to bring them to friends. Yet he was not happy. His wife by then had become an SED doctrinaire. Pinske too was in the SED but he sent his sons to school in the West sector. The Hurwitzes met him when Pinske decided to open a socialist reading club to which he invited both Social Democrats and members of the East Berlin Communist party, the SED. The first two meetings took place in the West sector (one of them was in the Leuschnerhaus). The Communists from the East sector sent observers to see what was afoot, among them the secretary of Wilhelm Pieck and a Soviet officer in mufti. Pinske saw that the Communists intended to control his club and to use it as a front organization for their propaganda when they began to ask questions like whether or not anarchist or Trotskyite literature would also be read. Pinske stood up and declared every Socialist should know Trotskyite and anarchist literature and that his own shop also stocked them. The SED people remained silent. The club was dissolved. Pinske after that stood under surveillance by the East German secret police (the SSD) and in 1951 committed suicide. I asked Harold his opinion of the Otto John case. Hurwitz: "If it is true that John went to the East voluntarily, he is the greatest traitor in history!"

After dinner we drove in his tiny Renault to the Kudamm for a stroll. He lent me an unpublished study of social conditions in Neukölln which he recently wrote for the FU.

Sunday, I August 1954

Klaus von Wahl called in the morning to ask me to lunch. Hanne Hiob and Rudi Getzke, the dancer, were at his apartment rehearsing a scene from *Lady Precious Stream*. I was mesmerized by their wonderful acting. Hanne has marvelous facial expressions. After divorcing Bert Brecht her mother married Paul Linge, an actor. Brecht also remarried, a certain actress named Helene Weigel, and the two daughters of this second marriage, Ursula and Barbara, are good Communists, but Hanne is not.

I was interested to hear Klaus talk about Mr. Gordon, the man from the Europäische Television Gesellschaft who has engaged Jay to act in his film. According to Klaus, Gordon is a charlatan, a dishonest fellow. When no one in the West wants to buy his awful productions, he has no compunction to sell them to the East German government for conversion into propaganda material. He once asked no one less than Yehudi Menuhin to play some excerpts of a violin concerto in his studio for him. Under the pretext of trying different camera angles and lighting, he got Menuhin to play the entire concerto and paid him only for the one short piece he said he would select from it for inclusion in an educational film. Only half a year later did Menuhin discover that Gordon had put all his excerpts together to make a full-length film called *Menuhin Plays*. Klaus von Wahl gave me a huge sunflower as a gift to take home.

In the late evening I drove to get some petrol for tomorrow's many errands and before I knew it landed on the Kudamm. I wanted to buy a *New York Times* to look for the Sullivan article, but there were no copies left at the newsstands. Lots of dubious, criminal-looking characters were hanging around the Joachimsthaler Strasse. I recognized the proprietor of that dingy little Imbisstube where I once had lunch. He was talking to an equally shady looking fellow.

2 August 1954

Met Herr Wilhelm Miethke in Neukölln, the founder of the socialist teetotaller society (Arbeiter Abstinenten Bund), a small man with a yellowish complexion and long white hair. He told me he was the son of a poor agricultural worker, and in the 1920s a great friend of Magnus Hirschfeld, the pioneer sexologist. He is also a member of the workers' society of atheists (Freidenker Bund) in the nearby Rollberg Strasse 9. I must come back here soon to look for documentary materials.

Telephoned Waldemar Jenny and arranged an interview with him at his trade union tomorrow. Jay called in the evening. Am reading Wheeler-Bennett's *Nemesis of Power*. A superb piece of historical writing.

3 August 1954

A busy day. I went to Dessauer Strasse 28/29 in Kreuzberg to see Waldemar Jenny, head of the textile and clothing union (IG Textil und Bekleidung). He has a very small office and I don't think his union is making much business. Jenny is a Swiss national, but he was raised in Germany and has spent many years as an organizer in the German workers' movement. We talked for over two hours. First he showed me a stack of old trade union books (from which I borrowed five), then we sat down and chatted. He told me he headed a municipal committee to investigate the conditions of the home workers in the clothing industry and to represent their interests. These home workers are mostly women. "They are stubborn, they will not organize themselves, they allow themselves to be exploited for the satisfaction of being unhappy in their own way." Their average earning is 80 marks per week, which looks fine on paper but in reality represents crass exploitation because they work far longer than 8 hours a day and are assisted by 5 to 6 family members who are not paid. In this industry work conditions have practically remained unchanged since before 1914. What frustrates him is that often these women refuse to let the union take up their cause. Jenny once sent out 1,800 invitations to home workers to attend a conference on their economic situation. Only thirty turned up. But he will try to put me in touch with some of these women.

Jenny also talked to me about his own life. Raised in Hamburg, he became a tailor and worked in Hamburg's biggest clothing factory. Though a Socialist the Gestapo during the war could not put him in a concentration camp because Germany wanted to stay on good terms with Switzerland. But they regularly sent him political pamphlets and Swiss fellow travelers (i.e., Swiss Nazis) came to his home several times to enlist him in the Swiss Freikorps. This was a Swiss unit of the Wehrmacht held ready for the eventuality of a German occupation of Switzerland. But, Jenny said, he stubbornly refused all entreaties. Then, in 1943, the British bombed Hamburg flat in 3 night raids. With most of the police files destroyed the authorities could not trace Jenny's whereabouts anymore.

Jenny gave me one of the most gripping accounts of air raids in the Second World War I've ever heard. He described how the British planes first fooled German radar by dropping thousands of strips of staniol paper and then caught the Germans unprepared for this first saturation raid on a German city, how the heat of the burning houses sucked people off their feet, how the streets filled up with dead bodies, and how a long darkness descended on the city because the smoke blocked out the sunlight for days and days. It was horrible, he said, and yet the population did not hate the British for it, they hated the Nazis instead. For by that time the defeat in Stalingrad had made it clear to many Germans that the war would end in a catastrophe. And Goebbels's speech in the Sportpalast, "asking" the German people to support total war, had only provoked yet more fear and desperation. After the British bombers destroyed 240,000 homes and killed 80,000 people in Hamburg the population turned on the Nazis, jeering: "There you have your wonderful total war!" The Nazis thereupon began frantically to evacuate the city and distributed quantities of red wine, butter, cheese, and milk to the people who remained behind. A brownshirt dared not go through the streets for fear of being beaten up.

And today? While Jenny had rejoiced at the Allied victory in 1945, he is disappointed with the new democratic regime in Bonn. At the end of the war he sat on a denazification committee for the textile industry. The small Nazis were punished, he remembers, and the big ones got off scot free. For a time all the Nazis went into hiding and non-Nazis were welcome to apply for public positions. Since then most of these positions are back in the hands of Nazis and the old military spririt is reasserting itself.

Had lunch in Potsdamer Strasse and then drove to the Berlin Public Health Office (Landesgesundheitsamt) in the Invalidenstrasse near Lehrter Bahnhof, where I was well received by the head librarian, Herr Lagermacher. Must go back there tomorrow. I also went to the French consulate to apply for a French visa, and finally bought a *New York Times* to read Sullivan's article on student duels, which he partly based on my diary account.

Spaghetti dinner with the Cerfs, then met Klaus von Wahl and drove with him to Wannsee to a birthday party of a friend of his named Peter. Peter lives in an elegant villa. Punch and sandwiches were served on the candle-lit garden terrace. The talk was mainly about theater people, anecdotes about well-known actors, and travel accounts about southern France, Italy, Spain. I found this conversation so refreshing because it allowed me to forget for a few hours the atmosphere of poverty and cultural deprivation which prevails among the people I meet every day. Among the guests was a young actress named Ursel Lyn who happens to be Jay's partner in the television film for Mr. Gordon, also a White Russian émigrée whose husband was kidnapped by the Russians in 1946 and whose whereabout are still unknown, some more actors (one very effeminate looking man, and an actress named Ruth who was really a born comédienne), and a French girl who knew no German and finally simply fell asleep. I also talked to a Fräulein Dr. Jäger of the Oskar Helene Heim whose dream is to be a doctor in India and who will be leaving for Iraq soon. Her parents, she says, are salon Bolsheviks who held leading positions in the East Berlin health autorities until one day they found an opportunity to escape to the West.

4 August 1954

Had photos made for my French visa, then spent the day in the library of the Landesgesundheitsamt (also called Senat für Gesundheitswesen). Had a prolonged talk with the librarian, Mr. Lagermacher. Can't figure him out yet. He is older than I first thought, since he remembers Paul Singer's funeral around 1910. He looks like Frederick the Great with big blue eyes that stare at you when he eulogizes the efficiency of Prussian administrators. He proudly (!) told me that the Landesgesundheitsamt could not make photostats of documents for me even if I wanted to pay for them because, though the equipment is here, no one knows how to enter such costs in the account books. I told him that, frankly, I found such bureaucratic pedantry very deplorable. All I wanted was copies of old photos showing Berlin women home workers. "Sure," he agreed, "very deplorable. And yet, German efficiency has always been the key to Germany's national strength! Hitler's power was founded on his control of the German administrative machine." I suggested that less discipline and less blind obedience by the German people might have prevented Hitler from doing all the harm he did. "Oh sure," Lagermacher quickly agreed, "Hitler has done tremendous harm to the whole world." And so he went on, eulogizing something Prussian at one moment, taking it all back when I disagreed, only to come forward with another equally provocative statement the next moment. "The American soldier is no hero," he said at one point. "He expects his commander to knock everything flat with bombers, artillery and tanks before risking him forward. We Germans, on the other hand, joyfully charge the enemy with loud cries of 'Hurrah!'" — "But isn't it commendable," I asked, "that the Americans place such high value on the life of each of their men and will spend thousands of dollars to rescue a shot-down pilot?" — "Oh, wonderful, indeed wonderful," Lagermacher quickly agreed, "I too am an individualist and respect every human life." — "Now," I said, thinking I finally had him cornered, "had Germany also possessed abundant war matériel, would she not also have preceded each attack by heavy bombardment to minimize her human losses?" — "Oh no," was the answer, and a smile appeared on Lagermacher's face and his eyes glowed, making him look more like the Old Fritz than ever. "Oh no! there are always Germans whose greatest wish is to die in a frontal assault at the head of their troops!" And he was proud as a frog. — Lagermacher, by the way, says he votes SPD. His father was a seaman and an old SPD party member. His grandfather was the captain of a sailboat that took Prussian officers who had participated in the 1848 revolution to America. He himself is a functionary of the union of civil servants of which there are over 100 members in the Senat für Gesundheitswesen.

I did some work here and drove home at 4 p.m. While I had a bath the telephone rang. Lagermacher called to say he had found a student named Sturzbecher, the son of an apothecary, who is also studying health conditions in Berlin. Sturzbecher lives in East Berlin but would meet me in one hour at Bahnhof Zoo. I must confess that though Sturzbecher gave me a few useful tips I found him a great bore and even rather annoying. What annoyed me was that he constantly tried to tell me what to do and what no to do. When I had to make a call: "Oh, don't go into a restaurant to telephone, it isn't done." He asked me to drive him to the home of Professor Zipfel (whom I had met at the Meinecke Institut) but when I wanted to come with him he said no, wait in the car, it is not done to arrive unannounced at people's door. I got very fed up with him and stopped paying him any attention. I walked past him to say hello to Zipfel's wife, and since Zipfel himself was not home she invited me to visit them both when they return from their vacation. Sturzbecher and I also disagreed over the student fraternities. He said he was against them, but then defended their ideals, including dueling as a test of manliness, with the old argument that saber duels were no worse than boxing in Western countries.

On the way home I stopped at the Bendlerstrasse to look at the old OKW building, in the war the office of the high command of the German armed forces and in 1944 the site of the unsuccessful putsch against Hitler. A high, massive building, painted a greenish grey, with lots of small courtyards. At present ordinary people live here. The Red Cross maintains some homes here for needy families, and small commercial firms have rented offices and workshops. In the first courtyard a bronze statue erected by the Berlin Senate after the war stands to commemorate those who took part in the 20 July 1944 affair.

I also stopped at Schlesisches Tor, which is another part of Berlin I have not seen before. I parked the car and went for a stroll. Had a fried fish and potato salad for 1 mark in a small restaurant which boasted an "Original Amerikanische Music Box." People were playing a game of dice at the counter. At one table, two working-class couples were celebrating by singing songs and dancing to the juke box. The juke box was American-made all right, but the records were German traditional folk tunes and marching songs. ("In der Heimat, in der Heimat..."). I then walked along the Schlesische Strasse as far as the sector boundary, and explored the side streets. It was a very warm, balmy night, and I was amazed to see how many people there were in the streets. This is a district full of tenement houses (Mietskasernen) for the poor. Young people were sitting on the steps in the doorways or hanging around at street corners, old men and women stood in the middle of the sidewalk doing nothing, and in the window, propped on cushions, grandmothers were looking at the passers by or talking to someone in the street. Most boys had long hair and sideburns and wore loud clothes: American jeans and "Texas shirts," and thick-soled shoes. Through the windows you heard radio music, but all of it classical: piano recitals and opera. I peeked into windows and saw old-fashioned, heavy furniture. A woman in a cellar sat next to the cooking stove knitting; I assume the kitchen was also her living room and her bedroom. Though it was past 8 p.m. in some shop windows you still saw people at work, sorting out wares or washing the floor. Some shops were quite elegant. But the courtyards were breathtaking in their melancholy drabness.

Jay called in the evening. He is going to be filmed tomorrow.

5 August 1954

Made my visa application at the French consulate. An old French-woman, Madame Dubois, was being bawled out for having cheated about her age in her passport application. She must have tried to appear "younger" than she is, for she had given her year of birth as 1874 instead of 1872. While I was at the consulate I also overheard a telephone call from a journalist who enquired about Josephine Baker's planned trip to Paris. (What? Josephine Baker??) But the consulate refused to give out any information on Josephine. I was also amused to hear the French consular official looking for his rubber stamp, crying, "Le *stempel*, où est mon *stempel*?" If a Frenchman must use a German word, what better word than Stempel?

Visited Prof. Dr. med., Dr. phil. Bruno Harms, former president of the Robert Koch Institut. It apparently is still done to call him Herr Präsident. He lives in Riemeister Strasse 42, Berlin-Zehlendorf. His father, he said, owned a carpenter shop (*Tischlermeisterei*) in Prenzlauer Berg. Now retired, he is writing a book on medical conditions in Berlin in the 17th and 18th centuries. Most of his material, he said, is provided for him by libraries in East Berlin.

8 August 1954

Today was lost because of my visit to the Göldners, Mehringdamm 51, rear wing, third floor. I was invited for 12:30. I was greeted by Mr. Göldner, who I thought was quite nice, a very simple and open man, but perhaps a bit too weak to stand up to his wife. Then there was the enormous Mrs. Göldner, as vulgar and gay as she was two weeks ago, 3-year-old Rosemarie, who was somewhat out of control, and Manfred who was away doing errands most of the time. Mr. Göldner said he never belonged to the Nazi party but he did show me old decorations from the Stahlhelm veterans' organization and from Nazi organizations. He is a worker but does not belong to any trade union. I avoided politics, feeling that it might lead to unpleasantness. A neighbor, a fat woman who is engaged to a GI (poor man!) and very proud of it, dropped in too. There was also an older son, Reinhard,

18 years old, who works as a truck driver's assistant for a moving firm. He left early because he had a date with a girl. Both parents reprimanded their children whenever they talked in Berlin dialect. "Why?" I asked. "Because when you go into a restaurant you are ashamed that your children talk Berlin dialect," was the reply. I was given an enormous lunch: soup (a kind of bouillon), meat, potatoes and cabbage, stewed prunes as dessert, then wine, and after that coffee and cakes. It is impossible to be moderate: your plate is heaped full again and again and all protests are in vain. "Eat, eat! You won't insult us, will you?" So you sigh and dig into more potatoes and cabbage. "Na, schmeckts?" Frau Göldner would then ask, beaming and smacking her lips, and perspiration breaking out all over her face since she too was eating away with relish and determination. Each time you touch your wine glass, everyone else immediately drinks too. "Zum Woh! Zum Wohl!" And when they emptied their glass they insisted that I also emptied mine. I finally left at 6 p.m. (they still thought it was too early) and was given a paper bag full of apples and a piece of cake to take home. I wonder whether they always eat so well on Sundays. I noticed that little Manfred had clapped his hands in anticipation of the meat course.

The talk had centered around America, traveling, and working conditions at Ullstein, where Göldner's job is sorting paper for 1.25 marks per hour. With overtime he earns about 60 marks a week. If I learned something from my visit today then it is mainly what it means to live very crowded together in a 2-room flat with a tiny kitchen and corridor on the third floor of an ugly house. I was told in the basement, there is an old locksmith's shop dating from 1904. The Meister was born there in this very house and expects to remain there until he dies. Outside the window the Göldners have the view of an industrial building. One floor is occupied by a printing press, another by a factory making ready-made dresses. The third floor has a carpet cleaning works. In the window, boxes of sorry looking plants. Soot comes into the Göldners' flat from the chimneys outside the window and everything looks very grimy. All the rickety shelves and nooks and corners are stuffed with junk: old papers, boxes, the broken bicycle. They have 3 books, carefully wrapped in silk paper. One is a big picture book on Adolf Hitler, and two are old-fashioned illustrated histories of the Wars of Liberation in 1813. In the chimney they also had an 19th-century Bible. The place was so small that little Rosemarie always got in the way of her parents. It seems on days when they don't have "hoher Besuch" (as they called me) Father Göldner takes his daughter to play in the court yard. The kitchen has only cold running water, the toilet is on the staircase.

9 August 1954

It rained all day today, but I enjoyed it after the heat of the last few days. Got up early to fetch my watch from the repair shop, but it wasn't ready. Then drove to the FU to borrow books from the Stein Bibliothek. Went to Charlottenburg, Pestalozzi Strasse 16, where Dr. med. Gustav Pölchau lives. He is an old *Sanitätsrat*, but too old (89) to let me interview him. His wife received me and showed me a list of Pölchau's publications, like pamphlets on the dangers of ice skating for schoolchildren. I'll see whether any of them are useful when I look them up in the library of the Landesgesundheitsamt. She then sent me to see a Dr. med. Ernst Umbreit nearby, an old welfare doctor, but he also turned out to be too old to give me much information. For some reason he always called me "Herr Jellinek," and when I corrected him he said, "Jellinek is a good Czech name." Why he insisted on calling me by a Czech name I don't know. Anyhow, the interview ended with the two of us assuring one another that Bohemia was a very beautiful country. I left Umbreit and drove to the Swiss delegation to file my application for a Swiss visa. Very courteous service. Had lunch at Aschinger's, drove home to read for a few hours.

At 4 p.m. I left for Rudow. I was to see Dr. Zadek in the Neukölln hospital at 5:30, and since it is a long ride to Rudower Strasse, I wanted to go early and look at the surroundings. So I drove to Rudow, past the hospital, and stopped close to the border of the Soviet zone. I sat on the bank of the canal that forms the border between East and West. It is open country here. On the west bank some old men were fishing and goats were feeding in the meadow. On the east bank stood a Volkspolizist with a rifle. The steel bridge across the canal had sentry houses at each end. The Western cops were laughing and joking, on the eastern side there were red slogans and a red flag. Lots of people on bicycles or on foot crossed the bridge in both directions; no one was stopped. I sat on the grass, sketching the bridge stealthily like a spy. It looked so symbolical of today's divided Germany.

I arrived at the hospital at precisely 5:30 p.m.. It is a beautiful hospital with an entrance fit for a castle. First I met Mrs. Zadek and her son who, having been born in England, claims British nationality, and who now studies medicine at Guy's Hospital in London. Then Prof. Dr. Ignaz Zadek, the internist, appeared. His father was an old SPD man and very interested in the sociological background of medicine. (His father's Christian name also was Ignaz.) By a great coincidence the Zadeks know Ma Shi-chen (Werner Ma), the Manchurian prince who was jailed by the Austrians for black marketeering after the war and who presented me with a violin when I met him in Vienna in 1949. Not only did they know him, but it turned out the violin which Ma gave me was bought by him with money that Ignaz Zadek had lent him years ago, when Ma was a student in Berlin!! I was glad when our talk turned to health provisions for workers in the time of Ignaz Zadek's father.[1]

---

[1]Ignaz Zadek senior (1856-1931) was the founder of the Association of Socialist Physicians (Sozialistischer Ärzteverein). His son, who headed the Neukölln hospital after the war, was SPD deputy in the Berlin city parliament. He died in 1955.

On my way home I drove past Buckow and again decided to stop the jeep for a walk. Buckow is a real village with ploughed fields all around and farms. Old men passed me on bicycles, and laborers and children returning from the fields in horse carriages. Some old farmers were sitting outside their cottages, smoking pipes. It had stopped raining and there was a beautiful peace and quiet.

When I got home Rena told me Carol had called. So I called her back. Jay had been at the film studio since 1 p.m. and Carol wanted to know whether I'd come with her to watch Jay perform before the camera. Of course I said yes. The studio is in Ruhleben on the Charlottenburger Chaussee. Jay had to go through several rehearsals before the scene was then shot 4 times. Gordon was there, Hanisch, Ursula Lyn (who was very nice), and a man called Fritz. Fritz, I was told, has lost his American citizenship because he broadcast for Radio Berlin during the war. Now he will never be allowed to go back to the United States. Jay wanted Carol to go to bed early so we didn't wait for him to finish. But Carol and I first stopped at the Kudamm for a "Komm morgen wieder" before going home.

10 August 1954

Today I went to the German Red Cross, Berlin Office (*Landesverwaltung*), in Bundesallee 73, where a Mr. Wittig led me into its very small archive. The only material of some interest was old numbers of the periodical *Das Rothe Kreuz*. After that I tried the Berliner Medizinische Gesellschaft in Charlottenburg, Meerscheidtstrasse 9-11, but found it no more helpful. However, the Berliner Ärztebund in Passauerstrasse 11, near the Memorial Church gave me the addresses of 2 old doctors I might look up. After lunch I went back to the Red Cross and read their old periodicals. Got home at 5 and promptly fell asleep until, suddenly, the door bell rang and there stood little Manfred with his father's 50-year-old bike. He was hungry, so I walked Manfred to Schlosstrasse, bought him a sausage and Coca-Cola from a street vendor, and sent him home.

II August 1954

Spent another morning at the archive of the German Red Cross. After lunch in Steglitz I found the Henningers had come home from their vacation. They brought me a little souvenir leather purse from Berchtesgaden made to look like a Lederhose. It still poured all day.

Interviewed Gustav Wiesner at his home in Morchinger Strasse 26 in Zehlendorf. Though we talked from 3:30 to 5:30 p.m. he was not a good interviewee, since he never stuck to one point. But I got a few interesting anecdotes from him.

Had coffee at my Stammcafé, ate a few Stullen, and then went to Gesundbrunnen (in the West sector), where the SPD women of

Prenzlauer Berg (in the Soviet sector) were holding one of their regular evenings. The meeting took place in a school building in Puttbusser Strasse and the topic of the night was "Knowledge and Truth." Miethke, the main speaker, had invited me to come. His motto, he told the audience, was August Bebel's old saying: "Socialism is the application of science to every facet of human life." We sat in a small classroom: I and about 15 women, all of them very aged. Miethke came in looking like a quack doctor and I am afraid his lecture, which lasted for $1^1/_2$ hours, sounded like it too. It started with a tirade against Christianity and the Roman Catholic Church in particular (he was fond of pathetic exclamations like "Jesus Christ is still on his way to heaven, he hasn't arrived there yet"). That turned out to be his main theme throughout the evening. Miethke ran through the entire history of Western civilization, listing all the past sins of the Church and interpreting every human misfortune (from medieval witch hunts to contemporary nazism) to forces inspired by the Church or supported by the Church. The women sat stiff and bored and in the end posed a few matter-of-fact questions like: "You say people are so short-sighted and will not live in flats with central heating. But such flats are so expensive!" In a way I was glad I had come. I suspect that the Socialist party meetings before the First World War may well have resembled tonight's event. The same ideas were certainly already current half a century ago, and from the looks of programs before 1914, many speakers must also have given what I call quack lectures. If these women ever talk on subjects like the decline of Western civilization they will probably repeat Miethke's theories as best they can, but I don't believe they they are likely to do so, nor that they really care very much about it.

Left at 9:20 p.m. and raced back to Zehlendorf to Hartel's place. Made it in half an hour as the streets were nearly deserted and the jeep was purring along beautifully. Hartel was giving a dinner party and he had told me to drop in after my SPD meeting if I could make it before 10. Among the guests were a Miss Mary Wilson, from the USIS formerly in Hong Kong, and the Cerfs, and later a Jerry something who also worked for RIAS and USIS. The conversation was very animated. There were two opposing sides, Jerry and Al on one side, Jay on the other. The Al/Jerry side contented that nazism has successfully been cut from its roots and that given a few more years it will have died out completely. Therefore the primary task of today is to fight communism and not some phantom resurgent nazism, and the West can safely go ahead with its project of establishing 15 German divisions— history will take care of burying the undemocratic Germany of yore. Against their view Jay maintained that nazism and communism are interrelated and can and should be fought together.

Hartel made a few strange remarks. In his view Prussia is still "essential for keeping order in Europe." He also argued that a

German army could not present a threat to democracy since the German officers would be trained in the U.S.A. and remain under U.S. supervision. (Yes, but how long?) Hartel spoke very optimistically about a future democratic Germany, provided Germany is absorbed in a united Western Europe. He also said the SPD was wrong in holding on to the Marxist Erfurt Programm because the world has completely changed since 1890. (How true!) Incidentally, Hartel also has the theory that Otto John may have gone to the East sector in the erroneous belief that he could land a big intelligence coup there for the West and later make a triumphant come back as a hero.

Drove the Cerfs home and had a cup of tea there. Jay and Carol assure me that people who work for the State Department show much more political sophistication than the USIS-RIAS set.

12 August 1954

Drove to Dessauer St. in Kreuzberg, where I had a very good interview with two old tailors in the rooms of the union of textile and clothing workers. One was called August Weicker (born 1874), the other Otto Kutzebach (born 1882). The history of the tailor's trade, as they told it to me, is both funny and interesting. For example, they said the confection industry began with a few shops buying up leftover scraps of material from the tailors to make a vest here or a jacket there, which explains why in the 19th century men wore such colorful suits put together from different materials.

It was lunchtime by the time I left. Still I first drove to Linden-strasse 42, one meter away from the East sector, to visit the Association of Insurance Doctors of Greater Berlin (Vereinigung der Sozialversicherungsärzte von Gross-Berlin), which is located in the Haus der Ärzte. I was well received by a Dr. Kindel, a very young man who just got his degree in economics from the FU. Like at the Red Cross, I had the honor to be the first one to use their library in ages. But there was nothing useful for me here. They have, interestingly, a few old copies of *Die Gesellschaft* edited by Hilferding dating back to the 1920s. I took notes on an article in a medical journal I found there and then left to finish reading *Das Rothe Kreuz* at the Red Cross Library.

Since it was so close to the Tiergarten, I went for a walk. At the Brandenburg Gate I saw a three-wheeled delivery van coming over from the East sector loaded with furniture. It looked like a family defecting to the West with all its belongings. I didn't know you could do this so openly.

Spent the evening with the Henningers. Nearly quarreled with them about Hitler and the Nazis. In Mrs. Henninger's eyes, Hitler's only great crime had been to persecute the Evangelical church. Otto

John, not surprisingly, was to her the eternal traitor who will always be on the lookout for a "better deal." The houses of the Nazi bosses in Berchtesgaden should not have been destroyed, she said, but left standing in all their pomp "as a reminder to the people that Hitler and his cronies had abused their tax money." I suggested to Mrs. Henninger that conducted tours through Bergen Belsen and Dachau would be more to the point. Mrs. Henninger insists she was against Hitler. One of his sins, according to her, was sending these awful workers on vacation tours on Kraft-durch-Freude ships. "The manners of these people were just abominable." Oh! — Mischa has also come back from his bike tour of $3^1/_2$ weeks.

13 August 1954

Today was Friday the 13th, but by no means an unlucky day. Went to see Dr. Walter Gaede this morning, whom Harold Hurwitz had telephoned on my behalf. He is 67 years old and lives in Wilhelmsaue 14a, Berlin-Wilmersdorf. Gaede is a philologist and Germanist, a retired schoolteacher and headmaster of a Gymnasium. Hurwitz knows him because he was a lifelong friend of Berlin's beloved socialist mayor Ernst Reuter.[1] I immediately liked this kindly, delicate old gentleman, who repeatedly excused himself for wandering off the subject. He was very anxious to help me and promised to find materials for my thesis.

Gaede told me that he knew Reuter from their student days together. When the war of 1914 broke out, Gaede, though a Socialist, became an officer in the Imperial Army while Reuter remained a simple private, a *Jäger*. One day they met in France and Gaede invited Reuter to the officers' mess in a French château. The light banter at the officers' tables quickly stopped after Reuter sat down and for the next two hours the officers listened intently to Reuter's discourse on the current world situation.

I used the opportunity to walk around in Wilmersdorf for an hour. Not unlike Charlottenburg, it reminds me more of the old Berlin as portrayed in Else Ury's novels than any other Berlin district. In a Mietshof an organ grinder was playing and a girl of about 12 was leaning in the archway listening. From a window on the upper storys, someone threw down a few coins wrapped in a piece of paper. The poor organ grinder was a cripple. While he turned the handle he raised his eyes to the windows above and around him with an imploring look that was pitiful. I also went into a junk shop in a courtyard that sold old sewing machines, grandfather clocks, suits of armor, and an old saber for only 3 marks.

In the afternoon I worked on old statistical yearbooks at the Bibliothek des Reichsversicherungsamts. In the street outside a film

---

[1]Ernst Reuter (1889-1953) was governing mayor of Berlin, 1951-53.

company was shooting a scene for some new Berlin thriller.

On the way home I thought I'd look up Herr Welle, the owner of the photo archive on Potsdamer Platz. I found him standing at the entrance of the building, calling out to the passersby like an *entraineur* outside a sleazy night club: "Come in and see this exhibition of Berlin's transformation since 1945! 30 pfennigs West or 30 pfennigs East!" What a come down for a man who before the war was an editor and a producer of cultural films!

Jay called. The man from *Life* magazine is interested in buying Jay's photos of the duel at the student fraternity and may also be interested in my drawings. Had a big dinner at the Cerfs' and did some reading there.

14 August 1954

Saturday. Esther played in my room in the morning. She took my pocket watch and asked me, "Can you cross your eyes for a whole minute?" I took her by jeep to the repair shop where her scooter and her roller skates were being fixed. Later took Carol grocery shopping and in the evening we all had dinner at Mr. and Mrs. Dennis (Reid and Betsy) in Zehlendorf. Present was also a German general Neweres, who formerly served with the German advisory team in China (1936-38) until it was recalled by Hitler. Fought in the battle of Shanghai, 1937. Expressed very right-wing opinions but was anxious to please, and assured Jay repeatedly of his very high opinion of the U.S.A.

24 August 1954

Jay and I had dinner with Hans Plehwe at the very posh Restaurant Aben on the Kudamm, where the waiters hover around you in bright red tails. Plehwe, 31 years old, is a German who speaks a flawless American-accented English without ever having been either to the States or to England. Formerly a Wehrmacht officer, he was wounded in the Russian campaign. He is now a correspondent for *Time-Life* magazine in Berlin and he borrowed my diary for a few days.

25 August 1954

The fan belt of my jeep snapped. The garage in Steglitz proposed at great expense to take the whole engine apart in order to get at the fan, but I said no. Fortunately they gave me the address of a shop in Leibnizstrasse 95, Charlottenburg, which specializes in jeeps, and there a mechanic fixed my problem in 20 minutes.

Went to the police to renew my residence permit. The officials were very courteous, but I also saw some very outlandish characters waiting on benches for residence permits. After lunch at Aschinger's, went to the civil registry office (*Standesamt*) I Berlin, Kuno-Fischer Strasse, Charlottenburg to see what information they had on working-class life. It is a very nice, friendly-looking brick building, with a public park and a small lake, the Lietzensee, behind it. I was led into a sun-lit room where I spoke with two officials, Teszmann and Kopp, both very friendly. Registry offices were introduced in 1874, they told me. Standesamt I, however, is not the Standesamt that supervises all the other Standesämter in Berlin, as I thought, but concerns itself with vital statistics for all Germany, registers marriages between foreigners, and marriages by Germans living abroad. They recommended that I visit a registry office in a working-class districts and ask to see its files.

26 August 1954

Spent the morning in Neukölln Rathaus reading on unemployment in Berlin. Then I called Janet Immerman, a former student of Carol's father, Professor William McGovern, in Chicago who had been at the Cerfs' on Sunday and who had wanted to see a real proletarian pub. I met her on the Kudamm and showed her Kreuzberg and Neukölln. But I don't think she enjoyed this trip very much. The romance of backyards and cellar dwellings didn't seem to appeal to her. As to the Bendlerstrasse, where Hitler's regime nearly was brought to fall in 1944, she decided to pass it up because she "hadn't brought her camera along." But we had one very good break. In a pub in Kreuzberg, located in a small side street, we joined a group of drinkers: a man and a woman who had started their "Bierreise" nearly 24 hours ago, namely yesterday, and were still going strong. Their aunt had joined them this afternoon. The man was an "Original." He called himself Nante, occupation: Nante, former occupation: locksmith.[1] Whenever he made a point he would lift his index finger and whistle. He wore his peaked cap the wrong way round and made tricks with it, cracked lots of jokes and drank quantities of beer. When I told him I studied history, he promptly proposed to give me a history lesson. History is divided into the history of nations, geography, and anthropology. Rome was built on seven hills. Napoleon and Bismarck were great men, they both wanted understanding between nations. Wilhelm II? I've seen him when I was a little boy in 1914. Zille? We used to paint pictures together! When I showed disbelief he ran home to fetch a few of his paintings. They were copies of postcards painted in oil on small pieces of wood, one representing Zille's favorite subject, the Restaurant "Zum Nussbaum," the other a street in a town near Bodensee. They were primitive and yet they had a certain naive charm. We

---

[1]"Nante" is the name of a popular Berlin figure created by the novelist Adolph Glassbrenner in the early 19th century.

bought both, and Janet gave me the "Nussbaum" as a present.

His wife looked very sick (she's got cancer) and had a yellowish complexion, disheveled bleached hair, and coarse, dirty hands. But also a strong and warm character, I thought. She wouldn't accept our beer until we allowed her to buy schnaps for the whole table. She felt hurt when everyone preferred my Pall Mall cigarettes to hers until I took a cigarette from her pack. "We don't take present without returning the favor as long as we can," she said. She is a home worker, making lamp shades for an electrical firm. She has worked for that firm for three years now and earns 50 to 60 marks a week. Tomorrow is delivery day, so she will stop drinking tonight to finish her work. Her husband helps making lampshades, too. But he is a do-no-good in general. He drinks up most of the wages. They have been married 3 years and this is not Nante's first marriage, of course. Janet wanted to know whether they liked Berlin or would prefer to live in West Germany. "Why should it be better over there?" Frau Krüger replied in a challenging voice. "Nee, ick bleib hier." She was born in Kreuzberg and intends to stay here too. She also expects to die soon. She is now 37 years old, her mother died of cancer at age 41, and she thinks she will *not* live as long as that. "That's why I drink so hard," she said. — The aunt was less interesting. A former factory girl (metal turner), she later became a lampshade maker like her niece. After the war she also was housekeeper for some Americans in Dahlem. Two years ago she got polio right after her husband and her daughter died. There is lots of sorrow among these people if you ask them about their lives. It was sobering to listen to the two women discussing dispassionately whether Frau Krüger's cancer had already reached the terminal stage or not.

At the beginning both Nante and the aunt declared they could understand English. So I tried slowly: "Do— you— like— beer?" A furious dispute between Nante and the aunt was the result. Nante said it meant "I should drink more beer." The Aunt thought it meant "You should drink less because of your weak heart."

I enjoyed the session immensely. Nante and I thumped each other on our backs, whistled with our fingers raised in the air, and "shared" our beer. ("Sharing" means that he drank $9/10$ of every glass and I the rest.) But while we were merry, Janet sat rather silently, though I tried to translate as many of Nante's jokes into English as I could. When we left at last, Nante suddenly grew serious and said: "You've been drinking with a simple worker, you know?" I shook his hand cordially and said, "It was a real pleasure," and I meant it. I had felt much more at ease in the pub than earlier in the afternoon when Janet and I stopped in one of the posh Kudamm cafes. Janet felt quite the reverse, I think. Nante had tried to make her talk while his wife had kept admonishing him for putting both elbows on the table so that Janet had hardly any room; his attitude was "Foreigners, sure, great. But we are people too."

27 August 1954

Nothing very exciting happened. I put in a solid day at the library of Neukölln Rathaus. Dropped in on Klaus von Wahl to have coffee on his terrace. He told me another of his many stories about theater people. Paul Hörbiger (the Austrian actor who played the house porter in *The Third Man*) was a guest of Hitler's in 1938. The party went on till the small hours of the morning, when Hitler suddenly asked his guests to see the latest newsreel in his private cinema. The newsreel however showed nothing else but what the guests had been seeing throughout the evening: Hitler, Hitler, and again Hitler. Hitler riding in a car, Hitler reviewing troops, Hitler greeting the crowds. Hörbiger (who by then was drunk) finally lost his patience and decided he'd start applauding next time Hitler's picture appeared on the screen— and did so. The other people, of course, had to follow his example out of politeness. Then, to their amazement, Hitler stood up, walked to the front of the audience and— bowed!

Later someone said to Hörbiger that Hitler's bow was no different from Hörbiger's after one of his performances. "Aber um Gottes Willen," Hörbiger protested, "doch nicht so devot, nicht so devot! Übrigens bin ich ein guter Schauspieler!"[1]

28 August 1954

Spent the day with the Cerfs. Took Carol to market in Steglitz and in the evening the three of us went to see Carl Zuckmayr's *Hauptmann von Köpenick*, with Werner Krauss in the leading role. Quite good. In the afternoon Jay and I had gone for a short bicycle ride in Dahlem and seen the Soviet city commander Dibrova and other Soviet officers arrive at the new U.S. city commander's residence, Major General George Honnen, in Pacelli Allee. We talked to the Russian driver and his comrade, peeking into their Zim limousine with its carpet-draped seats and blue curtains. The Russian driver laughed but said nothing. We went home to fetch Jay's camera and returned to stand in front of the entrance together with a young army photographer, a few German newsmen, and an honor guard wearing silver-plated helmets. But we waited in vain for we had to be back by 6 p.m. and Honnen's guests wouldn't leave. The guard of honor was pretty lax. One soldier played with his gun, some others smoked. The officer in charge didn't seem to care. He simply asked the army photographer to be their lookout so he could order his men to snap to attention when the door opened.

31 August 1954

Had gone to bed fairly early yesterday, so that I woke up before

---

[1] "Good God, but not as servile as that! Besides, I am a good actor!"

6 a.m. I heard birds chirping outside my window and the sun was just rising. I spontaneously decided that this was the ideal morning for me to observe the workers of Neukölln on their daily way to the factory. So I got up hurriedly and left before Rena could bring in my breakfast. Driving towards Neukölln I passed many people hurrying on foot with satchels, briefcases, knapsacks, tin cans and thermos flasks. Some were riding bicycles or bicycles with an auxiliary engine. There seemed to be a slight frost; it was quite chilly. I parked the jeep in Hermannstrasse and went for a long walk in direction Görlitzer Bahnhof. Actually I was surprised not to see masses of workers converging at factory gates or pouring from underground railway stations. People walked alone or in pairs, each seemingly bent on his or her own errand.

It was getting hot as the sun rose higher. I stopped at a bakery to buy two buns for breakfast. The old lady told me that she arrived each morning at 4:30 a.m. to help with the baking and that the shop usually opens by 7 o'clock. I walked as far as Görlitzer Bahnhof, which is a region still unknown to me. The station is quite big, but it has stood empty since the end of the war. There is no roof left, otherwise it looks intact. Only the layers of dust and rubbish show that it is no longer in use. On my way back I stopped at a bridge where a construction site was screened off by a wooden fence. And as I stood there, watching the fence for about 15 minutes, I saw that everyone who had to pass it stopped for a moment and peeped through a hole or a crack. Some people watched for a long time, others moved on after only a brief pause, but no one walked past.

I also saw one of the funniest advertisements painted in gigantic letters on a fire wall: "Otto Weber's Trauer-Magazin...Kann jede Dame welche farbig gekleidet eintrat, in passendem Traueranzuge verlassen."[1] I wondered when it was put up— it sounded so old-fashioned. As I sat down underneath the bridge of the elevated train to sketch it, schoolchildren stopped to peek over my shoulder.

Spent the morning working at Neukölln city archive. When I went out for lunch Fräulein Ditzner of the library, who had heard that I had a strange machine called a "jeep," asked me for a ride to Potsdamerstrasse, so I took her there. Then I went to sit at the Brandenburg Gate for a while. Saw Russian officers strolling with their girlfriends "on the other side." On our side an American MP car stood in readiness in the middle of the street as if waiting for an important visitor from the East.

Went to the Cerfs' for tea and glop (their expression for a simple supper) and did some translation work for Jay. At home I found that Mrs. Henninger had put a little cupboard for my books in my room. What a pity that my room should begin to look really nice when it's almost time for me to leave Berlin.

---

[1]"Otto Weber's magazine of mourning attire. Any lady can walk in here in a colored dress and leave properly attired for mourning."

I September 1954

Frau Schmidt called in the morning to ask me over for breakfast tomorrow. Did a hard morning's work in Neukölln going through a big batch of documents concerning the unemployment here in 1905-07. After lunch, dropped in at Frau Göldner's to say hello and "goodbye." Though I still have one month left in Berlin, I have no desire to see the Göldner family again. She gave me a cup of coffee and a piece of bread with pork dripping (the famous Berlin Schmalzbrot) and also a glass of lemon liquor. Then she showed me old photos of herself with her first and second husbands. Returned to the Rathaus and after finishing my work went for a walk in the Grunewald before turning in.

Friday, 3 September 1954

Yesterday Mama Schulz and Syke were having their breakfast in the garden. Mama Schulz once more attacked Heine "who never said one good word about Germany!" but agreed that few Germans did have an objective view about themselves as a nation, with the exception, perhaps, of the author of a "wonderful book" entitled *Deutschland, Deutschland über alles.* I was amazed to hear her say that because the only book of that title I knew was Kurt Tucholsky's, and that book is a scathing indictment of the German character. I said so. But as soon as I mentioned Tucholsky's name she blew up and spat out: "Tucholsky! That Jew! Jews are an uncreative race, they are incompetent to criticize the Germans."[1] She also complained about the Americans who in 1946 had so brutally evicted the owners of the villas here in Dahlem. The compensation they had paid had been terribly low. Syke this time played the role of appeaser and softened some of her mother's harsh words. She pointed out the Jews' contribution in music and science, and excused the American behavior as understandable after a long war.

After breakfast I worked in the Former Prussian Secret State Archive. Thanks to Director Dr. Bellé I could start right away on the old records of the former Imperial Ministry of Health. In the evening I did some translation work for Jay and spent the night at his place.

This morning, I worked at the Hauptarchiv, then drove to Kreuzberg, Dessauer Strasse, to return a pamphlet to Herr Jenny. Otto Kutzebach, the merry old tailor, was there too. He told me how he had become a member of the SPD after listening to a speech by Lily Braun, the famous woman socialist, in a pub in Naunynstrasse way back in 1905. Then drove to Rudow to meet Emil Wutzky again and noticed many U.S. Army vehicles driving around Rudow today. Ironically they drove past posters advertising the German veterans' organiza-

---

[1] Kurt Tucholsky (1890-1935), German publicist who went into exile after 1933.

tion "Der Stahlhelm." Spent the rest of the afternoon and the evening doing translation work for Jay. The Häkers and Gunar Hering were there, testing Jay's questionnaire for FDJ refugees on each other. It was a very busy place. We didn't finish till after midnight.

Sunday, 5 September 1954

Stayed home working on my notes. Esther tried to beg a jeep ride from me by using every device she knew from being cute to grabbing things from my table and refusing to give them back. My resistance broke down in midafternoon and I drove her to the corner for an ice cream cone.

Bought a *Neue Zeitung* from the young man at the corner of Schlosstrasse. We fell into conversation. He told me that the *Neue Zeitung* was the paper most widely sold in Steglitz, Zehlendorf and Dahlem, "where the better people live." *Der Telegraf*, on the other hand, was more popular in Neukölln and other working-class districts. "Oh, then I'll have to buy a *Telegraf*," I said, "since I don't belong to the better people." He gave me a quick look over (I wore dirty, creased khaki trousers and no tie), and then showed his teeth in a short, sneering laugh.

In the evening I dropped in at the Cerfs' place. Horst and Christine had been helping Jay for the last two days straightening out the German of his questionnaire and now everybody looked tired. I helped Carol bathe Randolph (which was fun), and went with Jay first to take the Häkers to Innsbrucker Platz to catch their bus to Reinickendorf, then to Kreuzberg to look for Nante. We couldn't find him, so we walked through the streets, peeping into windows and backyards and finally stopped in a pub where people were drinking, and playing cards and dice. The atmosphere was friendly and not too noisy. Some wives were present too. Jay got stuck in a corner with a man who was interested in him because he was an Ami, and I begged permission of the people around me to draw them.

Before going home we made a quick dash to the very badly destroyed area around the Alte Jakobstrasse, Berlin's old newspaper center. Jay says this is an area of vice and crime since the streets are deserted at night and many cellars underneath the rubble make perfect hideouts for criminals. We came across an old man with a stick and a flashlight who shone his torch at us and asked us what we did there in a gruffy voice. We asked him whether he was a nightwatchman but he just ordered us to move on ("Gehn Sie ruhig weiter!"). When we got back into the jeep we drove back to where he stood. Jay pulled his wallet to show his Connecticut driver's licence and said that here were his credentials, would he now tell us who he was? Jay's belligerent look and American accent plus my jeep did the trick, for the old man became very polite and admitted being a nightwatchman. There are many dubious elements in this neighborhood, he explained. Jay later said to me that he was sorry for having frightened the old man. We drove back to Dahlem where Jay and I finished off a pot of spaghetti with meatballs.

Monday, 6 September 1954

Work at the Hauptarchiv in the morning, lunch with the Cerfs, and in the afternoon coffee with Christine at the DGB Kantine in Schlüterstrasse. A certain "Manny" joined us, a big boy, former Hitler Junge, who tried to explain to us his reason for espousing pacifism with sentimental clichés like "I killed a Russian soldier on the Eastern front, yet he could have been my friend." Christine argued for defending democracy and freedom even with arms if necessary in the emphatic voluble manner she has. I stopped my car in Britz on the way home to watch people coming home from work. On the dot of 5:30 p.m. the streets suddenly became very quiet, as if a curfew were on. This is what the Germans call "Feierabend." In this rural area all the families seem to sit down for supper at the same time.

Poor Frau Henninger lost her purse to a pocket thief on Saturday when she went to the fair.

7 September 1954

Drove to the Tiergarten in the morning to get my Swiss visa. It costs nothing because there is a consular agreement between China and Switzerland dating back to 1931! In the center of town I followed two organ grinders who were making the tour of all the inner courtyards in the Hardenbergstrasse. The one played the organ and whistled the tune, the other was just a flunky who stood around to pick up the pieces of money. They told me that they lived together and rented the organ from a store. Next week, they added with a touch of pride, they will get an organ that plays the latest hit tunes.

At 11:15 I went to the Evangelischer Oberkirchenrat in Jebensstrasse 3 to look up President Dr. von Arnim, a friend of Mrs. Henninger. He gave me some addresses of old priests I might want to look up, including that of Pastor Rackwitz, West Berlin's one and only communist clergyman, who lives in Neukölln. According to Arnim, the Church has a very difficult time retaining some influence among industrial workers.

I had lunch at the Mensa Library, where I was joined by a Japanese professor from Tokyo University who spoke only a little German and a little English and sat down at my table because he thought I was Japanese. He had just been to international agricultural conferences in Copenhagen and Edinburgh. He thinks Japan needs the emperor in the same way Germany needs a Führer. Today Japan does not want to have an army any more. "What if China and the Soviet Union were to attack Japan," I asked, "would Japan not want to fight?"— "We shall stay out of the war," he answered, unperturbed.

After lunch, returned to work in the Hauptarchiv, then dropped in at the Cerfs' and stayed for tea and dinner. The jeep's starter has finally broken down and nothing Jay and a group of street boys did to help me worked. We stopped a huge Packard and asked for a push. Two American civilians got out and looked at my jeep. Then one of them exclaimed excitedly that he recognized it as the same jeep he drove in the Italian campaign in 1944!

8 September 1954

Wednesday. Went to the garage in Steglitz and found the jeep already fixed. Drove to Neukölln, first to the Rathaus and then to look up Pastor Arthur Rackwitz of the Philip Melanchton Church, Kranold Strasse 16-17, West Berlin's only communist pastor. I came unannounced and just introduced myself as a student recommended by Präsident von Arnim. Rackwitz was sitting in a large, comfortable study. He is 58 years old, a big man with much white hair and, as I soon found out, he is a very lonely man. One wall of his study was completely covered with books, mostly theological works but also Chevalier's *Clochemerle*, Stalin's *Gedanken zum Leninismus*, and a book on Mao Tse-tung. On a little table next to a couch lay Hemingway's *The Old Man and the Sea*. Through the window of his little alcove you saw the shabby front of the small, dingy working-class houses that are so predominant in this area.

Pfarrer Rackwitz did not seem to be busy. Dressed conservatively in a dark suit and black tie and slowly smoking his pipe, he sat hunched over his desk and started talking to me in a deep, melodious voice. He looked at the table top most of the time, but now and again he looked up and smiled sadly. He gave me the impression of a man making a confession but who isn't quite sure how his words are received. I sat very still and just let him talk.

Rackwitz's father was a pastor in a little town somewhere. He called himself a liberal, though in fact he stood on the side of the bourgeois state and against the workers. The young Rackwitz must have had socialist leanings from an early age; as a schoolboy he remembers slipping into a grimy local bookstore that sold SPD party literature and buying books with his paltry pocket money. Though not a socialist yet, he felt that the ideas of the Social Democrats needed to be taken seriously. This was in 1913. In 1914 he went to war as a volunteer. On the battlefield of Flanders he decided that there was no possible compromise between the teachings of Christ and soldiering. The Church saw nothing wrong with offering blessings to men going off to slaughter other men. Rackwitz however decided to quit the war—fortunately, he said, he fell ill.

After the war he became a clergyman. In 1925 he joined the Christian Socialists. He also joined the SPD, which for a pastor was nearly as unforgivable—and it did cause much uproar—as is joining the Communist party today. In 1929 he came to Berlin-Neukölln. On the personal level he got on fine with the workers, he said, but he was not successful with them as a clergyman. "The simple fact is that workers dislike the Christian Church. And the fault lies primarily with the Church, which has always sided against them." Rackwitz's popularity among the workers grew after 1933 when he joined the anti-Nazi resistance group around Otto Dibelius (after 1945 bishop of Berlin) and was thrown into Dachau concentration camp. At the end of the war he was liberated by American troops (here he gave me a queer smile). The SPD resumed its work as a legal party and he joined it. But the SPD had always struck him as too weak, too ready to make compromises. So when the Sozialistische Einheitspartei Deutschlands (or SED, the Communist party in the Soviet zone) was founded, he gladly switched his party allegiance. He is still a card-carrying member of the SED today, though he does not accept all its principles without criticism. As a matter of fact, he has many quarrels with the Party. The SED wants him to leave the Church or face expulsion from the Party. But he knows it will not do such a thing because having a communist priest in West Berlin is a valuable propaganda asset for the East. The Evangelical church, too, tolerates him to prove that it stands above politics. The American authorities have repeatedly asked for his removal but the Church authorities always refused. (Bischof Dibelius once said to Rackwitz: "My dear old fellow, you are not without your prejudices." Whereupon Rackwitz had answered: "My dear Bishop, if 99 clergymen are prejudiced in favor of the bourgeoisie, let one clergyman be prejudiced in favor of the workers!")

Rackwitz's situation today seems to me quite sorry. Among his congregation of about ten thousand churchgoers all the workers are against him. They will no longer visit him in his home because he is SED. I asked Rackwitz what he would do if all the working people rejected communism. "You can't force communism on the people," he answered, "but you can still teach and enlighten them." Rackwitz regularly goes to the East sector to attend Party meetings, but these meetings more often than not end in quarrels. For example, the Party would ask him to give a talk on Christianity and social justice, and he would say: "Yes, I'll talk about it if you let me talk about Christian love and Christian humility also." So they prefer that he not talk at all. He does not think the SED is bad, only foolish. And the Russians exert too much influence over East German communism. The method which the Soviets used in Russia may have worked fine over there and seem to have produced a wonderful new society where people love their work and know they are bringing about a better future for all mankind. But the same methods won't work in Germany.

Rackwitz also said he cannot denounce the horrors of nazism knowing that similar things are happening under communism. Only the horrors under communism are aberrations that need not be! Communism is a radical form of Christianity, down to and including the principle of loving your enemy. Because of the mistakes made by the Russians and the stupidity of the SED, the chances for communism in Germany today are very slim. Communism no doubt will triumph eventually, but he unfortunately has no means to help bring this about. Maybe he will write a book on "the political consequences of Christianity" in which he will argue that the only solution for the problems of the world lies in Christian communism.

I asked him his opinion of Martin Niemöller: "Ich freue mich über ihn" (It makes me happy), Rackwitz answered a bit cryptically. True, Niemöller once was a ruthless U-boat commander, but you can't blame a man forever for the sins of his youth. He is really for peace now and for international understanding. Rackwitz agrees with Niemöller that West Germany is beset by resurgent nazism and he wants EVG to fail in order to prevent the return of militarism. In his view, neither West Germany nor East Germany are free countries.

Finally, Rackwitz told me he thinks highly of Chinese communism, and as I took my leave he advised me to return to China. I left him wondering whether everything he had told me about himself had been entirely true. Do I respect him as an idealist or do I feel sorry for him as a failed existence?

After lunch I went to visit the Tabor Community in Kreuzberg, near Schlesisches Tor. Drusedau, the Superintendent, was away on a holiday, so I spoke with Pfarrer Schiller, an old man who had once traveled to South America. He offered me a pear and talked to me for a while about the workers' attitude towards the Church. "The Church has failed to take good care of the workers," was his basic conclusion.

Later this afternoon I got terribly soaked in a big thunderstorm which caught me quite far away from my jeep, near Buckow. I saw an MP jeep which had rescued a cyclist by letting him ride under the canvas roof while one soldier towed his bicycle alongside. I myself was besieged by 4 village girls who wanted to be taken to the local cinema. This is the third big storm this week. I raced home to change my drenched clothes and then went to the Cerfs' to take Carol to see *Johnny Belinda* at the Filmbühne am Steinplatz.

IO September 1954

In the morning I had an interview with Sozialpfarrer Dr. Harald Pölchau in Zehlendorf, Am Heidenhof 30. A very interesting man in his 50s, who talked to me about his efforts to win the workers for the Evangelium. Three years ago he brought together about 500 workers from all over Berlin who were true Christians and asked them to spread Christianity among their colleagues in the factories. He gave up when he found out that Christian workers are not accepted as comrades by other workers but seen as members of the bourgeoisie. Now he has theologians working in the factories for half-year periods instead, and they are much more effective. They take workers to the cinema, to the theater and to concerts or go with them on hiking tours. Sooner or later they find occasions to discuss with them such things as literature, art, and of course religion. I am to meet two of these theologians tomorrow, and get the address of one old Christian worker.[1]

In the afternoon interviewed Pfarrer Bleier in Charlottenburg, who looks like a kindly, pot-bellied country pastor. Pfarrer P. Bleier is the "socialist priest" of the Trinitatis community in Charlottenburg since 1915 and lives in Arco Strasse 1. He joined the SPD in 1920. He told me that he had testified in court on behalf of the artist Georg Grosz when the Nazis put Grosz on trial (later the Nazis made Bleier pay for his temerity), which I thought funny because Pfarrer Bleier looks just like a Grosz caricature of the well-nourished bourgeois shopkeeper.

Before my visit to Bleier I had gone to the French consulate for a transit visa because my ship next month will leave from Cherbourg. I was a little early and the consulate was still closed. I saw a woman come up the stairs. She looked very tired, had red eyes (as if she had cried) and immediately started talking to me (thinking I surely came from Indochina and so must know French). She is a Parisian newspaper vendor, it turned out, 32 years old, of Russian origin but a French citizen by marriage to a French peasant son and now she no longer speaks Russian. Ruth Jardot is her name, born in Mannheim, and, as she proudly told me "a partisan of the communists." But "I have done something stupid" (j'ai fait une bêtise), she confided to me, sniffling. Because her husband's family and her own parents disapproved of her politics she had decided to run over to the "democratic side" as a political refugee. The Soviet consulate in Paris gave her a permit to travel to Leipzig in East Germany to visit the fair there. But instead of going to Leipzig she had taken a train to East Berlin and reported to the police as a political refugee. Three days they had kept her there, interrogating her first at the police station for $2^1/2$ hours (she thinks that was very long) and then in some ministry. Finally she was told to leave East Berlin because she could not prove that she had supported communism all her life...she had never joined the Party. Now she must go back to Paris to ask the French Communist party for an affidavit, but since she has no money she hopes the French consulate will pay for her trip.

---

[1]Harald Pölchau belonged to the Kreisau circle in the anti-Nazi resistance. As chaplain of Tegel prison he attended to many condemned resistance people in their last hours.

A pathetic case. Madame Jardot wore a coarse corduroy jacket and no stockings and her fingernails were dirty. She chatted with me for a while. She hates Germans ("Comme je déteste cette race!") including the East Germans and she wants to live in Poland, Bulgaria, or Hungary. To prove to me the evils of capitalism, she took out an old, dirty clipping from *Humanité* telling the story of some workers who were cheated out of half of their wages by a French factory owner. I asked her whether she hated all bourgeois irrespective of their personal character (her answer was "Oui!"), and whether she would prefer a dishonest Communist to an honest bourgeois? "Mais il n'y a pas de communistes malhonnêtes!" (Dishonest Communists don't exist!), she simply replied. Such people would not be admitted into the Party. I asked her whether she would approve of children denouncing their parents and sending them to jail ("Ah, non!") as they do in Red China ("Ça m'étonne!— I can't believe it!"). England to her was not a democracy since she has a royal house. I did not bother to ask her what she thought of the United States. But I did tell her that I had studied in England and was now a student in America and that if I now returned to China my previous studies in the West could be held against me. This seemed to perturb her. I also told her of my visits to factories in Berlin and of the social provisions that the workers get from the employers and the city. That must be in East Berlin, she exclaimed. No, I said, here in West Berlin. She was perplexed by that, and probably wondered whether I was telling her the truth.

Poor Madame Jardot is incredibly naive and ill-informed. When the consul called her into the office I waved to her and said "bonne chance." But I don't really know what a "bonne chance" for her means. A safe return to Paris? Finding refuge in Eastern Europe?

Saturday, II September 1954

Went in the morning to the meeting of the Evangelische Akademie Berlin, near the Reichskanzlerplatz. It took place in a beautiful villa belonging to the Workers Welfare (Arbeiterwohlfahrt). About 30 people were there, mostly theologians but also teachers from various professional schools. I was duly put in my place by a pastor who approached me as I entered the house, offered me his hand and smiled: "You must be the young man Pölchau told us about, the one who didn't know the meaning of the word *Numinose!*" I only stayed to listen to the talk by Vikar Mundt, a young theologian, who talked about his observations as an apprentice at the Borsig machine works. What he had to say was not particularly profound, and Pölchau later got up and more or less plainly said so. The ensuing debate was quite lively. People talked very openly, and didn't bother to make polite compliments to each other.

Drove to Dahlem to take Carol and Randolph to the market near

Kaufhaus Held. After a quick lunch, we all went to Wannsee, where Jay had rented a Scherenkreuzer sailing boat. Ulli Morgenschein and Wolf Müller had come on their motorbike and we had a wonderful trip on the lake with a stiff breeze yet plenty of sunshine. After dinner, did some translations for Jay.

Monday, 13 September 1954

Since this is the last week that I shall have my jeep, I plan to make all my remaining visits in the next few days. First I tried my luck with the Superintendantur of Kirchenkreis Berlin II in Alt-Moabit, but with little success. So I decided to give up further inquiries into the religious life of workers and drove to Utrecht Strasse 27 in the Wedding to visit the Touristen Verein "Die Naturfreunde," an old socialist hiking club. I was introduced to the chairman, Franz Maspfuhl, who lives in Brüsseler Strasse 14. He readily let me interview him when I told him the former Reichstagspräsident Löbe had sent me, and though the interview was short, it was very fruitful. The workers' hiking movement was apparently not the politically innocent recreational undertaking that I thought. Maspfuhl is a printer by occupation.

I also met Richard Bowitz, the manager of the Touristenverein, who lives in Utrecht Strase 27. I spoke to him for about quarter of an hour sitting in his bedroom. He was quite nice, but I didn't want to stay long since a family party was under way in the living room next door and I didn't want to keep him from his guests.

I had had lunch in Müllerstrasse and also took a long walk through the Wedding district's "Afrikanisches Viertel." It is not especially colorful. Much open space, many new housing projects and relatively few people in the streets. It rained. People look poor, but not downright miserable as they do in the Soviet sector of the Wedding. I stopped the car near the sector boundary and following a sudden impulse, I stashed all my notes and identification cards under the seat, locked the jeep, and walked across the border into the East sector.

It was a wonderful walk. I changed DM 1.15 West for a 5-mark bill (East) and had a great time. I crossed the sector boundary near Nordbahnhof, bought an ice cream cone (rather fluffy) for 15 pfennig to give myself a particularly innocent air. Near the railway station loudspeakers blared out communist songs, but the choir singing was good. To my astonishment this time I did not get a nervous feeling in the stomach as on previous occasions. I felt perfectly at ease. I entered a tobacco shop to buy cigarettes (they are so much cheaper here than in the West), but when I saw a sign asking all customers to produce their identity cards, I quickly changed my mind. Seeing that the shopkeeper did not sell any pipes, I asked for pipe cleaners, was told he had none, and thus made a graceful exit. (Later I bought a pipe for only M 1.95 (East) in another shop. I told the saleswoman I had left my passport in my hotel room and was too lazy to fetch it. And she let me off.)

Across the street was a "Tageskino," a movie house where, as in the United States, you can walk in any time. I bought a ticket and a program for 1.35 marks and saw an old film made by Helmut Käutner and based on Gottfried Keller's 19th-century story *Kleider machen Leute*. I guess it is about as tendentious as is Dickens' *A Christmas Carol* or *Oliver Twist*, and the film was really quite good. According to the previews some Western films are shown here too (for example *Moselfahrt aus Liebeskummer*, which West Berlin cinemas showed one or two months ago). Before the main film was shown, there was a short satirical skit on bureaucracy called *Das Stacheltier*. The newsreel showed the Leipzig fair, Otto Grotewohl making a speech, horse racing in East Germany (horse racing in a socialist state?) and a report on the suicide of President Vargas of Brazil. The pictures shown were the same as those shown in Western cinemas, only the commentary was different: here the public was told Vargas was the victim of American imperialist plotting and that the new president is a puppet of U.S. dollar imperialism. The scene showing soldiers guarding the American embassy was explained as troops holding back angry workers bent on venting their fury against the Americans.

I left the cinema at about 6 p.m. and started walking through the side streets. Fascinating little crooked streets with small, curved houses, and picturesque pubs. The streets crawling with Zille-type urchins. It just itched in all my fingers to draw these people and their houses but I had left pencil and notebook in my jeep. The poor people in East Berlin (and who is not poor here?) seem so much more miserable than in West Berlin, but the setting in which they move is much more colorful. Appropriately enough, I found the Zille Park here in the middle of all these drab tenement houses. On a small piece of greenery a stone figure of Zille, sketchbook in hand, is surrounded by dozens of little children.

It is not difficult to see how Zille got children to pose for him in the Wedding. In Ackerstrasse a group of tots looked at me curiously, so I said "Tag," and immediately they all came running after me. I told them I was Chinese (puzzled looks), whereupon one small girl, divining that Chinese must be a very odd language, asked me to say something "differently" ("Sag' mal was auf anders"). Then they ran after me, wanting 20 pfennigs. They were not begging, for the 2 girls who asked me were comparatively well dressed and they were beaming at me as if doing me a great favor. I gave them my last 5 pfennig piece and they disappeared in a bakery.

In fact, not long before that I had gone into a bakery myself to buy a crumpet. Suddenly I was greeted by no one else but Frau Hubert from the SPD Frauensekretariat, whom I had interviewed in West

Berlin. "Ja, was machen Sie denn hier?" (What are you doing here?), she asked. She was just making the rounds of all her friends, distributing illegal Western newspapers to them which she carried in a big black bag. Her son also carried a briefcase stuffed with Western newspapers. So I went along with them for a while, climbing staircases and slipping forbidden literature under kitchen doors.

Intermezzo in the Ackerstrasse. A woman shouting after a man: "Das ist meine Wohnung, ist das klar? Von mir aus kannste weiter herumhuren, aber in meine Wohnung kommste nich mehr!"[1]

On a housewall, I saw the remains of a Soviet military order dated 17 June, 1953.

14 September 1954

I spent this morning in Gruntaler Strasse 5, which is a trade school for electricians. I was introduced to three teachers, Herr Botzelmann, Herr Rjosk, and a Herr Brennecke. Botzelmann told me that the Nazis forced him to break an engagement to a Jewish girl but that he was lucky and finally married her in 1945. Herr Rjosk offered me an apple and promised me some old catalogues of trade schools for workers. Brennecke was an 82-year-old artisan, anti-SPD and also suspicious of me. Afterwards I walked around in the Gesundbrunnen area. Oddly enough, it reminded me of the miserable condition of the poor in wartime Chungking.

15 September 1954

A very busy day. I started off by visiting a large consumer cooperative, the Berliner Genossenschaft in Germaniastrasse, Tempelhof. This is a big building complex with lots of warehouses, a bread factory, and busy with the traffic of lorries and delivery vans. I spoke with some officials who promised me materials on the history of the workers' cooperative movement by tomorrow. I also called on the Catholic church authorities in Stresemannstrasse in Kreuzberg where I was given the address of Pater Klausener, the son of Ministerialdirigent Dr. Erich Klausener who was shot by the Nazis in 1934. Maybe he could help me with information on catholic workers in Berlin, they said.

I went to the Möckernstrasse to look up Frau Ida Wolf, the chairwoman of the Workers' Welfare Agency (Arbeiterwohlfahrt).[2] She is a small but stout woman with a strong face and huge, dark eyes. She patted me on the shoulder like a schoolmistress patting a good pupil, and told me she was very pleased that I was interested in the Arbeiterwohlfahrt. I was then lectured on the history of this or-

---

[1]"This is my home, understand? You can whore around as much as you want for all I care, but don't you ever come into my home again!"
[2]Ida Wolff (1893-1966) held the title of city elder of Berlin.

ganization which, she said, began as a volunteer commission to combat the abuse of child labor (Kinderschutzkommission) half a century ago. We were joined by a Herr Protz who told me about the Arbeiterwohlfahrt's activities since the end of the war. It also operates— illegally— in East Berlin and in the Soviet zone.

I also found the main office of the Arbeiter-Samariter Bund in Joachimsthaler Strasse 41, near Bahnhof Zoo. This is a socialist parallel organization to the German Red Cross, also dating from the turn of the century, which the workers founded because they considered the Red Cross under the patronage of the empress too far engaged on the side of the employers in the class struggle. A Herr Schock, a bit young and timid, gave me the issues of the ASB's periodical publication for 1910-13 to thumb through, and his secretary gave me a cup of Nescafé.

After lunch at Aschinger's I met a Mr. John Flachmeyer at the office of *Time-Life* magazine on Kurfürstendamm 12. Flachmeyer (a former U-boat commander in the German navy) told me *Life* magazine might be interested in my drawings of the student fraternity duels.

Had tea with the Cerfs. Jay has been to RIAS and Peter Herz has got him some FDJ high school boys from Kladow for tomorrow to serve as guinea pigs for his questionnaire. I went on to visit Herr Rjosk in Alte Allee 14-16, Berlin-Eichkamp, to ask him questions about trade schools for working-class boys. But he mainly wanted to talk about his personal life. He told me that he had joined the NSDAP in 1942, largely under the social pressure of his neighbors and colleagues in the small town where he worked as a teacher in a trade school (*Berufsschullehrer*). This Party membership caused him much difficulty after the war. For a time he worked as a cow attendant on a farm, later as an unskilled factory worker. It has taken him close to eight years to resume his career as a teacher, and he only got this nice modern flat with piano and radio four weeks ago. To supplement his income he wrote two textbooks in his spare time this year. I found him not a very intelligent, but certainly a resourceful man.

In the evening I was invited to supper with Frau Trapp. Her nephew Günther was there, a young student of physics who wants to become an atomic scientist and strongly sympathizes with Anglo-Saxon ideas of liberty (he spoke fondly about a brief visit to England and Scotland), and a hot-headed, slightly crippled Frau Dr. Höhlmann, who is a judge at the labor arbitration court (*Arbeitsgericht*). It was a very lively evening, filled with heated political discussion. I opposed Höhlmann's peremptory assumption that all the Russian atrocities in Germany, which she described as "genocide," took place with the foreknowledge and so with the approval of the Americans, and that the U.S. had a business interest in the postwar partitioning of Vietnam. But it was fascinating to listen to the two women tell about their resistance work in the Third Reich. Höhlmann worked in a publisher's firm that employed almost exclusively people who were in trouble with the Nazi regime. These people were used by the anti-Nazi resistance for small but nonetheless important functions like carrying messages camouflaged as greetings from Mr. So-and-So to Mr. So-and-So. They provided that essential communications network between the highly placed government officials, lawyers, doctors, and also Army officers (she mentioned no workers, I noted) who sought ways of overthrowing the Hitler regime.

I asked Frau Höhlmann whether she would have helped the Allied cause by sabotaging the German war effort had she concluded that the Nazi Government could not be overthrown in any other way. Her answer was a categorical no. "This would have hurt our own boys." She also said that the atrocities in the concentration camps were known only to a minority of people, namely to higher ranking Nazis and to certain people in the Resistance. The average German would have refused to believed it.

Frau Trapp had not directly worked in the Resistance, though many of her friends did. As a prominent SPD woman she was too closely watched by the Gestapo and her participation would have jeopardized many an underground undertaking. But she told us how some factory managers improved the work conditions for foreign slave laborers during the war by calling on the factory inspectorate to step in and enforce certain work laws. In this connection Frau Trapp visited penitentiaries (where labor conditions for inmates differed little from those in concentration camps) and also factories around Berlin using women prisoners. Conditions had been so abominable that often the management agreed with the factory inspectors that shorter hours, better washing facilities, and bigger food rations were absolutely mandatory. But their efforts more often than not failed in the face of SS opposition. In one workshop employing only women Trapp saw an SS woman whipping the working women and cursing them. She impulsively tried to intervene but in the last minute was held back by the manager: "Wollen Sie Ihr Leben riskieren?" (Do you want to risk your life?), he whispered to her.

16 September 1954

This morning I was so tired I slept till 9 a.m., then raced to the GVG (Grosse Verbrauchs Genossenschaft, or Grand Comsumers' Cooperative) Berlin to meet Messrs. Pump, Lips, and Jürgeit, three members of the Aktiver Vorstand (executive committee?). We had a very lively session that lasted all morning. I was treated to "home made" (i.e., coop-made) wine, cheese, sandwiches, and cigarettes and later had to enter my name in a guest book. Lips is a former Wehrmacht captain, of bourgeois origin and on the extreme right wing of the SPD.

After lunch in Gesundbrunnen, looked up Horst Häker because he lives practically next door to two persons whom I wanted to interview. Horst had just come home from teaching school and was making himself lunch in the kitchen. (I've never seen a man doing household chores in Berlin, come to think of it. Horst belongs to a generation that is becoming more democratic.) He accompanied me to Herr Maronde, a Christian worker, and to Vikar Mundt, but both of them were complete flops as interviewees.

Then I took the U-Bahn from Seestrasse and went into the Soviet sector, back once more to Nordbahnhof. Alas, I came too late to see the Zille festival, but I nevertheless enjoyed my walk immensely. It was late and raining softly. The street lights were dim. Very shabbily dressed people were rushing home from work. I saw no Vopos in this part of town, and scarcely any propaganda slogans. Only dark, winding, sinister looking streets with cobblestones glistening in the rain. Coarse laughter emanated from a dark doorway and an old man with a limp chased all the women in the street, sending them scurrying off with screams. I could imagine myself walking through Dickensian London. I bought cigarettes and a copy of *Neues Deutschland* in a dimly lit store and enquired about the Zille festival. The shopkeeper told me to go and ask in the information office (*Aufklärungslokal*) in the Ackerstrasse not far from his shop, which is a communist agency for the "enlightenment" of politically inept comrades. I went there and peeped through the window. It was dark inside with only a small lamp burning on a table. But there were people inside engaged in an animated discussion. I did not dare go in for fear I might be asked to show identification papers, so I went on, up a very sloped street lined with tall, old houses on one side and piles of war rubble on the other: this was the Veteranenstrasse with the Zionskirche on top of the hill.

I entered a small pub to have a sausage and a bowl of soup. At the entrance a young lad was sleeping with his head on the table. At another table two men were arguing loudly over the merits of buying on the instalment plan. The younger of the two cautioned against it because you run the risk of defaulting on your payments when you incur "other obligations that you cannot openly admit to the authorities." He was asked to explain this cryptic remark, but he refused. Three very grimy men came in and sat down at my table. They ordered beer and schnaps, and each time they downed a glass of schnaps they first rapped the table in unison with their knuckles. So I asked them why they did that. "Schnaps is dead matter," was the prompt reply of the oldest of the three. Maybe he meant that rapping on the table would wake it up? Soon we were all chatting together. I was amazed at the self-assurance of these men, their frankness and fearlessness. Here I was, an obvious foreigner smoking an East German cigarette and reading a communist paper, and they started talking against the regime in front of me! The oldest man told of a drinking bout in the West sector not long ago during which, he claimed, he drank 3 bottles of cognac. "Western schnaps is better than what we have here," he said. "If you but drink 5 to 6 glasses over here you end up serving 15 years in the penitentiary."— "Why is that?" I asked naively. "Because when you are drunk you tell the truth," was his reply, "and that is not what is wanted here. In the DDR only drunkards and children tell the truth."

Since I saw their political views were pro-West, I admitted to them that I studied at a Western university. They nodded approval.

Then they went on to criticize the Volkspolizei. These people have everything, they complained: free public transportation, free use of telephones, etc. And what do they do? Precisely nothing. "Had I been thought politically reliable," said one man who had long white hair and penetrating eyes, "I too would have wanted to become a policeman." Their next criticism was directed at the socialist style of production, which they thought so very inefficient. The Leipzig fair is nothing but eyewash, according to them. None of the things exhibited there can actually be bought. A new car design seen last year is still not in production. Two years ago the old man had made a down payment on a new "Vulkanisiermaschine" for repairing rubber tires in his workshop. He has so far neither seen the machine nor got his money back. "Your order could not be met," he sarcastically quoted a letter he received from the firm, "due to *over*production."

It turned out that the three men at my table were self-employed artisans, hard-working and— to my surprise— religious. The oldest man owns a small tire repair shop around the corner. The man with the white hair owns a tractor which he uses to provide transportion jobs for people. The third man was his partner and tractor driver. They work from 6:30 a.m. till about 10 p.m. almost every day. For the last 4 weeks they have not even taken a rest on Sundays and have hardly seen their families. "Sure, we are independent," one of them said to me, "but we must work very long hours if we want to earn enough to live." (Each of them makes about 1,000 marks a month.) Often they go to bed too tired even to wash up. The oldest man, who is 65, is a Roman Catholic. He never wanted to join the SPD or the trade union movement. "Nischt mit Politik!" To him the Roman Catholic church was the foundation of his outlook on life, and the white haired man, who was Protestant, likewise assured me that religious faith was stronger than any political conviction. Hitler was defeated because he turned against the people's religion, including the Jewish religion. They had a heated debate on art too. A fourth man, who joined them for a short while told about the art objects he had seen in a castle in Mannheim and then the old man talked to me about the architectural marvels of Würzburg.

They invited me to watch them repair the tire of a tractor in their workshop, which was situated in a small cellar around the corner from the pub, lit only by a naked electric bulb. I left them after first enquiring about the Zille festival. "I have seen it," the old man replied, "it was wonderful. Unfortunately this has been the last one."

I got back to the Western sector without incident, though I did steal a communist paper flag from a kiosk on the U-Bahn station platform, which was almost totally deserted. Very stupid of me, of course, for had I been caught it would have meant great trouble. I dropped over at the Cerfs' after that. Jay was just back from running interviews on FDJ boys in RIAS. He said they were wonderful boys.

17 September 1954

A full day. At 9:30 in the morning I met Horst Häker outside the DGB offices in Schlüterstrasse. We went to see Pietsch and had a delightful conversation with him. Opa Pietsch tried to get me in touch with Senator Kreil, a Catholic who is well informed on Christian unions. We also talked about China which Pietsch wants to see once more before he dies. I am invited to his home for coffee on Sunday week.

In the Möckernstrasse Herr Protz lent me 2 small pamphlets on the Kinderschutzkommission of 1903. I tried to interview a Herr Reuschler in Moabit, a Christian worker, but he was not in. A Pfarrer Holzmann of the Evangelische Gemeinde in Charlottenburg tried to tell me that there had been no Socialist party in Germany before 1914! Finally, after lunch I met Kaplan Klausener in the Morus-Verlag, Arnimallee 11. Klausener is the editor of the clerical paper that the Roman Catholics publish here. A very nice, energetic young priest, who was all smiles, dashing around all the time to find me materials. In the end he asked the Morus Verlag to give me as a present a book, Ernst Thrasolt, *Eduard Müller, der Berliner Missionsvikar.*

Monday, 20 September 1954

Went to Reinckendorf to visit Horst and Christine. They served me a delicious Wiener Schnitzel. Then Horst came with me to interview Fritz Maronde, a Christian worker recommended to me by Pölchau because he is one of the few who still believes in the monarchy. ("The Kaiser?", Maronde said at one point, "he personnifies the divine order!") Maronde was exceedingly friendly compared to last time. He smiled and gave me short and precise answers, so that these $1^1/_2$ hours turned out to be most profitable.

Afterwards, Horst took me to Lindenweg 38a, the home of Christine's parents because they wanted to meet me, and to interview Christine's aunt, Frau Schulz, who was a factory girl at the AEG for 40 years. The

interview with Else Schulz was also quite good. True, Christine later
told me, Tante Else has a very strong sense of family loyalty. That's
why she hadn't told me that her father had cursed the Church all his
life, and that her whole family was very poor. (To me Else merely said,
"We were not rich but there was enough to live on.") We had coffee
and cakes, and then, to my great pleasure, Christine's mother
allowed me to help at the counter of their little drug store. I sold 4
sweets to a little boy for 5 pfennigs. Other customers were more
difficult because they asked for particular articles by their brand
names, and I didn't not know whether they wanted soap, tooth paste,
medicine, or something else. After this amusing interlude we got still
more Stullen to eat and looked at family pictures of the Häker family
before going on to Prinzenallee.

At Prinzenallee the Sozialistische Deutsche Studenten were holding a meeting in the same Jugendheim where Jay and I had met FDJ
youths during the Whitsuntide rally. The boys and girls whom I met
today looked rather rough. They were not students but young
workers, who (Christine later said to me) felt shy in the presence of
a foreigner like me. There was not much talk; only a movie was
shown. I invited the Häkers to coffee in a nearby pastry shop. I was
interested to hear Horst say at one point that the ideal country in the
eyes of a German liberal today is Sweden, followed closely by
England. What about America, I asked? "Very dark grey, to say the
least," was his answer.

21 September 1954

Spent the morning with Jay in the Friesenstrasse police office,
transferring ownership of the jeep to him. The afternoon was spent
in the Hauptarchiv. On my way home I noticed for the first time on
a telephone pole outside the Steglitz Rathaus a sign with a wreath,
reading "On 24th April 1945 a German soldier was hanged here by
inhumane National Socialists." And walking home from the S-Bahn
station I marveled how much reconstruction work has been accomplished in Birkbuschstrasse over the past few months. There are
things you don't see when you drive by in a car.

22 September 1954

Worked in the archives, then made a visit to Prälat Adolph in
Arnimallee 11, to find out more about the Catholic church and the
workers. I was a bit astonished at how little the good Prälat knew
about the labor question. After some general remarks about the state
of the world today, he made the pronouncement that "History is the
greatest power on earth, no one can resist it."— "What about God?"
I asked, thinking to give him a cue, "cannot God shape history?"—
"God also is in History," was the answer. When I asked more

questions along this line he qualified himself: "God plays a guiding role in determining the course of history. We do not know why he allowed Hitler to come to power but we know that His ways always serve an ultimate end that is good." At this point I asked what ultimate end God has in mind: Is He shaping history to benefit mankind or is there a higher good yet? "Partly to benefit mankind," the Prälat said. "And the other part?" I insisted. "Maybe to benefit the angels," he suggested.

This afternoon I was stopped in the street by 2 men named Müller and König who want to film me tomorrow for a documentary film, *Geburt der Vernunft*, which deals with the international exchange of students. Dinner with the Cerfs. Peter Herz had also been invited but he didn't turn up.

23 September 1954

It's already becoming miserably cold in Berlin. My fingers are stiff and it rained on and off all day. I was filmed on the sidewalk in Steglitz this morning and was paid 5 marks just for standing there with a load of books in my arm.

Interviewed Dr. H. Brauweiler of the Katholisches Arbeiter Sekretariat, in Nymphenburgerstrasse 9, Schöneberg, at 11 a.m. He lives in a spacious, old-fashioned Berlin *Wohnung* and told me some very interesting facts about the Catholic workers' movement in Berlin before 1914. Had lunch nearby and spent the afternoon in the Hauptarchiv. Got sopping wet and cold waiting for a tramway to go home. Rena made a fire in my room. Sitting over my books wearing 2 sweaters and munching bread and apples as my frugal supper, I felt as if I were back in the good old November days when I first got to Berlin. The crackle of the fire made me think of the approach of Christmas. It has almost been a full year.

24 September 1954

Friday. I got up early and went by tram to the labor arbitration court (Arbeitsgericht) of Schöneberg, in Babelsbergerstrasse 14-16. Frau Dr. Höhlmann had seen to it that I could be present at three different trials. Many cases like the ones I observed were being heard throughout the building in little rooms resembling schoolrooms. Very few people attended as spectators. Where I was, room 111, the plaintiff and the defendant each had 2 lawyers. A judge presided, assisted by 2 assessors (*Beisitzer*), and one recorder (*Protokollistin*). A bailiff (*Gerichtsdiener*) was there too. The proceedings were pretty informal. The judge and the Protokollistin always wore gowns and caps, the lawyers only sometimes. People stood up when the judge and his Beisitzer entered the room and when he read the verdict. The judge usually urged both parties to come to a settlement (*Vergleich*); failing that he withdrew with the Beisitzer and not long afterwards returned with a verdict. When the verdict was read out the judge stood with his cap on and everyone else in the room also had to stand. Immediately afterwards the judge sat down and read out an explanation of his verdict. The atmosphere was matter-of-fact, serious, and calm. Every verdict was pronounced as emanating from the will of the people ("verfügt und anerkannt im Namen des Volkes").

The first case I heard was that of a tailor who was suing his firm. The tailor had made a number of coats for a clothing firm, but the firm had refused to accept them because they were too small. The case was adjourned because several witnesses had failed to show up. The second case was against the leader of the RIAS dance band, who was accused of witholding payment from his musicians. He lost. The third case was that of a young employee, Schneider by name, who had suffered an automobile accident a year ago and whose employer, the grocer Malone, refused to pay him the regular 6 weeks' wages for invalidity as laid down by law on the grounds that Schneider himself had caused the accident by drinking. The judge urged a "Vergleich," but on the stubborn refusal of the grocer, finally sentenced him to pay the 6 weeks' wages plus the cost of the proceedings.

25 September 1954

My days in Berlin are almost over. I'm leaving in about a fortnight and without a jeep and with plenty of books still to read I doubt whether I'll meet many more people or see much more of Berlin. After a morning spent in the Hauptarchiv, went home to find my room full of smoke because the new stove wasn't working properly and I had to cough a lot. In the end I had to leave my room. Went to Steglitz to see a movie (awful wartime propaganda about fighting Japanese in the Philippines) and had dinner at the home of Otto Brinkmann in Sodenerstrasse 38, Berlin-Wilmersdorf. The Brinkmanns' little daughter was there too. We had a good old-fashioned Berlin "Abendbrot" with beer, a nice informal conversation, and finally listened to some records (*Tosca, Heimatlieder*).

29 September 1954

I haven't kept my diary for the last few days. Without a car and going no further every day than to the archive in Dahlem (where my work is practically finished), the Innere Mission, and the Free University, life seems pretty uneventful. Yesterday visited Klaus von Wahl. There was a movie actress there, Vera Friedmann, who is married to an American FBI man, and Eckhard Duchs, another actor whom I already met at the party in Wannsee several weeks ago. They left soon, and I spent the rest of the afternoon listening to Klaus telling me, in his masterly way, of his experiences in the German Army, first as an ensign (*Fähnrich*), then as a prisoner of the Russians. His best story: a conceited German officer was instructing

Klaus and other recruits how to throw hand grenades. This officer was a pest because of his verbosity. On this occasion he talked too long after pulling the fuse. Off the grenade went, the officer was dead, and the reaction of the boys who were lying in the trench was..."Ha!" (What a relief). Had supper with Klaus.

After the archives went to visit the Cerfs. Carol was slightly ill. Had dinner and left early. Jay drove me home, taking some detours through the streets of Schöneberg and Steglitz. Many candles were burning in the windows in all the streets in memory of the death at 7 p.m. one year ago today of Ernst Reuter, Berlin's beloved lord mayor in the most difficult years immediately after the war. The DGB and the Berlin Senat had both asked the population to show their solidarity with Reuter's democratic ideals by this gesture. We stopped at the gas station where the attendant (an active SPD man and trade unionist) spoke highly of Reuter. By contrast the new mayor, Schreiber, is a "reactionary nonentity." Jay and I stopped at my Stammcafé. The proprietress here was anti-Reuter. There were candles in the window, but she told us, "I didn't put them there. The girl did this to give the place a Christmas-like air!" There were only two other guests in the cafe, an older lady and a younger one. The older one challenged the proprietress on account of her remarks about Reuter. Jay and I also didn't like the proprietress: she claimed to be English (?) but spoke English with an awful accent, and her views seemed like those of an unreconstructed *Volksgenossin*. When I got home I noticed the Henningers also had no candles in the window, but Frau Henninger said she had forgotten. Oh, really?

2 October 1954

Tea alone with Dr. Theo Schmidt. All his family is away on various travels and we sat alone in his luxurious villa. He gave me an excellent tea, prepared all by himself. Outside the weather was wintry: foggy, cold, and by late afternoon it was already dark. Schmidt first told me of a school he had attended as a boy in the Swiss Engadin, then we talked politics and history. His theory is that if the Americans had adopted German as their national language (which he says they nearly did during the Revolution) they would have inherited German culture and that would have been spared them the materialistic money culture they now have and which they owe to the British. In his view the British are the eternal profit makers, the nation of shopkeepers. You have always found agents of the Bank of England in the remotest little town in Russia, making money. Schmidt is sure that even today there are British Red Cross agents in Russia doing that sort of business. He has a certain sympathy for Russia— he admires Russian peasant craft— but Bolshevism has sterilized Russia's native cultural vitality. Her present leaders are mostly Georgians and Jews... He also criticized the U.S. for adopting a moralistic view in world affairs. It's wrong not to recognize Red China on moralistic grounds. What government a nation chooses to have is its own affair. The atrocities of the Chinese Communists were the inevitable accompaniment to any revolution. America also committed atrocities in the Civil War and there are still atrocities being committed in Chicago today. Then there were the British massacres in India and the British concentration camps in the Boer War, the French atrocities in North Africa, and "let us admit it, some of the things we have done ourselves in Germany." He violently attacked the French and Mendès-France. The French people are scared of German industrial competition. At this point Schmidt raised his voice: "Our former Generalstabsoffizier, General Halder, has declared, and quite rightly so, that instead of paying the European Defense Community 9 million dollars for a German contingent of 12 divisions, the U.S.A. should simply give Germany half that sum, and Germany will provide an army of 50 divisions to help defend the West." "Wow," I said, "No wonder the French are afraid of Germany!" (I was thinking of 50 German divisions independent of EDC control.) "Of course they are right to be afraid!" Schmidt answered, "their industry will never reach our level of efficiency!"

Schmidt is in favor of rebuilding the German armaments industry. Only leftists (Socialists, etc.) cling to the ridiculous idea that armaments mean a declining standard of living for the people. Hitler raised the standard of living in Germany, but arms production remained a small part of her national output in the Third Reich. Krupp mainly built heavy machines. During the war Schmidt had belonged to a government commission that urged Krupp to increase its arms production from 8% to 15%, but Krupp had insisted that its exports were vital for the German economy and raised arms production to only 12%. So, Schmidt concluded proudly, Germany fought the war with only 10% of her economy geared to the making of war equipment.

3 October 1954

For once, a beautiful, sunny day. Since it is Sunday, Rena didn't wake me up until she brought in my breakfast. After a hurried cup of tea, I went by S-Bahn to the Wedding to sit down for a last time drawing pictures of tenement houses. It was close to lunchtime and the streets were almost deserted. In a nearby park I watched old people throwing bread crumbs to sparrows. Then I went to the house of Gustav Pietsch to say my farewell and to thank him for all the help he has given me in my work. His wife, I found out, was an employee of the railway workers' union back in 1919, and she was born in the Wedding and grew up here. The Pietsches live in Ostender Strasse

11, a newish-looking building owned by a building society. They have two and a half rooms, very modest but modern and comfortable. So one of the top officials of the DGB is shaving every morning at the kitchen sink because his bathroom has no washbowl.

Pietsch was in a very good mood. The Häkers had also come and we all first ate cake and drank coffee, then took a ride in Pietsch's car touring the Wedding. We visited the Ernst Reuter settlement in the Ackerstrasse (lots of Berliners from all over the city come here on Sundays to see it), some courtyards in Hussitenstrasse, the Schillerpark and the Rehberge, a youth hostel in Am Dohnagestell (very good indeed) and a newly erected obelisk near the local museum in Müllerstrasse. This obelisk, made entirely of bricks and stones collected from bombed houses, is meant to stand for the destruction and subsequent rebuilding of Berlin.

There is an odd story that goes with it. This obelisk was inaugurated not more than a few months ago. The SPD mayor of Wedding was asked to make a dedication speech, but the Catholic priest of the church across the road furiously rang the church bells throughout the ceremony (Don Camillo fashion) because he opposed socialism. How strange, I thought, since the occasion seems so innocent.

We sat in Opa Pietsch's living room for another two hours after the tour to look at his photos taken in China (1911-13), Japan (1913) and U.S.A. (1949). The Häkers and Pietsch then talked about some unpleasant elements in the DGB who oppose any German contribution to the defense of the West and prefer German reunification through negotiations with the Communists. To the Häkers and Pietsch the Communists stand for a reactionary political system, irreconcilable with the traditional ideals of social democracy. They are frightened of this vocal minority of Socialists who are ready to deal with the Communists and whose arrogant bearing intimidates the younger TU members. Worse, insofar as they do have a following, they owe their power to their authoritarian behavior.

II October 1954

I am leaving Berlin for Frankfurt by Pan American Airways, flight 185, at 9:30 a.m. today. The last ten days were spent mostly with Jay. Carol and Randolph left Berlin to return to New Haven on the 7th. Over the past few days I still read a few dossiers in the Hauptarchiv and the Innere Mission in Dahlem, and spent hours with Jay walking around downtown Berlin near the Gedächtniskirche. I am not really sorry to leave Berlin for I think I have exhausted the city just as the city has made me exhausted. I shall always remember the Putlitz Bridge and the towering chimneys of the Bolle Brewery which I saw each time I drove north to the Wedding, symbolizing the gateway to Berlin's poorest working-class districts. I also will remember the friendly, quaint streets of Neukölln, where I have found most of the material for my thesis. I will often think back to the contrast between the glamor of the Kudamm and the desolate fate of Berlin's many destitute refugees and old pensioners. And I will think of the East sector with its bright posters, blaring loudspeakers, and grey, forlorn emptiness. I don't think I want to come back to Berlin very soon, but eventually I will surely want to see it again because this is where I was born and where I now have a hometown.

Epilogue

The thesis on working-class life in imperial Berlin (1890-1914) was written during 1955-59 while I held my first teaching jobs in history in America. I continued my interest in Berlin history in the 1960s by writing a book entitled *The Berlin Police in the Weimar Republic* and an article in German entitled "Die Chinesen in Berlin," which told about the various Chinese who had come on official missions to Berlin between the two wars.

Jay and Carol Cerf settled in Washington, D.C., and later moved to Cambridge, Massachusetts, and I had the honor of being named their second son Christopher's godfather. Jay was very successful as a specialist in international trade and briefly served in the Kennedy administration. He died very unexpectedly in 1974. Brigitte Hagemann ran the Wasmuth bookstore in Hardenbergstrasse for many years. She married an architect, Hans Hensel, and the two now live in retirement on the shores of the Havel river. Jürgen Brandenburg made a good career as a biologist at the Free University. I saw him last in 1977; shortly afterwards he died of cancer. Peter Herz entered Berlin city politics and in recent years has devoted his energy to helping refugees in Berlin from Southeast Asia.

Street figures in Charlottenburg. 10 a.m.

On a short visit to West Berlin in February 1985, I dropped into the Landesarchiv. I was told that Herr Siewert was about to be given a retirement party by the staff— did I want to come? Of course I did, and for the first and only time in my life, I made a brief speech in German:

Dear Herr Siewert. Ladies and Gentlemen,

I think I speak for countless visitors to the Landesarchiv Berlin— and in particular for the foreign visitors— if today I say to you: there is many a Berlin book that would never have seen the light of day but for the energetic assistance of our Herr Siewert, his friendly advice and encouragement.

I must be one of Herr Siewert's oldest *protégés*. Our friendship goes back to the year 1953. I was still a young man then— so was Herr Siewert— and Berlin surely the most interesting city in all Europe. Berlin in those days could fatally ensnare a foreign student who is keen on exploring the many different worlds to be found in West Berlin and East Berlin. But I was lucky to have a guardian angel in the Landesarchiv. Herr Siewert's devotion to duty and his tireless industry were a good influence on me, and so the research for my thesis did get done in the end. We old Archiv users of the class of 1953 keenly remember the strict work discipline in the reading room in those days. None of us ever dared to reach for our sandwiches until Herr Siewert, on the dot of noon, broke the silence with the words: "So! Now we can have lunch."

Dear Herr Siewert: I thank you for all the academic assistance that you have given me over so many years. I thank you for your many marks of friendship. I owe to you the love for Berlin which grew in me 32 years ago while you and I worked together on the history of this city. I think of you as I say with pride (and with a bow to the late President Kennedy): "Ich bin ein alter Berliner...Landesarchiv visitor."